Social Media Marketing

Become An Expert Influencer Using Facebook, Youtube, And Instagram; How To Use Social Media For Business; How To Build Your Personal Brand

---

BY

Chris Marshal

CONTENTS

Introduction

The advent of online social media has allowed one person to connect with hundreds or even thousands of people around the world. Social media has exploded as an online discussion category where people create content, share content, bookmark it, and vastly network. All forms of social media give diverse communities and individuals who may be interested in an opportunity to introduce themselves and their goods.

Technological advances have a major effect in a number of ways on every organization. Digital technology's advent has revolutionized marketing operations worldwide. There is today a high degree of competition on the market, and consumers have incentives to make smart choices on the variety of products and services available. Companies need to be cautious in this competitive environment to maintain consumer loyalty. Reducing the contact gap between the business and the customer may be a positive way to build a stronger relationship that can be of more benefit in creating a deeper understanding of the needs and preferences of customers. Throughout this way, social media plays a key role, and the businesses take advantage of the friendly approach of social media to create brand relationships. Social networking platforms are forms of contact used to link people together. Research has shown that people are moving to use social media to access knowledge, ideas, and opportunities. Social networking technology has changed the ways the brands and consumers handle their relationships. Social media's popularity lies in the fact that it has created a means by which people communicate. They managed to establish ties with each other. The advertisers use social media platforms to promote brands. They use social media to understand customer expectations, and then develop appropriate strategies for promoting their marketing goal offers. Commutation is very important and useful for the initiation of dialogues. Therefore, contact is the only mechanism used to establish, grow, and sustain the two-person relationship. Communication opens doors to understanding uncertainty and to eliminate it. Social networking acts as a forum for a wide number of clients to connect and interact with. Via this channel, companies may raise awareness of their brands. They can also promote their brands by distributing their specialties and parity points.

Social networking platforms have made engagement and collaboration so simple that the different businesses can communicate with their customers and learn about their interests, which are then used offline to establish an effective brand marketing strategy. Because of the variety of apps, social media offer versatility to handle large target market traffic. Although face-to-face contact and communication are strong, social media has the potential to provide an efficient communication substitute. It lets the brands and consumers handle instant message contact and dialogs. Such platforms can store the interaction between the brands and the consumers and can be used for further development. Brands can also be able to flash their advertisements on social networking sites. Flashing the ads on the target public's pages is like winning a tender. Brands have to realize that when they show their advertisements, they will win the bid. They need to state their target market clearly and position the highest bids. This results in the creation of publicity for many consumers, which can indirectly result in a large number of sales and a massive fan for a brand to follow. Social networking sites are not just a phenomenon to keep up with. Rather, they have demonstrated their value in developing a business-to-customer relationship, catching potential customers, retaining customers, fostering a high-end network, and potential business development. Companies can not afford to neglect such a vitally critical forum for their brand growth. Conrad said that social media and blogs for social networking are the most common marketing contact basis. The platform offers a more transparent and unrestricted means of contact for the marketers. The modern generation of websites offers more integrative facilities for consumers, and these facilities are used by advertisers. New website protection is growing, and this also increases consumer trust in digitally buying the product from the organization. The website of social networking likes Facebook, Twitter, and LinkedIn and many others draw millions of users. On these social networking sites, the advertisers are searching for their clients and use them as marketing and contact channels with the consumers. Here consumers collect information from social networking websites while actively checking and sharing the information with one another. The reliability and authenticity of this knowledge are more so as consumers more trust each other than conventional marketing methods.

Social media comprises a variety of applications that allow consumers to post, tag, dig, blog, etc., using technical terms. This content created by social media is a type of newly generated online information resource which is created, disseminated, and used by consumers who wish to educate each other about products, brands, services, and issues. Sources include Facebook, MySpace, Digg, Twitter, Google+, and LinkedIn. Social media was the trendsetter in subjects ranging from climate, politics, and technology to the entertainment industry because of its ease of use, speed, and scope. In this distribution of users, social media is basically self-promoting. The viral content of social media makes the promotion of goods and services an enticing resource for corporations. Social media is now an emerging marketing trend. Marketers are starting to recognize the use of social media as a part of reaching out to consumers in their marketing strategies and campaigns. Promotions, business intelligence, opinion analysis, public relations, digital strategy, and product and consumer management are business sub-disciplines that can use social media. -- social media network (such as blogs, online discussion boards, and online communities) has an impact on marketing success (sales, for example), so knowing their relative value and interrelationships is important. Additionally, social media users are now highly engaged Platform customers. State of the Internet: Social Media shows that 70 percent of social media users are engaged in online shopping, as Nielse (2011) reported. Consumers can easily get what they want by simply sitting in front of the computer screen and visiting websites online. While social media marketing has tremendous benefits for both customers and advertisers, it also has negative impacts on both. It inevitably favors many threats and cyber criminals due to its simple way of getting access to information, lack of monitoring, and control. We will address the benefits and drawbacks of social media marketing in more depth in the upcoming chapters.

What Is Social Media?

Social media is basically the online content developed by a variety of people who are open to access over the internet. In other words, social media is the shift of people`s attention on the online platforms where people share, discover, and read information and gain knowledge. Conrad believes that social media is a sort of synthesis of sociology and technology and creating an environment or platform on the internet where people share experiences with each other and develop networks for a variety of different official and unofficial reasons. Social media has become an important platform and has gone so important that nearly every business uses social media for the marketing and promotion of its business, products, and services. Social media is also used for sharing information and getting in touch with their customers and society at large. Ahmad suggests that social media can be divided into three main components:

- **Publishing Technology for everyone**: Social media is free and open for publishing for everyone, and the technological advancement has made it even more convenient. Social media is online; therefore, they are not restricted to any physical set up. Previously social places used to be like pubs, clubs, gardens where people used to interact with one another and share information. Advancement in the technology and the development of virtual social platforms enable people to interact and develop a network with one another; online social media has become the new talk of the town. On online social media, everyone can be the publishers and generators of the content for which the information is shared.

- **Information Diffusion**: The rate at which social media diffuses information, no other medium is capable of doing so because other media like TV, newspapers, and magazines are not that faster in filtering and spreading information. Online social media like Facebook, Twitter are faster in the transmission of information and relatively far less expensive than the rest. Barefoot and Szabo suggest that previously companies used to market their products or services through advertising on TV and newspapers, making it a one-way communication. Through the development of online social media, companies interact with their customers and take feedback and suggestions from them for further developments. Social media has made the information open and equally accessible for all. Online social media has bought democracy in the sharing of information.

- **Relationship Building**: Social media has become a powerful medium for the development of relationships through sharing valuable information and creating wonderful ideas. Social media helps people in connecting with one another. A person is connected and shares information from the UK with a man in New Zealand, all because of online social media.

Gunelius states that social media has gone so powerful that it is now used for not only business and personal relationships but also for political developments. All this clearly highlights the various dimensions and importance of social media. The rise and advancement of technology and the shift from traditional media to online social media has made it more significant. There are many other reasons due to which people, businesses, and even the political parties are shifting and using social media for the development of the achievement of their objectives.

Social Media Marketing

Marketing through social media is the latest and popular trend in the market. Traditional marketing tools such as TV, newspapers, magazines have been very expensive and cover a limited, targeted market. The traditional marketing strategies were based on focusing on specific markets individually. Even now, it is difficult for businesses to target and market their products and services to the big geographical position through one single campaign, such as covering the entire Asia through one newspaper advertisement; because not every country in Asia watches the same TV channels. The social media has entirely changed that approach towards marketing. When we see the basic definition of marketing, it says to maximize the usage of resources of the business and develop products and services to satisfy customer needs. Social media marketing has, in reality, enabled the businesses to take the feedback, comments, and suggestions from their customers through blogs, pictures, and ratings and improve their products and services so that customer needs could be addressed in a more proactive manner. So advertising and marketing have entirely changed due to social media. Jaoker, Jacobs, and Moore state that through social media, customers are building information about everything from insurance to career, from pet food to electronic appliances, and through this, customers are beating out marketers in their game. They are sharing their experiences with one another, which nowadays is directly making an impact on the business. This is the era of information; therefore, it has become necessary that there is a spread of positive information about the company offerings out in the social platforms.

This positive word of mouth at the social platforms will help them to retain customers and generate more sales. Kabani and Brogan say that the biggest comfort with social media is that it helps the businesses in marketing their brand to the wider 'global' community. The social media platforms are open and accessible for everyone from every country, and therefore they provide companies with tremendous opportunities to communicate with communities and build relationships with their target audience. Social media marketing is different all together than traditional marketing. Social media in marketing is all about using the natural conversational platforms of people to build relationships with them in order to satisfy their needs. Social media platforms are helping businesses to spread positive word of mouth for themselves and their goods so that customers' needs could be addressed effectively. Social media involves a number of different social channels, as traditional media has offline channels. Social media keeps changing over time, and therefore it gets better and better. Social media is highly participative, and the participants of the conversation are the key people that generate the content. In traditional marketing on TV and newspapers, marketing and communication are one-sided, whereas social media is a collective approach that enables the collection and sharing of information. This information becomes essential for businesses to actually revise their business and marketing plans in order to maximize customer attraction and retention.

Social media operate as a digital platform upon which social interaction occurs. Social networking platforms help in building virtual communities, or social networks, for individuals with similar attitudes, interests, education, opinion, and lifestyles.

Social Platforms And User Behaviours

Burke defines social networking platforms as: "... a loose affiliation of people who interact, communicate, and share content through platforms, building relationships among communities of practices. Social platform management is a social and technological process that enables the development, deployment, use, and management of social media solutions and services. In social aspects, a 'social platform' enables communities of users in, posting, editing, and sorting, co-creating, and sharing a variety of contents. Thus it enables us to communicate implicitly or explicitly with a specific person or broadcast to all. Its other features aid in adding friends into the network, setting privacy controls, and other native social media network features. In its technological aspects, a social platform consists of dimensions of social mark-up language for creating native applications, an application programming interface (API) for third party application integration and a backend admin console for managing the entire user base and preferences, etc. It provides continuous visibility and persistence to people and content.

Thus a social platform enables creating social media websites and services with complete social media network technical, user-specific, and social functionality. These are second-generation (Web 2.) websites/platforms that provide users the ability and tools to create and publish their own mini web sites or web pages using the "bottom-up approach" — using a many-to-many model. Such platforms provide features such as; user-created contents, a high degree of user participation in communities of practice, and the ability to integrate with multiple sites or networks. Thus a social platform include things like social networking (Facebook, Google+

MySpace, Twitter, LinkedIn); photo and video sharing sites (Flickr,

Vimeo and YouTube); blogs (such as Blogger, WordPress, Typepad), social bookmarking (Delicious, Stumble Upon) news sharing (Digg, Yahoo! Buzz). The networked social platforms can attract traffic by managing touches of 4Ps; Personal, Participatory, Physical, Plausible. The companies have used social platforms for internal and external communication and branding. Its use can be attributed to demand-side factors (the fact that social media give us that we can't get offline and let us meet our social needs) and supply-side factors (websites such as Facebook, Twitter, and LinkedIn have more than 1.2 billion users and account for almost 25 percent of Internet use). To get full advantage of social media, companies need to develop and harness their social strategy. Over 1.7 billion people use social platforms on the Internet. Some social platforms, such as Twitter, MeetUp, and eHarmony, enable strangers to connect. eHarmony alone is estimated to account for one in six new marriages in the U.S. LinkedIn helps one expand business relationships. Other social platforms, like Facebook or Renren in China, create more relationships with other known peoples. In fact, Facebook boasts a staggering 750 million users and valuation in excess of $100 billion. Different platforms have different levels of restrictions on users' choices. This is puzzling that some platforms like e-Harmoney (dating site), WhatsApp (social one to one texting on the phone), headhunting (recruitment), etc., are successful even with restrictive access and a user fee. On the other hand, platforms like Facebook (social networking), Monster (job hunting), Lastminute.com (travel and tourism), YouTube, etc. that offer unlimited free access are also successful. The understanding becomes more complex when even platforms with the middle ground on access like twitter (limited in words with unlimited access to the network) and

LinkedIn etc. are also growing. Therefore, It could be argued that the value of participation in a social platform often depends on the number of choices offered, and a platform offering unrestricted access (yet in user's control) could quickly displace a platform that restricts choice or provides restricted access.

In June 2014, Ebiz/MBA ranked the top 15 platforms by comprehensively average of integrating rankings from other ranking evaluators (Alexa Global Traffic, compete and Quantcast).

In 2013, a study carried out by Pew Research found that in the US, around 73% of online adults use a social networking site of some kind, 42% of 2% of online adults now use multiple social networking sites, but Facebook at 71% remains as the top platform of choice. The study by Pew research also found that user segments of different platforms are not the same. Facebook is preferred by a diverse mix of demographic segments and who also visit the site daily many times. Pinterest has four times high appeal to female users; LinkedIn has more college graduates with higher-income households. On the other hand, the segments of Twitter and Instagram are overlapping with younger adults, urban dwellers, and non-whites. Further, 90% of Twitter users, 93% of Instagram, and 83% of LinkedIn users also use Facebook. A small number of users use only one type of platform; 8% LinkedIn, 4% Pinterest, and 2% Instagram or Twitter only. This pattern shows a high level of similarities between user needs to visit social platforms on the one hand and also put forward a question that why people visit many platforms if one platform can meet their social needs!

Do people have different motives at each platform, or do they have a different network of connections at each of the platforms, or they want to exhibit different personalities and roles at different platforms?

The features of different platforms are used to segment platforms. There are a variety of Social Media platforms that are in use with their corresponding features. Nearly one in four people worldwide (1.7billion people) use a social network site. There can be seven kinds of social media users. The Deal Seeker follow a company for bargain or value deals, so companies should always offer them deals along with a request to refer more friends to the brand; the Unhappy Customer has potential to do harm to a company by creating a stream of negative words of mouths, so the company should solve their problems immediately; The Loyal Fans spreads positive word of mouth and recommend the brand to their network and even defends their brand, so the company should reward their behavior; a Quiet Follower neutral and is just there because his friends are there, so the company should call them to engage in actions; The Cheerleader is a top fan of the brand and likes everything a company does; hence the company should keep him fresh and inspiring with updated information, and lastly the Ranter goes for virtual fights with strong opinions about everything, so the company should react cautiously and very selectively. Hence in overall, the company should have a customized social platform strategy, and the contents of the messages should be engaging with a sense of community, inclusive in action, newsworthy, and contents from all followers are allowed and recognized.

Facebook

Facebook is the biggest social network of the current era, with 1.1 billion registered users and an estimated 750 million unique monthly visitors. Facebook can be utilized by companies to build a strong base for getting in touch with potential customers. The business needs to develop its brand profile through creating a stellar Facebook page that is worth the attention on the platform and then shares information with the people that are interesting and newsworthy to the consumers. Then the content can be enriched with information related to the products and services, new launches, or company happenings, etc. make sure that Facebook is not a broadcasting media; rather, it is a social platform for consumers, and you can be guest there with invitations only. The company needs to help consumer meet their social needs and let them fulfill their other needs. Do not intrude or be pushy like a salesman, be societal oriented marketers, and act as facilitators for a community of practitioner -prosumer. Those with an account on Facebook can conveniently join the company profile and exchange information and updates provided, but it is important that you first invite your close friends or missionary customers, they can create budge. Do offer incentives or recognition for new needs. Do act according to the kind of Internet users, as mentioned in the preceding sections. It gives a great opportunity to enhance a company`s visibility and image in the virtual world. Do respond to comments and weave into your comments and posts to continually extend this. Individuals interested in the company can easily share ideas with actual or potential customers. They can also create discussion forums to have feedback about their products and services.

Twitter

Twitter is a very popular microblogging site amongst celebrities and Politicians, due to which it attracts a wide variety of fans of such personalities from around the globe. It has 500 million registered users, and 400 million tweets are sent each day. It permits each user to post messages of 140 characters or less at one time. A business should create its unique profile. People at twitter share their ideas and link with one another. So it provides an excellent opportunity for businesses to market their brand. Companies have also created their profiles on Twitter in order to get in touch with the audience. The message or tweet can be personal thoughts, quotes, news and picture links, brand, and product and service links. The users start a Twitter account in order to follow, and feel connected to, their favorite celebrities, media personalities, opinion leaders, role models, sports figure, politicians, etc. business can sign up for a Twitter account to keep up-to-date about industry leaders, stakeholders and keeping customers updated with newsworthy tweets. Invite friends or brand cheerleaders and follow opinion leaders or media channels that are of interest to your customers & followers. Each user that's registered has an average of 208 followers that can retweet if your content is relevant to them and touches their life or something they care about. The chain can grow exponentially, provided tweet is worth tweeting repeatedly. Everything that can be applied to Facebook can also be applied here with some alteration. Your followers are following you as role models or reference groups or your power authority due to rank, expertise, referrals, coercive, etc. ensure that you continuously perform your role. Tweet yourself and retweet from higher-ups in industry, media, consumer groups, government reports and news channels, etc. sensible uses of hashtags (# brandname) are very important to create brand budge. It is about what is happening right now in the world? So keep up to date but avoid controversial content.

LinkedIn

LinkedIn is a social networking platform that mainly focuses on professional and business networking segments. It has 225 million registered users and, on average, 110 million unique monthly visitors. This platform strategy also starts with creating a LinkedIn company page. The accounts on LinkedIn can help in expanding business or professional or employment-related connections, thus ultimately a platform to gain access to customers and professionals.

Remember to follow principles of AIDA – attention- interest- desire and action. Request cheerleaders and opinion leaders for testimonials. Promote the company through the 'follow' button and remember to link your other social media accounts to your LinkedIn Company Page. Make the information engaging and varied, but also remember pictures speak more than words. The primary functionality of LinkedIn allows users (workers and employers) to create profiles and "connections" to each other in an online social network, which may represent real-world professional relationships. Users could invite anyone so as to become a connection. Though, if the invitee picks "I don't know" or "Spam," then this would count against the one who invited, and If he gets too many of such responses, the account may be restricted or closed. This list of connections could then be made use of in many ways:

- Obtaining introductions to the connections of connections (termed second-degree connections) and connections of second-degree connections (termed third-degree connections);

- Clients can secure positions, individuals and business openings suggested by somebody in one's contact arrange;

- Employers can list occupations and quest for potential up-and-comers;

- Job searchers can audit the profile of recruiting directors and find which of their current contacts can present them;

- Users can post their own photographs and view photographs of others to help in distinguishing proof;

- Users can follow various organizations and can get notices about the new joining and offers accessible;

- Users can spare (for example bookmark) occupations that they might want to apply for;

- Users can "like" and "praise" each other's updates and new occupations;

- Users can also see those who have visited their profile page.

YouTube

YouTube, with 1 billion registered users at which videos are viewed 4 billion times per day, is the largest media sharing site in the world. With its inception in 2005, this platform has been used to entertain, educate, share thoughts, provoke, and inspire people. It is accessible to everyone, with or without registering an account. A business can register as a corporate account using Google mail only. Once registered, a business can upgrade with a fee to get YouTube's 'branded channel' option. It is important to bring in traffic use SEO keys and tags that are consumer segment and your brand-related. A business can add as many relevant keywords using the auto body example from Pinterest. If one cannot create a video to start with, the business can upload loyal / missionary customer videos or can search YouTube for your brand relevant videos from other channels or industry or education, etc. and link them to your site or social platform pages. A business should stay current and follow the rules of movie making and education. People like seeing more than reading, but it must be something for them.

Google+

Google+ has 343 million registered users who visit 65 million times per month. This social platform includes a number of features that are very relevant to social platform marketing. For instance, the share button can be used to share links, videos, and photos with segmented and filtered Google circles. One more feature is the option for bigger and clear cover picture. A business should use keywords strategically. Businesses can link this with other websites and social platforms and invite contacts. Other features like story, events, hangouts, Google+ community are really worth utility for a business, but it is the responsibility of the business to be responsive, empathetic, and trustworthy to your community. Google+ profiles will be used as the background account for several Google services starting November 2011, including YouTube, Gmail, Google Maps, Ios, Google Play, Google Music, Google Voice, Google Wallet, Google Local, and more. As of January 2012, Google Search is personalized with a feature called Search Plus Your World, which inserts content shared on Google+ profiles and brand pages under the results of Web Search, if one is logged into their Google+ account while using it. The app, which is opt-in, has been received with controversy over Google+ profiles' reliance on other social networking services. The feature builds on the previous "Media Search" app, which indexes material posted or published by authors; A Google+ user profile is a publicly available user account linked to many of Google's assets. It includes basic elements of social networking, such as a profile photo, section, background photo, past work, and school history, interests, places lived, and an area to post status updates. It also includes several parts of identity services, such as a contributor and other profiles, allowing one to connect their "online assets." Optionally, this section links to other social media accounts that one has, any blogs that one owns, or has published or places on which one contributes—using this field for Google Authorship. Starting on 29 October 2013, personalized or Vanity URLs have been made available to the public for any account that was 30 + days old, has a profile image, and at least ten followers. Google removed the photo of the author from the search results in June 2014, and in August 2014, Google would stop displaying authorship in both photo and author name search results.

Circles

Circles is a key feature of the networking network Google+. This helps users to organize people into groups or lists that can be spread across various Google products and services. Circle management is achieved by means of a drag-and-drop interface. When a circle has been formed, a Google+ user can share unique private content for that circle only. For example, work-themed content should only be shared with colleagues at work, and more personal content and images may be seen by one's friends and family. The choice to share Public or with Others is still accessible. Since the September 26, 2011, users can share Circles; this is a one-time sharing, and if the Circle maker replaces participants, the shared copies of people will not be changed.

Circles another function is to monitor one's Stream content. A user can click a Circle on the left side of the page, and only posts shared by users in that Circle will be included in the Stream portion of the page (the center). Every Circle has a "slider" configuration element with four positions for the unsegmented Stream (includes information from all the user's circles): nothing, some items, most stuff, and everything. The Nothing location allows the user to specifically select (click on) the name of the Circle to display user material in that Circle. The all environment as its name implies filtering nothing out in the Circle from men. The remaining two positions control the number of posts appearing in one's mainstream, but there was no disclosure of the algorithm determining what displays.

Stream

This occupies the centre of three columns on the tab, users see notifications in their Circles from those. There is an input box that allows users to sign in to a message. There are icons to upload and share images and videos, in addition to the text entry area. You can filter the Stream to display only posts from different circles.

Instagram

Instagram is a very popular photos and videos sharing platform and recently purchased by Facebook. It has 130 million active monthly users. The business can upload photos or videos and can link with other social platforms and invite people to click for favorite ones. To keep always in the trend, continuously upload new action photos about your actions that would be of interest to users. That addresses their social, rational, emotional, and epistemic needs. Promote photo-sharing contests of different themes, offer discount codes, invite testimonial, and use hashtags.

Blogs

Blogs can be updated on a frequent basis. Blogs can also be regularly developed for a variety of different purposes. They are an active source of promoting products and services and spreading information. There are many different blogs that cover and attract people from a specific industry. Marketers generally develop their profile and carry on updating them so that the fans and connected users are kept well informed.

Tumblr

Tumblr is one of the blogging platforms that also allows sharing photos, videos, quotes almost everything. It is more images driven; interest focused rather than personnel oriented and offers many choices to the users. Tumbler has 300 million registered users and 216.3 million monthly visitors. There are many options for formatting and layouts etc. that can be customized and focused as per your customers' needs. The Admin option allows adding users, opinion leaders, experts, and so on that can add blogs to your pages. Try a variety of photos and videos with themes, and things like bloomers, how-to, behind the scenes, etc. try to make it as close to the personal site as possible but make sure that company's social media strategy should lead to more contents from others as compared to from the company. Just like other traditional marketing platforms, these mediums also require consistent time and effort. Marketers generally develop their profile and carry on updating them so that the fans and connected users are kept well informed. Tumblr's production started in 2006 during a two-week contract gap at David Karp's software consulting company, Davisville (housed at Karp's former stay at Fred Seibert's Frederator Studios, a block away from Tumblr's current headquarters). For some time, Karp had been interested in tumblelogs (short-form blogs) and was waiting for one of the existing blogging sites to set up its own tumble logging site. Karp and developer Marco Arment started working on their own tumble logging app, as no one had done so after a year of waiting. Tumblr was launched in February 2007, and the site had attracted 75,000 users within two weeks.

Blog Management

Dashboard:

The dashboard is the primary resource for the average Tumblr user. It is a live stream from recent blog posts they are watching. Users can comment, reblog, and like posts from other blogs that appear on their dashboard through the dashboard. The dashboard enables the user to upload text messages, photos, videos, quotes, or links to their blog with a click of a button at the top of the dashboard. Users can also link their blogs to their Twitter and Facebook accounts, and it will also be sent as a tweet and a status update anytime they make a post;

- **Queue:** Users can set up a schedule to postpone posts they upload. They could spread their posts over many hours or even days;

- **Tags:** They can help their audience find posts on certain topics by inserting tags for each posting that a user makes. If anyone were to upload a photo to their blog and wanted their viewers to find images, they would add the # photo tag and their viewers could use that word to search for posts with the # picture tag;

- **Template editing:** Tumblr enables users to change the HTML coding style of their blog to monitor their blog's appearance. In addition, users can use a custom domain name for their blog.

MySpace

MySpace (stylized as MySpace, formerly stylized as MySpace) is a social networking site operated by Specific Media LLC and pop music singer and actor Justin Timberlake with a heavy music accent. Myspace was founded in August 2003 and is located in Beverly Hills, California.

Myspace had 1 million unique visitors to the US in April 2014. Myspace was founded by Chris DeWolfe and Tom Anderson in 2003 and was later purchased for $580 million by News Corporation in July 2005. It was the highest visited social media site worldwide from 2005 until early 2008, and in June 2006, Google surpassed it as the most visited website in the United States. It was taken over by Facebook in the number of unique visitors worldwide in April 2008, and surpassed in the number of unique U.S. visitors in May 2009, while Myspace generated revenue of $800 million during the 2008 fiscal year. Since then, following many redesigns, the number of Myspace users has gradually declined. Myspace had been ranked 982 by overall web traffic as of May 2014, and 392 in the United States. Myspace had a major influence on pop culture and music and created a gaming platform that, among others, launched the successes of Zynga and RockYou. The platform also started the trend of creating exclusive URLs for businesses and artists. MySpace is a wide majority of businesses market and promote their products and services on MySpace and target its users. The network also provides a variety of other options like gaming, music, videos, etc. Social Bookmarking

There are many such platforms of social bookmarking, such as Stumble Upon. StumbleUpon discovery engine has 25 million registered users. It searches and recommends web pages to its users and can also be shared by others to 'like it.' This also recommends users other related sites or sites that your network has liked or submit industry-related sites and blogs or create a stumble upon channel.

Social Media Marketing And Its Features

Social Media Marketing is a new phenomenon and a fast-growing way for companies to meet targeted consumers with ease. Social media marketing can be described simply as using social media platforms to promote a firm and its products. This form of marketing can be seen as a subset of online marketing activities that supplement conventional web-based promotional strategies, such as email newsletters and online advertising campaigns. Social media marketing has injected a new term of exponential distribution and confidence into mass communication and mass marketing by empowering consumers to distribute messages to their personal contacts. In this modern approach to outreach and marketing, new resources are being created and, in effect, increased for companies. Social media marketers are now gaining a deeper and more successful perspective by incorporating predictive applications across official website channels on the social network. There are many different social media platforms, and they take many different forms and have different characteristics. The most social networking site that comes to our mind is without doubt Facebook. First launched in February 2004, Facebook was owned and run by Facebook, Inc. As of May 2012, there are over 900 million active users on Facebook. Users must register before using the site; when they update their profile, they can create a personal profile, add other users as friends and exchange messages, including automatic notifications. Additionally, users can enter user groups of common interest; organize their friends into lists such as "People From Work" or "Close Friends" The main mission of Facebook is to give people the power to share, and to make the world more open and connected. Other social network sites like Twitter, Google Plus, and LinkedIn that vary in some respects, but they operate basically on the same principles.

Marketing that uses social media like these can take several different forms. In particular, the traditional Facebook model involves replacing a human "friend" with a brand or a tangible product or creating a page or group. A person who wants to "like" a product or organization advertises that links to their own private communication network. The principle also applies to other types of social media. Facebook is a mix of microblogging and the social network, according to Bernie Borges. Youtube also helps users to receive small alerts and advertisements from favorite companies. Twitter offers its users the ability to engage in real-time messaging. Typically a tweet is no more than 140 characters and can be used by user followers. These two outlets of social media are now among the most common and widely used alternatives, but they are far from being the only ones. As Kaplan and Haenlein observed, several platforms have been established that fall under the social media group, each of which has opportunities and specific advantages for marketing use. Collaborative projects like wikis or editable data-sources are especially poignant communication avenues. Indeed, trends indicate that they are increasingly becoming the predominant source of knowledge between consumers. Blogs are another widely-used communication platform, operated either by individuals or organizations. Businesses may foster brand awareness through blogs by sharing insider details, educating consumers on new products, and providing links to the key distribution channels. Fans will be updated on any special activities, competitions, or a new promo coordinated by the company or product from time to time. Blogs also encourage comments and feedback to be posted, enabling fans and critics to post thoughts and questions to producers. This promotes the peer-to-peer exchange of ideas, and can also promote honest dialogue between individuals and businesses to enhance their defaults. Approaches to social media ought to be addressed in order to ensure the best likelihood of social media marketing success. Emphasize the need for a social media strategy and diversify and ensure that messages reach appropriate audiences; there is no simple, right solution.

Advantages of Social Platform Marketing

Many organizations, including those in tourism, now routinely use publicly available social networking and microblogging sites for innovation, marketing, and after-sales service purposes. This resulted due to the fact that social networking offers many opportunities to address challenges and improve affordances to its users. The challenges of locating opinion leaders or experts find users' motivations to share knowledge and capitalize on social network connections and can address with help from transactive memory, public goods, and social capital theories. The social media enables different ways to engage in publicly visible knowledge and conversations through different kinds of affordance. The affordance offered are; visibility, persistence, editability, and association, metavoicing, triggered attending, network-informed associating, and generative role-taking. However, there are still some challenges, like governance, an abundance of information, interpreting quality, tensions of accessibility, contextual cues, leaky pipe, echo chambers, and intrinsic interest inherent in the information that needed to be addressed. The online social media platforms have become so powerful and popular that they have proved to be very excellent for marketing activities too. Social network marketing could be really advantageous for businesses. As it can help find talent and customers, build brand awareness and intelligence, create word of mouth or viral marketing, create a community of customers, and market research. It also helps customers communicate effectively and allow review or see reviews during the decision-making process, protect speaking to outside strategies for information, and thus decreases the cognitive load on the shoppers. Businesses can create user relevant contents, which can increase brand visibility. Social strategy can become a core capability if properly managed. It is a trendy, much low-cost supplement to other contents.

It is multiple to multiple connections that create opportunities for customers to know, demand, share, and participate and complaint about experiences of products, services, brands, and other interests. The customers can get better products and services as they can participate in the design, development, and consumption of products and services. It provides an opportunity for publicity in the contest to a paid advertisement. However, there are certain challenges that the business needs to address; it demands a commitment of resources, continuous visibility, difficulty to measure ROI, and if it goes out of control, then it can cause huge damage in the least time. It can make use of faster diffusion of innovation by using the pressure of opinion leaders, early adopters, and social pressures. The company in the tourism sector can use say 'Trip Advisor.' The company can understand target consumers' behavior and profile, interact with potential, current or exiting customers, identify brand advocates and WOM leaders, improve customer experiences through all phases of the consumer decisions making process, participate in trade competition, and scan moves of the competition. Social network platforms work in various different ways, such as:

Innovation:

Social media provides insight into customer experiences and ideas, which helps businesses to generate ideas for further development and innovation. The use of social media is also becoming very popular, especially in the context of marketing that it provides the opportunity to fetch some excellent ideas from the market without paying even a single penny;

Purchasing Decisions:

The consumer decision-making models guide the buying behavior results from consumer involvement and engagement in multistage problem-solving tasks.

The stages are: need recognition, information search, evaluation of alternatives (evoked set), evaluation result, and when buying, post-purchase evaluation. Marketing communication using social platforms provides consumers information, so they become able to support the learning process by which they acquire the purchase and consumption knowledge. Consumers' learning, attitude, and motivation can change due to any newly acquired knowledge gained from reading, observation, discussions, and virtual or actual experience. A social platform can affect consumer perception about evaluating the desired and actual state and can drive active or latent 'problem recognition' and also offer a solution to the problem. During the second stage of 'the information search,' social platforms can aid in the learning process by helping to search either internal or external memory sources. The evaluation of the alternative stage is conditioned by the type of consumer's choice and discussion on the social platform, which can aid by influencing consumers' learning, motivation, and attitudes with the help of augmented reality experiences. In the last stage of consumer decision making process-post-purchase evaluation, the consumer compares the real product performance with his/her expectations, and right discussions and word of mouth on platforms are useful in setting right levels expectations at well above consumers' minimum noticeable threshold levels and by reducing any uncertainty in offerings or services.

Right evaluation not only sets evokes set and helps in making a choice of brand offerings or destination but also can create positive word of mouth, customer loyalty, feedback, and cross-product buying.

The social platforms can provide conditions for a high level of customer involvement and engagements with the product or the services. The level of customer involvement in the buying process means the amount of psychophysical energy spent by the consumer in the buying process. Higher levels of involvement are associated with greater use of affective and cognitive decision making strategies across different cultures. During buying or consuming highly involved individuals compared to lower involved individuals will use more criteria search for more information, accept fewer alternatives, process relevant information in detail, and will form attitudes that are more resistant to change. Involvement levels, therefore, can have an impact on the information processing decision-making and responses to advertising. Lack of proper management of touchpoints/customer encounters can cause a churn among the firm's existing customers. The social platform not only increases customer relations but also enhances loyalty, satisfaction through customer involvement and encounter management, socially, emotionally, visually, auditory, and kinaesthetically. The social media marketing platforms are useful for businesses to spread a positive word of mouth through which they could influence them and exchange information. These platforms also provide an opportunity to clear any misunderstanding that could have become a hindrance to the purchasing decisions of customers.

Singh states that because of the sharing of instant information, the developed societies have got in the habit of creating awareness, sharing it on the

Internet on social platforms and then making purchasing decisions

Monitoring:

Social media also helps marketers to monitor what is going on about them amongst the people. It also provides them an opportunity to develop a strong basis for the business through which they could inspire individuals. The social platforms also help in interacting in real-time. A business could clearly watch out of any incorrect information and take appropriate actions accordingly;

New Customers:

Social media marketing provides you the opportunity to reach new customers efficiently. Through social media, you can also study and research people who could be your potential customers in the future. This also helps businesses to devise strategies that could target people in a more effective manner;

Referral:

The social media also helps businesses to promote themselves through clearly targeting people who prefer to be with your company and like your offerings. This easily helps in increasing the referral for the business;

Fan Clubs:

The rise of social media has actually helped businesses to create fan clubs for their businesses. People who are crazy for your businesses can easily get closer to the company. The fan clubs work tremendously for the creation and spread of positive word of mouth;

Feedback:

Marketing through social media actually helps businesses to get in one to one contact with the target audience and let them share their experiences with you so that you could work on them to improve your offerings. Companies by getting involved in such platforms can actually gain information about their products and services and take corrective measures in order to address the issues.

When people use a product, they then share their experiences of the internet with others on the conversation on social media platforms, and this makes others revise their purchasing decisions.

A business can effectively take advantage of such a platform and interact with its customers in order to help them satisfy their needs by addressing their issues promptly:

Connections and Access:

For marketers, social media provides an excellent opportunity to gain access to individuals in an informal manner without even making them feel different. Databases of customers from platforms give businesses opportunities to mine social network information and contacts. Furthermore, social platforms help in finding suppliers or employees too. It has been observed that social people are more comfortable and open in sharing information and experiences on social platforms and over the Internet than in face to face;

Brand Awareness and Image:

Businesses have been actively involved in sharing information for the enhancement of their brand name and in improving the overall position of their brand in the market. Marketing on social media has also revised the concept of a brand. A company can carry out brand Intelligence, thus collect consumer feedback, establish a brand presence, get insights about the way its brands are perceived and discussed. Through continuous interaction with customers a business can address their needs and thus build long-term brand relationships;

Product Launching:

It has also been noticed that social media also plays a pivotal role in the launching of the product. A wealth of word of mouth information regarding the brands and products, on social platforms, leads to its use as a new channel that has features of search engines, review sites, and price comparison. It directly acts at least two marketing mix elements place and promotion which aids in other 2 Ps Price and product strategies;

Sites:

Online social media platforms give the opportunity to market products and services and make people aware of upcoming products and services. Social media is a great way of giving details about your company, its offerings, and its operations. It also helps businesses to create hype in the market for their products;

Coverage:

The social media platform provides an excellent platform to cover a wide range of individuals from various segments of society. As described earlier that these platforms are open for all and do not restrict anyone from anywhere. This makes it convenient for companies to target a wider global market;

Cost:

Marketing through social media is very cost-effective as compared to traditional offline marketing media. This is an inexpensive way to promote business more efficiently. Previously Costs on MySpace ($25in 2009), Facebook ($5 daily + $0.01 in 2009), and LinkedIn (a $25/1000 clicks in 2009) was very competitive and enticing in the US. In 2013 in UK costs per click on Facebook (£0.25-0.57), Google Ad (£1.50), Linkedin ((£1.50), Twitter (£0.75) was still attractive and lower than traditional media channels (Bryan, 2013).

With digital marketing's popularity on the rise, several companies are exploring how social media can help them promote their products and services to potential and existing customers. Social networking sites like Fb and Twitter have changed the way some companies think about advertising. Some companies steer customers more towards their social network pages than to their own websites. Marketing via social media has certain benefits, but there are also associated disadvantages. The primary benefits of social media marketing are cost reduction and expanded visibility. A social media platform's cost is typically lower than other marketing channels, such as face-to-face salesmen or intermediaries or distributors. Additionally, social media marketing allows companies to target consumers who may not be available due to the temporal and locational constraints of traditional distribution channels. Social media platforms expand the scope and cut costs by offering consumers three areas of profit. Firstly, without human intervention, the marketing firm can provide infinite knowledge to customers. This is an advantage over other modes of interaction, as the amount of information that can be received is significantly greater than in any other form of communication. In addition, and more critically, the information may be given in a form that can be easily interpreted and understood by clients. Airline scheduling and booking processes, for example, are very hard to create and manage to meet individual needs. In addition, in this sense, the options in any format that is better than web-based format are wide and difficult to provide. Second, a social media marketing company may create connections by customizing details for individual customers that allows customers to design products and services that match their specific requirements. Online screening and assigning of seats can be done on the Internet, for example. Finally, social media platforms may facilitate transactions between consumers and businesses that would typically require human contact, as in the case of successful companies such as Dell and amazon.com. To better understand the benefits of social media marketing, there are five major advantages to achieving success in this field:

I. Cost-related

The key cost-related benefit of social media marketing. Compared to others, the financial barriers to social media marketing are fairly low. Most social media sites have free access, profile design, and posting information. Although traditional marketing strategies can cost millions of dollars, many social media instruments are free even for business use. Businesses can use a limited budget to execute highly successful social media marketing campaigns. The benefit of targeting your targeted market for little or no cash investment is significant, and you are willingly joined or followed by the audience that wants your content. Pay-per-click ads on sites like Facebook are "geo-targeted" to reach the right audience, according to specific criteria. The open nature of social media means each person reading your posts has the ability to spread the news further within their own network, so in a short time, knowledge can reach a large number of people.

II. Social interaction

One of the new media's most prominent phenomenon is how it has evolved and formed new forms of social interaction. People tend to spend more than a quarter of their time online engaging in networking activities (e.g., emails, IM chat, and social networks), which is equal to the total amount of time spent online for general entertainment and leisure activities. Social networking sites have become so ubiquitous that they are the Internet's most popular destinations. Not only has new media demonstrably changed how often people communicate online, but it has also widened the pool of individuals they communicate with, leading to new ways of shaping behaviors. Studies of consumer behavior show that individuals offer greater consideration to online shared advice and information, spend more time with websites that provide third party evaluations, and other studies suggest that such knowledge can directly influence buying decisions, even though it is obtained from solely 'virtual' sources. Indeed many of the documented benefits of new media use (increased credibility, expected reciprocity) are directly related to its aspects of social interaction.

III. Interactivity

New media interactivity lets users become more than just passive stimulation recipients, unlike watching television or listening to the radio. Interactivity can be generally defined as the degree to which users are engaged in real-time modifications of the form and content of a mediated environment. Interactivity is one of the defining features of new media platforms, providing greater access to information as well as fostering increased user control and interaction with content on social media. The interactivity is context-dependent.

Interactivity refers to a user-centered interaction with computers, messages, or other users in an online social networking setting, concentrating on the experiential dimension of networking operation. Although interactivity can be easy in some ways (e.g., simply filling out forms, clicking on links), it can also be more involved and complex, such as allowing individuals to create content online. Studies show that higher interactivity rates can lead to higher engagement and more positive attitudes towards websites along with greater credibility of the source. This user interactivity allows users to engage in personal social networking by choosing the content, timing, and act of communication.

Specific social media technologies allow customers to take active control and conduct bidirectional communications. Active regulation takes place within the context of social networking and involves the involvement and participation of all interested participants, including individual users, networked individuals or societies groups and brands.

IV. Targeted market

Social media offers advertisers the ability to target viewers and customers based on the personal interests of the website users and what their friends want. List country music as one of your passions, for example, on a social networking site; you'll most likely see advertisements for country music concerts and musicians. Advertising on some pages will also highlight which country artists your friends like to make a personal connection to. Marketers successfully reach the people who are most interested in what they have to sell with such "smart" ads and advertisements. In addition, social networking enables word of mouth to promote products beyond just what advertisement does.

A well-cited example of viral marketing blends market-oriented networking with implied advocacy: the free email service Hotmail appended the hyperlinked advertising to the bottom of every outgoing email message, "Get your free email at Hotmail," thereby targeting the social neighbors of every current user thus taking advantage of the implicit advocacy of the user (Montgomery, 2001). The traditional methods of marketing do not appeal to some customer segments. Apparently, some customers enjoy the appearance of being on the cutting edge or "in the know" and thus gain pleasure from promoting new, exciting goods.

V. Customer Service

Customer Service is another critical field in the marketing of social media. Website designers sometimes can not escape any degree of complexity within a website's architecture. Hence, a proactive customer service system is required. Links to Frequently Asked Questions (FAQs) and links to online representatives are useful in helping clients with the search or purchasing process. Not only should a marketer have online assistance. In many cases, contacting a service is more convenient for consumers. Therefore, consideration should be given to using a toll-free telephone number for clients. Order fulfillment and fast delivery systems are just as important to the growth of e-loyalty as the other factors. A thoughtful logistics system that ensures a quick delivery after the checkout process contributes to customer satisfaction, which in turn contributes to loyal conduct. In addition to delivery speed, the logistics system will allow for multiple ways to deliver goods. Some consumers, including FedEx and UPS, choose to get the product shipped by parcel service. Others may want to pick up a product in a physical store to have someone talk to. A consumer who buys something on the internet has one major drawback compared to a real-space user. Internet clients can't touch, feel, or experience the positive before buying it. This makes a shopper uncertain about purchasing a product. To mitigate this uncertainty, a social media marketer should be providing well-known, good product quality brands and, of course, guarantees.

Challenges For Organisations In Using Social Media Marketing

L ike any other media, the social platform also offers challenges to the business. Challenges such as an invasion of user privacy, aggressive advertising, lack of e-commerce abilities, lack of brand controls, and certain legal pitfalls can be major disruptions to social platforms. The consumers do not like intrusive advertisements and communications, and they are not ready to share their privacy that can be pervaded on an online platform. Aggressive advertisements are a definite no-no in an online platform. The consumers are there on the platforms to talk to their friends and do not like strangers being intrusive, aggressive communications, and overselling. The businesses need to be careful against legal frameworks related to data mining, research, and selling online. As social platforms are user created contents and users are free to take actions and comments, so with a single mistake from a business may lead to the brand campaign going out of control. The biggest challenges are treating the social network as a broadcasting media instead of a social platform for communities of practice.

The online world creates not only opportunities for the social media marketing process but also problems and challenges. Web openness makes online information accessible to all stakeholders, which emphasizes the need for continuity in online marketing communication preparation, design, execution, which control. There are five major drawbacks to remember when it comes to social media marketing, which are:

I. Time intensive

As the name suggests, social media is interactive, and the two-way conversations are productive.

The essence of social network marketing shifts, with an emphasis on creating long-term relationships that can translate into further sales. Someone has to be responsible for monitoring each network, answering comments, answering questions, and posting customer important product information. It will be difficult for companies without a company to handle such social networks to compete. The first and perhaps the most critical, preliminary consideration is that social media marketing requires a substantial investment in time. As a general rule, it's fanciful to simply dabble in a few social media platforms and expect to achieve big returns. A business must meet the time commitment necessary and either approve or deny the commitment as realistic for its service.

II. Trademark and copyright concern

When using social media to advertise their brands and goods, it is of utmost importance for businesses to protect their own trademarks and copyrights. Brands and other intellectual property in a business are also just as important as the goods or services they sell. The power of social media to enable casual and impromptu contact, often in real-time, can help businesses promote their products and disseminate copyrighted content, but it can also encourage the infringement of the trademarks and copyrights of a company by third parties. Marketers will periodically track the use of their trademarks and copyrights while using social media, whether from a third party channel or the company's own social media channels. Companies should track their own social media accounts as well as social media channels from third parties to ensure that those delivering content through the media outlets does not abuse their intellectual property. Web monitoring and scanning tools are available to detect the use of the logos and copyrights of your business on third-party sites, including reviewing profile or user names on social media platforms that are identical or significantly similar to your company's name or trademarks.

Where left unchecked, this type of business impersonation can harm the brand and credibility of a company; such monitoring can also serve as a positive indicator of business performance. Companies should consider reserving usernames that suit or closely imitate their trade names and marks on various social media platforms. Therefore, businesses will provide terms and conditions for their own social media sites, with clauses outlining whether the products or intellectual property of third parties are to be properly used. Marketers undertaking those forms of social media marketing campaigns, particularly promotions and user-generated content campaigns, should have laws in place that include strict prohibitions on infringement and impersonation of trademarks and copyrights.

III. Trust, Privacy, and Security Issues

Social media can also include trust, privacy, and data protection issues to promote one's brand, goods, or services. Companies need to be aware of these concerns and take reasonable steps to reduce their exposure to the liability related to the collection, use, and preservation of personal data. Trust, particularly the specific transactional security and privacy dimensions, plays a critical role in generating consumer loyalty to social media marketers. A Ratnasingham study has shown that fear of online credit card fraud was one of the key reasons consumers didn't make more comprehensive online transactions. In addition, privacy issues for some big social media campaigns have contributed to a public relations crisis resulting in significant degradation of the brand image. Social media sites like Facebook and Twitter typically have their own privacy policy regulating their use of user data, and third parties execute personal data on the social media site. Marketers using social media platforms from third parties should ensure that their marketing strategies do not enable customers or any other party to participate in activities that would breach the privacy policy of the social media business, and marketers should also ensure that they abide by the policies. Companies running their own blogs or other social media sites should also maintain detailed policies that document the company's data collection, usage, and storage activities, as well as any third-party obligations with respect to privacy and data protection. Trust, which is closely linked to health, is a very important factor in the behavior of the online buying process. You can't feel, smell, or touch the drug, in general. You can't look through the head of the salesperson. Such forms of building trust are also removed on the Internet. The brand trust typically helps to reduce confusion. Further, trust is a part of the attitudinal loyalty system. It is also clear that loyalty in general and brand trust, in particular, will help overcome some of the drawbacks of the Internet, such as overcoming perceptions that the Internet is an insecure, deceptive, and unreliable marketplace. Such biases actually also prohibit some potential customers from doing business on the internet. A "third-party approval" is a trust-building device.

IV. User-Generated Content (UGC)

Users have spent more time and exchanged more information, thoughts, and opinions with each other easily over the Internet over the last few years. There have also emerged new ways of content creation, communication, and collaboration on the Internet. Marketing campaigns involving social networking sites or other social media also integrate user-generated (UGC) content into the market. UGC enables Internet users to comment in different ways, such as images, videos, podcasts, ratings, comments, posts, and forums, for example. Whether it's a website-shared video or photo, or messages that website users disseminate to network members, UGC holds a lot of promise as a marketing tool. Furthermore, user-generated content comes with a fairly high degree of consumer legitimacy, particularly if, for example, someone created the content or a tweet between friends. Requesting user-generated content in conjunction with a marketing strategy involves some risk of incurring legal liability for content produced by a person engaging in the campaign. However, marketers may take certain steps to mitigate legal risks associated with marketing campaigns involving the distribution of user-generated content through social media.

V. Negative Feedbacks

Social media, in a way, turns customers into marketers and advertisers, and customers may generate a positive or negative impact on the company, its goods, and its services, depending both on how the business is portrayed online and on the nature of the products and services provided to the customer. Consumer-generated product reviews, photos, and tags, which serve as a valuable source of knowledge for consumers making online product decisions, have increasingly increased across the Internet and have had a significant influence on electronic commerce with the advent of Web 2.0 technologies. One aspect of social networking, which is especially detrimental to marketing campaigns, is the negative post reactions. Unhappy consumers or industry rivals may post frustrating or offensive images, articles, or videos, and not much can be done by a marketer to avoid such occurrences. Even, it is difficult to ignore negative or other non-constructive reviews. Social networks must be handled quickly enough to respond immediately, and offensive messages need to be neutralized, which takes longer.

Halligan and Shah identified that there are a variety of things that businesses believe to be unimportant because of which they fail to take the benefit form social media marketing effectively:

Not Developing a Marketing Strategy:

Some businesses do not take social media seriously and believe that just creating a page would be enough. Just like other mediums, social media platforms also require a workable marketing strategy;

Gathering Followers not Networks:

Some companies are only busy in generating users and people who could join their company page. They fail to focus on developing networks of people who could benefit them; customers who could strategically benefit them etc.;

Focus Only on Social Media:

Social media can be of great help and support if it is aligned with other offline marketing tools.

Some companies only focus on social media for marketing and do not invest at all in other marketing mediums;

Abusing:

Some social media blogs do not give proper attention to their blogs due to which sometimes people even start using negative or abusive language for one another. This does not only distracts people from coming to your blog but will also create a negative impression about your business.

The online marketing world offers social media marketing professionals a variety of rewards and also challenges. The consumers are more divided and constructive, but, on the other hand, the organization has the ability to incorporate various modes and knowledge categories in a dynamic message. Social networking also helps businesses to collect, track, evaluate, and use customer data and reviews to better target and customize online audiences. In reality, Internet and social media applications' unique characteristics make incorporating integrated web marketing both unavoidable and effective for a web approach. The cost-related considerations, social networking, interactivity, targeted business opportunities, and customer support are excellent features for companies to take a proactive-reactive approach and thrive in social media marketing. On the other hand, the drawback of social media marketing such as time-intensive issues, trademark and copyright issues, trust issues, privacy and security issues, user-generated content (UGC), and negative consumer reviews are major obstacles that social media marketers face. Those characteristics can be implemented according to designing and implementing a particular model of implemented social media marketing. The message conveyed online should first be infused with the core corporate principles, then tailored to the organization's online strategy and strategies, and finally personalized for a particular mix of the targeted audience and online platform. Selecting the right communication-mix must take into consideration the characteristics of social media marketing.

Working With Social Media

Companies initially establish their priorities and ambitions for the future, in particular with regard to marketing and promotion, and then create pages or make profiles on social media sites such as Facebook, Twitter, and so on. They keep updating them with the latest details, images, company news, latest innovations, product and service details, accomplishments, revenues, optional information. The profile is tagged along with search engines like Yahoo, Google, Bing, and so on so that the link and profile can show up at the top when people are searching for business. The corporation also advertises on the general social media areas from which people often come to learn about the business's happenings. Furthermore, businesses develop interesting ideas, commercials, competitions, promotions, and a number of other activities in which people get involved. Such events also encourage more people to enter the company and get linked to the company—further tracking and review of feedback, reviews, and consumer happenings by companies. Via social media firms, they often build various blogs in discussion forums where people share their thoughts, helping businesses gain healthier thoughts and innovative tips that are also really helpful to them. Such social pages and forums are also linked by businesses to their main websites and portals through which they also get people into the habit of visiting their websites and getting knowledge about the various products, features, and happenings. Zarrella suggests online communities have become so strong they can make or break a corporation, person, or society. As previously mentioned, social media marketing is about developing relationships, and such relationships can be preferred, or potential rivals may also create their own network to split different businesses.

These are some of the notable mistakes that companies make as a result of which they miss out on the social media benefits, particularly in the marketing context. Personally, the researcher believes that it is important for companies to first develop an effective marketing plan in order to gain the full value out of social media for marketing and promotion. The approach should comply with the priorities and objectives of the organization. The researcher further analyzes that it is also necessary for the company to actively monitor and maintain all of its social media pages, blogs, and accounts and respond promptly to the queries and comments from the people.

Tools And Services Can Be Used To Magnify Presence In The Digital Realm

L ive online consumers of today. Anything happens over the internet, from product analysis to purchase. However, as a small business, reaching the connected public isn't always easy. Moving and responding in the online world is hard enough for big brands – it can seem very daunting to smaller businesses.

Yet there is good news. You can quickly nail down a more detailed image of what your business needs to survive and succeed in the digital world by breaking your efforts down into manageable steps and asking some basic questions.

Move 1: Assessing Basic Connectivity Needs

With the growth of the mobile workforce and cloud storage solutions, high-speed internet has become a requirement for most small businesses, rather than a luxury. Take the time to answer these four questions to help you narrow down your Internet Service Provider (ISP) options:

What Internet speed do I need for my business?

Consider the number of people who can use the internet concurrently, the size and extent of your uploads and downloads, and the essential services you frequently use. Plug those numbers into an online speed-gage device to decide what speeds to check for.

Will I use VoIP Telephones (Voice over Internet Protocol)?

The bandwidth required for VoIP service depends on how many calls you will be making at the same time. VoIP services shouldn't be much of a hassle for small companies with minimal phone use. It can not be said the same for call-heavy enterprises.

What's my contingency plan if we go down the internet?

Many small business owners do not know that a few minutes of downtime every day can be as much as thousands of dollars wasted each year. If your company is still able to perform vital offline operations, you probably won't need a comprehensive backup plan. However, if your company is reliant on running the internet, look for plans with more extensive offers of help.

How high is my estimate?

Small business Internet pricing varies depending on the form of link-cable, DSL, satellite, or fiber. Additional features such as service and infrastructure and the size of the network can also affect costs. Before you start shopping around, look at your internet budget to stop signing up for more bandwidth than you can afford.

If you would like to further simplify your quest for an ISP, do not hesitate to ask around in your field. Nothing beats learning stories from fellow small business owners right away.

Step 2: Study online customer engagement software

You can start identifying programs to boost internal efficiencies and customer relationship engagement (CRM) using a secure internet plan in place. There are many resources out there, and many small businesses are fairly inexpensive. Ask the following questions to select the best CRM system and free up more time for you and the rest of your team:

What tasks or processes could help me with the online CRM tools?

To find out which resource suits you best, figure out the specific tasks you need help with. When you regularly send newsletters online, check for automatic messages. If you rely heavily on revenues from outbound sales, consider a program that helps collect consumer information.

Will I look for solutions based on the Cloud?

On-premise CRM systems house servers and data in customer offices while cloud-based applications house information remotely, providing users with internet access to that data. Although both solutions have their own pros and cons, cloud-based services are by far the better choice for companies seeking flexible access to safe, reliable storage.

How high is scalability?

One enormous benefit of online CRM tools is that they typically evolve and scale faster than conventional solutions. Even if you don't expect much growth over the next year or two, it's worth looking at smaller annual fluctuations – particularly during the holidays – to find out how much scalability means to your company.

Phase 3: Protect Important Digital Information

Once you've found out and resources you're going to use in the digital realm, you'll need to set up some security protocols for how to use those programs.

Every year an unprecedented number of companies fell victim to cybercriminals, and data theft and small businesses are no exception. Indeed, according to the Internet Security Report from Symantec, 43 percent of all cyber attacks reported in 2015 were aimed at small businesses. Consider these questions to help ensure safe communications within your organization and determine the level of readiness for information security at your business.

Which kind of details do I need to protect for customers/clients?

The confidential information varies from small business to small business. For example, a retail corporation might need to protect transaction information and financial records, while a healthcare sector entity would need additional protection to manage private medical information.

Need Cybersecurity Insurance for my business?

Many small businesses are unable to afford to face litigation that comes with data theft and loss – a breach may spell disaster for a limited-resource company. When you do not have the money to cover legal bills in the case of data theft, it is worth considering cybersecurity protection.

Is there a formal policy on the protection of information in place?

Strict password policies, steps to optimize firewall safety, download/streaming rules, and antivirus software regulations should be part of your security policies. Don't hesitate to spell out the implications of breaching the policy created.

Step 4: Plan Digital Marketing and Outreach

You can start developing your digital presence once you have successfully laid down ground rules for online processes and security. Social media is a hit-and-miss affair, for many small business owners. Some don't see the point of putting a lot of work into it, while others have tried but haven't seen the good results they'd hoped for.

The reality is that social media marketing has everything to do with establishing relationships with prospects and clients. Results require time and effort to see. To help decide how social media will fit into the broad picture of your brand, find out the answers to these three questions:

What are the basic objectives of social media marketing for my company?

Small companies have multiple reasons to dive into social media marketing – from customer experience to brand recognition to lead generation. By keeping your targets concrete, you will have a better image of the tools and strategies needed to keep your social campaigns running like well-oiled machines.

What audiences should the firm target?

Understanding the preferences, desires, and pain points of your prospective customers will make it easier for you to recognize the social networks which can provide the most leverage. It can also help to pinpoint what kind of content your customers care about.

Who is responsible for social media marketing?

Examining the online marketing strategy will help you decide if you can recruit someone to do full or part-time social media. Several small businesses have already outsourced their ads on social media.

The Takeaway

Whether it's finding the perfect ISP or stepping up your information security steps, the above questions will help you easily and efficiently decide the digital needs of your company. Only allow yourself plenty of space to explore your choices and set up your company for online and offline long-term success.

There's a lot of stuff that needs your attention as your startup develops. Using a project management tool is one way to ensure you are able to handle the marketing projects on growth efficiently.

Let's take a deeper dive into these developments and how your company can profit from them.

1. Authentic marketing on content is on the rise.

Content marketing is nothing new, but it is and remains a strong marketing tool tight on resources for small businesses. You can build interest in your goods by adding a blog to your website while establishing your brand as the industry's leading think tank. Writing about subjects your customers are interested in is a perfect way to create brand recognition and customer loyalty. You'll create confidence by demonstrating that you care more than just selling to your customers.

"Authenticity is possibly one of the most important attributes a brand can inherit from the experience of its larger customer," said Shoperr CEO Aviram Kadosh. "This value has a direct correlation with other essential brand health metrics, such as confidence, reliability [and] readiness for trials." With content marketing gaining prominence, being authentic in your content is crucial. Whether it's a social media post or your blog, make sure your clients get a good balance between selling goods and taking the time to help them develop their company through actionable therapy.

2. The demand for chatbots is rising.

Sixty-five percent of U.S. millennials choose to use chatbots when interacting with brands, according to a Capterra study. Yet, most of the small companies surveyed didn't use the technology. You want to build the best online customer experience possible because consumers continue to migrate online. A chatbot running on your website means consumers are able to answer their simple questions at all hours of the day or night, even if you're working on various tasks.

"AI-powered chatbots can be used for customer service, significantly extending the communication strategy with a guided message," said Joey Penick, CenturyLink's vice president of marketing. "These chatbots have become so lifelike that many consumers don't even know the difference, but provide the added advantage of being able to collect, evaluate and provide actionable data that can be used to enhance the customer experience."

3. Voice quest gains traction.

With mobile apps and voice services continuing to grow in popularity, such as Amazon's Alexa, voice search is being increasingly used. If your company is online, in 2019 and beyond, there's a chance people can find your website or digital marketing materials via voice search.

"We had to adjust to the increasing usage of the smartphone a few years ago," said Blog Hands owner Chris Hornak. "And now, according to

Google, smartphone searches are more than 50 percent [of searches.] Marketers will need to start adjusting to voice searches, which already make up 20 percent of mobile searches, and that is expected to continue to expand similarly to web searches." From the viewpoint of Hornak as a digital marketing professional with experience in developing blog content for small businesses, the company organizes the quest.

"Digital marketers will need to change their marketing strategies to be conversational and address questions directly in plain terms," said Hornak. "One easy tactic they should implement in 2019 is to provide their website with FAQs – [responses to questions] that consumers frequently have about their product. Remember to be informative and conversational about the responses."

4. Software analytics tend to be key to performance.

Any company with an online presence knows how important it is to use consumer data to make business decisions. Most brands are beginning to make data analytics a priority, but marketers still have a way to go when we interviewed him in 2017, said Curtis Tingle, CMO of smart media distribution company Valassis. His remarks for 2019 hold true.

Access to client data goes far further than simple demographics, Tingle said. Today marketers can control online and offline advertising habits and preferences of customers, locations all day long, history of sales, response to marketing, etc. This, he said, helps you to personalize texts, photos, and deals through platforms, including at-home level.

"Marketers need to know how to make better use of the data they collect," Tingle said. "Consumers are continually feeding personal information to the businesses they engage with – from shopping habits to favorite items to the best ways to reach them through ads and marketing campaigns. With this exchange of data, consumers are searching for some kind of return, whether in the form of more personalized commercials or targeted coupons/deals."

Observation by Tingle is important. Marketers need to do more than just collect data. The data must be valid, and businesses must use the data to enhance marketing strategies. It is not necessary to gather details alone.

"It's going to be more focused on collecting and using data from purpose," Penick said. "Intent data is information directly regarding the actions of an individual or business. This can be gathered from a company website by looking at which sites a customer accessed, how long they remained on those sites, and which links they clicked on or received from a third party. Intent data can be used to target the best consumer opportunities and develop more targeted strategies to achieve better sales."

5. AI is to be the best mate of a marketer.

For years to come, artificial intelligence is expected to play a significant part in marketing. While AI has been discussed for years, we are reaching a point where small businesses could benefit better from its use. AI's ability to process data rapidly and turn it into actionable information is one primary advantage.

Take Fizziology, for instance. The agency, which is specialized in customer understanding, likes to combine human intelligence with AI.

"While artificial intelligence remained a top buzzword of 2018, we'll see it grow from a 'hot subject' to an actionable resource in 2019," said Ben Carlson, co-founder, and Fizziology co-president. "As part of this development, we'll see companies applying human intelligence to AI to make it more relevant and actionable to specific business goals." For example, as Nike's new face, we've done a study on the reaction to Colin Kaepernick. There were more than 3 million brand mentions on Twitter on the campaign's first day. While updates on blacklists of the brand, consuming and crushing product drove features, those discussions just made up 3 percent of notices the day of the declaration and under 1 percent of notices during the time after the declaration." With internet-based life responses to the obliteration of product driving the sequence of media reports, it would've been simple for an advertiser to miss the genuine marking sway. Rather, the information was gathered and deciphered through crafted by both the Fizziology staff and AI. "While AI amassed the notices of Kaepernick from internet-based life, it took a human to comprehend the genuine brand sway, contextualizing factors running from bots attempting to influence the discussion to occasional patterns in social notices," Carlson said. Fizziology's model is somewhat extraordinary for independent ventures, as the Kaepernick ad crusade was one of the most-discussed battles of 2018. Notwithstanding, the possibility that your business can profit by innovation helping sort and carry significance to information is an important one for organizations all things considered.

The main concern

These five tech patterns are required to impact promoting in 2019 and past, however that doesn't mean you have to promptly begin utilizing unique and further developed innovation to showcase your business successfully. "The fundamental standards of how you market and construct a brand haven't changed – in spite of what everybody says – in the previous 10 or 15 years," said Allen Adamson, an assistant educator at New York University's Stern School of Business and fellow benefactor of Metaforce. "What innovation has done by, and large is amplified what was in every case valid." Adamson clarified that, while extravagant new showcasing apparatuses appear every year, verbal promoting still issues. Decades back, shoppers may have asked their companions face to face where they ought to go for the best burger around. Presently, Adamson says, individuals "ask every one of their companions" by playing out a snappy web search and perusing surveys of burger joints in the zone. The expansion in innovation doesn't change the center ideas of promoting. However, the new innovation magnifies each triumph and disappointment. Previously, serving a terrible burger to one client may prompt the despondent client to advise their companion not to eat there. Presently, a furious Yelp audit can deflect many forthcoming clients. Seeing new mechanical instruments can enormously profit your business. On the flip side, if you don't see how the innovation can support you, there's no utilization, including new instruments in with the general mish-mash. Adamson, who filled in as the director for North America of Landor

Associates when it assisted with marking for significant brands like Marriott and HBO, says numerous organizations have issues getting found the best in class advertising instruments. "It's similar to watching 8-year-olds play soccer: It's only a ball, and nobody is on guard," said Adamson. "Everybody is pursuing the gleaming new article. Regardless of what technology you purchase, if you don't know how to use it very well, it won't give you a competitive advantage in the marketplace. "You do not need to act on any of the trends mentioned in this article. On the other hand, adding a chatbot or more genuine content marketing to your company will bring your business to a new level of customer experience and interaction. They have to ask the following four questions:

1) Who are my audience?
2) What are my business gaps, and where?
3) Will this technology help to close the gaps in my business?

4) Do I have the ability to maintain this technology in the long term?

"Using Gould's questions as a test will ensure that you don't blindly leap into a marketing trend that isn't suitable for your company. Be aware of the 2019 marketing trends, but before you act, take a careful look at where your company stands. Asana Asana is, by far, the most commonly used project management tool for startups. It's a really flexible and user-friendly framework that makes it simple to get started.

GSuite

Gsuite is another platform for project management that you can use for your startup, particularly if you're just starting. All of the features found are free to use, and a Google account is required.

What makes this a better alternative to Asana is the fact that many of the different features like

Google Docs, Google Sheets, Gmail, and even Google's calendar are very familiar to people.

At the same time, it helps you to store your files in Google Drive, so your team members can easily download and have access to them anywhere.

The minute you sign up for your Gmail account, you'll get 15 GB of free file storage. What's cool about that is that you just access the storage space for the files.

That means it will not take your storage space, even if you create a huge Google Doc file. If you need extra space, you can register for a paid account. The monthly rate is very competitive, so it will not be a burden on your budget.

The only drawback to Gsuite is that when you view them, even if it provides you with a dashboard, each will open up to a different website. When you have opened a lot of windows or tabs, it may eventually cause your browser to look so cluttered.

Marketing Automation

The marketing automation tools and systems are the best friends of a start-up. They can also compensate for routine processes that tend to take time. That means you have more time to concentrate on those critical to growing your startup.

Zapier

Essentially, Zapier allows two or more devices or programs to communicate with each other. In addition to the numerous ready-made tasks you can use (called "zaps"), Zapier also allows you to create your own zaps that are specific to what you require.

IFTTT

IFTTT functions in the same way as Zapier in that it acts as a bridge for interaction between devices and programs.

One advantage over Zapier is that it isn't just about software programs and phones. IFTTT also integrates with various consumer-facing applications, and you can use this to help you change your office lighting and temperature. It can even make ordering the favorite pizza of your team really simple, perfect when you need to punch in a few extra hours to meet a deadline after work.

Another is that it comes with an interface built specifically to cater for the usual tasks that you do on your cell phone. Such apps (known as DO apps) make it easy for you to snap a photo (DO camera) or take down notes and store it in your cloud (DO Note) storage.

Because IFTTT follows the format "If-This-Then-That" (hence the name), each function (so-called "recipes") involves just one stage.

HubSpot

HubSpot is more than just a versatile CRM. It's packed with a variety of tools allowing you to plan and share your blog posts automatically on your various social media platforms.

At the same time, in your email folder, it connects all social interactions to real people. This way, you can keep track of the conversation in your database with each of the people and prioritize those who are more likely to convert to paying customers.

eClincher

The eClincher is a social media marketing automation tool that enables you to handle multiple social media profiles, pages, and groups effectively in one dashboard.

Aside from offering the standard features, you find in most automation systems for social media marketing; it also comes with features to make it easy to communicate with your marketing team and delegate various tasks to complete without leaving the site.

EClincher can also recommend web-based trending content and various social media platforms. Not only does this feature help to reduce the time you spend doing inbound marketing, but it also makes it easier to come up with ideas while you develop your marketing strategy for content.

Crowdfire

Crowdfire is an advantageous online marketing tool to use to promote the brand and products of your startup.

Crowdfire will monitor your Twitter and Instagram accounts once you specify your specific marketing goals, and give you suggestions to help you achieve them. Thus, the name of your company stays before your target audience and keeps them interested in your brand and products.

Content creation

According to the Digital Marketing Center, one of the key challenges faced by marketers is producing digital that is high quality and useful.

Here are some useful tools for easing the project.

SEMRush

SEMRush does more than just help you study keywords. This online resource provides you with insight into how well your website does with your keywords.

It also allows you to take a look at how the sites of your competitors work. So you can see which keywords and content appeal to your target market and use them on your website.

Zerys

Zerys is a strategy, planning, and development platform for all-in-one content. The user-friendly interface and free tool suite lets you prepare and create a comprehensive content strategy for your inbound marketing campaigns.

What sets Zerys apart from other sites is that by delegating the content writing to skilled authors, it lets you save more time on your inbound marketing tasks. You post the title and kind of material that you need. The writers then offer their price for creating the material for you. You can then review the draft they produce and pay only if you 're satisfied with what they submit.

HubSpot Blog Ideas Generator

This free tool will create a list of title ideas to help you get the juices flowing. If you have picked a specific keyword, but don't know what subject to write about.

Usage is straightforward. All you're to do is type your chosen keyword in the given space and then click the "Give Me Blog Ideas" button to get a list of suggestions.

HubSpot's Blog Name Generator has been helpful to me in developing titles not just for blog posts on my website, but also for successfully accepted guest posts.

CoSchedule's Headline Analyzer

Is a handy resource to help you gauge how eye-catching your chosen blog post title is. A title with a minimum score of 70 is a strong title.

Although it offers you insights into which parts of your title need to be changed, it does not provide any practical suggestions to boost your ranking. Yes, when you check various versions of your title right, you will need a bit of patience.

Grammarly

I don't know about you, but nothing more bothers me than reading through an article that has a lot of grammar and punctuation errors. Even if the material is packed densely with details, the mistakes are sufficient to distract me.

If you can't afford to employ a proofreader and editor right now to review your content before it's written, the next best choice is Grammarly.

Although the free version is good enough, I personally prefer the paid version, as it advises you on your document to avoid important grammar errors depending on what type of content you are publishing.

Another factor I want to go with the premium edition is that it contains a checker on plagiarism. This ensures that the content I create is not only error-free but original as well.

Also, it comes with a browser add-on that tests the content that you plan to post or send via email to your social media accounts.

Hemingway

One drawback I find with Grammarly is that it has no features to help you test your content's readability ease. Here's where Hemingway comes in handy, particularly if the product of startup is very technical.

This free online tool tests not only your content for grammar errors, but also tests which sentences and paragraphs in your content are difficult to read and frustrating to understand. It also tells you what approximate time your reader would need to finish reading through your post.

Crew.co

If you need a web- or mobile-specific developer or designer for your startup but can not afford to get one in-house, Crew.co has a pool of skilled developers and designers that you can select for your projects.

After you've submitted your project to Crew.co, you'll get a list of the best-fit developers or designers to complete your project.

Venngage

More people prefer documents to visual content such as infographics since they are easier to understand.

Venngage is an online platform that allows you to create beautiful infographics quickly based on the data you've been researching. You can choose from any of their models, or you can create one from scratch.

Camtasia

Video has become one of the fastest-growing marketing trends for content today. Currently, video accounts for 74 percent of all internet traffic. Furthermore, 83 percent of marketers say they want to make more videos if their marketing budget allows.

Camtasia is a video editing application that can be of use to you and your company. Its drag-and-drop dashboard makes your video content quick to capture and edit.

It also has an extensive library so you can include a host of different effects such as captions, cursor highlights, and call-to-action buttons to use to improve the effectiveness of your video in lead generation.

Lead Generation

That Generating Leads in Inbound Marketing is important. Without it, you're not going to be able to collect the information you need to cultivate and turn the tourists to your platform into clients.

InstaPage

This is an electronic platform where you can quickly create eye-catching landing pages, which will help to increase your conversion rate for visitors to lead. Easily integrate these landing pages with several third-party apps like SalesForce, MailChimp, and even Facebook.

Its "what you see is what you get" easy-to-use landing page editor comes with a built-in A / B check tool. This tool lets you see the success of your landing page once it goes live. These can help you get the most conversion from the landing page you build here, along with real-time analytics and the capacity to add team members.

Wistia

You'll need a place to host this other than your website if you are making videos to generate leads for your startup. But, your website does not slow down, which can have a dramatic impact on your search engine rankings.

Wistia is a video hosting platform that many startups prefer, even if you have to pay for their hosting services. For example, your embedded video loading to your site is faster than other sites for video hosting. Wistia also offers a variety of elements and services to its users to help you create more leads.

Wistia also offers you a more detailed analytics analysis of your various videos. In this way, you can see in more detail how each of your videos works, and how they help you achieve your marketing goals

Chatfuel

Chatbots quickly becomes one of the most powerful resources used by brands when it comes to leading generation and conversion of sales.

Chatfuel is a startup that provides a variety of services that allow you to create a Facebook Messenger chatbot quickly based on your inbound marketing objectives. The best part of their services is, you can make your company a very own chatbot for free.

Learnable online courses are a good choice for offerings for lead generation. Teachable is an online platform that offers you practical strategies for successfully completing and launching your very first course online.

What sets Teachable apart from other sites for creating courses online is that it offers a host of content videos that will direct you through each process of creating an online course.

In addition to this, those who want to go with their Professional Plan receive live coach calls where they can get expert advice and feedback on your particular challenge in designing your online course.

Influencer marketing

The marketing influencer remains an important inbound marketing tool in 2018. These tools will help you use that to promote the brand and products of your startup.

Ninja Outreach

This is a robust blogger outreach platform that helps you to quickly search your niche for bloggers and influencers. If you find them, the details can be saved to ordered lists.

The platform also has a robust library of templates that you can use to create drip email campaigns to reach out and communicate with the influencers you like. So, you should keep track of who you have reached, and you don't risk turning them off by coming across as a nag.

Tap Influence

Tap Influence is another forum inside your niche, which you can use to reach out and communicate with influencers.

Like Ninja Outreach, the website features micro-influencers primarily at Tap Influence. These are influencers on some of their social media pages, which have less than 100 K followers. Despite having a lower base of followers, marketers tend to partner with them, as they have a more dedicated group of followers. Its asking price is also considerably smaller than macro-influencers and celebrities.

BuzzSumo

This is an electronic platform where you can find within your niche which content is trending based on your chosen keyword.

Around the same time, if you are trying to incorporate influencers into your inbound marketing campaign, BuzzSumo is a fantastic resource to use. That's because BuzzSumo also offers you a list of main influencers as well as their Twitter information and, more importantly, their levels of engagement when it comes to sharing content written by others.

Affiliate Marketing

Even if you run a startup, there is nothing wrong with receiving any extra profit from delving into the marketing of the affiliates.

Weave Social

Is an affiliate marketing network that links you to online retailers so that through the content you post on your web; you can earn money.

Whenever you sign up for a free account, you can select from a vast catalog of the products and brands with which you want to partner. Weave Social will then provide you with a connection that you can now insert into your blog. Clicking on this link in your content and making a purchase from your readers will give you a commission from the sale.

ECommerce

If your company sells physical products, it's only fitting for your site to have an online store where your target market can search and buy your products conveniently.

BigCommerce

This is the leading eCommerce platform that facilitates the development and integration of an online store for your products on your website. The feature list includes solutions that make it easy for you and your company to handle payments and ship your goods to their customers.

In addition, BigCommerce offers solutions that allow you to sell your goods on Facebook, Amazon, and eBay. Such services make discovering and purchasing your goods much more convenient for your target audience, thereby helping you to increase your sales.

Analytics Marketers need to have in their arsenal of different resources; none is more important than analytics. Such tools give you a direct and measurable insight into how various elements are performing in your marketing plan, and decide which ones are working and which are not.

Google Analytics

The first thing that comes to mind when it comes to analytics is Google Analytics. It is not surprising, particularly because this remains today as the most widely used platform for analytics. That's because it's not about supplying you with results information for your website. It also offers perspectives that come from smartphone phones and even offline platforms.

DataBox

DataBox is a versatile KPI tool for enterprise analysis. It gathers the data for each of the metrics and presents it on a single dashboard, not only making it easy to track but also to interpret. You don't have to think about wasting time looking for them all over your CRM, that way.

What's great about DataBox is that it not only integrates seamlessly with a host of different CRMs and tech systems but also delivers the new metrics instantly on your computer or through their mobile app. This makes it much more easier to track and monitor the overall success of your campaigns.

Personal development

The field of online marketing is changing rapidly. That said, making sure you stay up-to-date with the latest trends and how to leverage these to improve your campaigns is crucial. At a similar time, being able to impart your aptitude and information to others will assist you with setting up yourself as the expert in your specialty and in your image.

CreativeLive

CreativeLive provides more than 1,500 online courses to help you learn new skills or enhance the skills you already possess.

Upon entering their site, you can find three separate class classes. The first one is its Air Class. These classes are free and will only be transmitted on a given date and time.

The second is online courses paid for by them. Some of the most recognized names in their respective industries pose certain individual classes. These classes are on-demand, so you'll be able to learn them at your own pace.

Then there are courses on Learning Path. Such online classes include a series of different individual paid online courses that CreativeLive has chosen to help you go deeper and quickly develop all the required skills.

Breathe University

They offer a host of personal and business growth training courses that you can complete right in the comfort of your home or office. The resource speakers are made up of young people who use their personal and professional experience to help others accomplish the goals they want.

Financial Peace University

As a company owner, the number one thing you need to help your business thrive is to be able to handle your money wisely.

The University of Financial Peace offers live workshops and online courses that teach you six principles to become financially stable and safe. While the principles here are geared to managing a household budget, I have personally applied many of the principles I have learned to handle the finances in my business, and it has been helpful to help me keep it in line.

Ads That Gives You The Right Investment Returns

"Half the money I spend on ads is wasted," was famously quoted as saying department store magnate John Wanamaker in Philadelphia. "I don't know which half of the trouble is." Wanamaker's dilemma remains today's bane of advertisers — especially small business owners on shoestring budgets. Like big names, advertisers like Pepsi, Adidas, Apple, and Ford, small companies can't afford to throw millions of dollars at Super Bowl advertisements or glamorous magazine advertising. If your ad budget is $5,000 or $50,000, you have to make a count for every dollar.

And that means doing the calculations to measure the return on investment for each ad campaign that you run.

What will be a return on investment?

Project Investment (ROI) tests the overall success of an investment, like an online advertising campaign. Relative to the initial expense, it explicitly links how much of the investment was returned.

Think about it like this: Let us say you're renting a targeted list of 100 dentists in your local zip code and giving them a package each with free samples of your groundbreaking new dental floss. Upon adding up the printing, post, rental list, and sampling costs, you can end up paying $3 for each package you send. This means that your campaign must bring in a profit of at least $300 to break even, and $600 to double your income.

Here's the good news: With the recession's double whammy and the Internet hitting conventional media outlets such as newspapers, magazines, television, and radio, there's never been a better opportunity to purchase quality ads at bargain-basement prices — even for a small business consumer.

The trick is to find the advertisement platform that suits your business and industry best and use it to get your buck's biggest bang. It's not just how much you pay at the end of the day, or how many eyeballs you get to. It's just how many people you can get in the door while still making enough money to keep your boat afloat. And while no promotional campaign is foolproof (there will always be some initial trial and error before you find out what works), if you do your homework in advance, you will get better results and spend less money.

"Electronicmail marketing, television, search marketing, and yellow pages usually deliver a better ROI for unknown or unbranded direct response deals," says Michael Weinstein, CEO of Primary Systems, South Salem, N.Y., Internet marketing business. "Banner ads, printing, and social media are better for current exposure businesses. Toyota, for example, would do better with banner ads when a one-time advertisement is better. For example, if you're trying to sell prepaid phone cards to Queens Indian immigrants or L.A. Mexican-Americans, local ethnic newspapers can be a low-cost way to reach the whole community in one shot and deliver discount coupons that will enable you to monitor your offer's response. Similarly, a targeted local or regional magazine may provide an affordable way to meet quilters or new relatives. Newspapers can usually charge $5 CPM to $25 CPM (cost per thousand impressions), depending on the size of the market and the size of the ad (quarter, half page or full page)— national magazine prices CPM 6 dollars average.

Broadcast

No media channel reaches more people than television, which is why it is still so common with advertisers but also why calculating ROI is so difficult. Although TV can be a fantastic way for the approximately 100 million people watching the Super Bowl advertise a new vehicle, it's not a cost-effective way to reach your target audience — even though you could pay $2.6 million for a 30-second spot. TV advertisement ranges from $10 CPM for local broadcast, to $35 CPM for a popular sitcom network commercial. That does not include the cost of spot production.

"If you need a general audience definition, TV can be fantastic," says Jerry Shereshewsky, a veteran ad agency and Grandparents.com CEO of New York City. "But as soon as you try to get narrower, you're out of luck." Direct TV is a better bet for small business owners, particularly inventors, with a blockbuster new kitchen gadget or the exercise machine that needs to be seen as credible. Both broadcast and cable TV networks deliver direct response advertisements of 30-, 60- and 120-seconds at a fraction of conventional spots' cost. Since DRTV spots typically include a "call to action," a toll-free number or web address can be flashed to allow you to calculate your ROI to the penny. If your product is hot, you could even land a contract with a DRTV production company in exchange for a share of the sales to cover the bill for your infomercial.

There's nothing like radio if you're trying to reach a particular audience when they're going to work in the morning or driving home at night. Radio is a low-cost way to attract loyal listeners of prominent DJs and talk show hosts with an average CPM of just over $4. More than just a pre-recorded spot, radio advertisement packages deliver. These also provide on-air introductions to your ad plus engaging competitions and giveaways, which can help you track and monitor your campaign's effectiveness.

Directory

Ads in the Yellow Pages may be old school, but if you're a plumber, electrician, locksmith, or another specialist of an emergency repair, you can't afford to be there. Ninety-six percent of U.S. households have at least one copy, according to the Yellow Page Publishing Association. If a pipe bursts, a toilet overflows, or at 2 a.m. someone locks himself out of his home, you want to be the first to get the call — even though no one knows the company's name is AAA Aardvark Plumbing.

But these days, in the Yellow Pages, there is more to ads than listing your phone number in large bold numbers. With customers and businesses increasingly turning to the Internet to find the service providers they need, online directories can also pay to list your business. AT&T's YellowPages.com reports that it produces more than 140 million monthly searches and that 55% of its customers have ordered a product or service from a retailer they find online. Merchants can incorporate interactive features such as video profiles, premium product lists, blogs, and search engine optimization to their lists.

Outdoor

Outdoor advertisement-the signs you see on buses, bus benches, subways, trains, airports, and elevators-is virtually impossible to measure in terms of ROI, but it can work well for dentists, attorneys, podiatrists and business schools trying to attract busy commuters. No, there's no better way to meet a captive audience at an average CPM of $2.26! But, while a small resort hotel does not have the ad budget of a Marriott or a Hilton, there's no better way to tell tired travelers about your hotel than with a sign that says "Pat's Bed and Breakfast, Exit 16."

Internet

This is no longer an unconventional ad medium; this year, Internet ads will reach $24.5 billion, up 4.5 percent from 2008, eMarketer research firm reports. In comparison to printing and broadcasting, Internet ads can be easily calculated thanks to tools that track web traffic and click-through. And it's also cheaper than conventional media since success is paid by many online sites, not conventional CPM based metrics.

Internet advertising falls into three simple categories:

banner advertising

The online print and broadcast sister, banners will give your constant advertisement visibility on a prominent website or advertising network, enabling you to connect your brand with a publication already trusted by your prospective customers. Banner advertising typically works well for e-commerce firms selling directly from their web pages and boasting well-established logos. Those are the types of businesses that can benefit from the fact that their next customer may be only one click away from them. CEO of Small Business Television, Susan Wilson Solovic, says, "banner ads work great for branding campaigns and set up products with a clear call for action." To get the most out of banner advertisements, it's best to run the banners on pages that reach the ideal demographic — working mothers, sports car fans, business travelers, or senior citizens. For example, if you're selling luxury vacations or expensive watches, an advertisement on The Huffington Post could be worth $7.50 to $15 CPM. You do not mind paying $25 CPM to $45 CPM to run your ad on AARP's platform if you're trying to target the wealthy baby boomer market. But beware: There are relatively low click-throughs on banner advertising, so make sure you don't spend more on banners than you can actually recover from sales.

E-mail Marketing

Unlike conventional direct mail with its high cost of sending, printing, and handling, you can blast out an e-mail marketing campaign for little more than the rental cost of the list alone — and start ringing up sales in minutes. You can pay a tenth of a penny to more than $1 per e-mail address for a targeted list of permission-based e-mail addresses depending on how narrow the market you're trying to reach (for example, divorced female fly fishermen, ages 35 to 45, in Jackson Hole, WY)

Once your list is selected, the rest is easy. Only whip up some copies, remember to pop up, and press send in a link to your web site. If you are sending your e-mail campaign to existing customers or hot prospects, you can easily track ROI by inserting a URL in your message containing a special tracking code or sending mailing recipients to a specific page on your website. A word of caution: "Spam lists" that include e-mail addresses collected from blogs, directories, and other sources without the permission of their recipients tend to circulate on the Internet. Beware of the bargain-basement lists offering millions of e-mail addresses — or else you might find your mailings blocked, and your business kicked off your ISP.

Search Engine Marketing (SEM)

Each store is just one click away on the Internet. That's why funding search terms on Google, Microsoft, AOL, and other common search engines is one of the most cost-effective ways to push clients to your site. In comparison to CPM-typically sold banner ads and e-mail marketing, pay-per-click marketing allows you to pay only when a prospective customer types in the appropriate keywords and clicks on the link to your website.

"Hunt is now the shoppers' method of choice, replacing both local newspaper ads and yellow pages," says Shereshewsky.

Even so, it's important to carefully choose your keywords and track your budget closely. Since common keywords like "toys," "shoes," and "travel" can be costly, endorsing more focused terms like "extra big women's shoes" or "luxury hiking trips in Nepal" is often more cost-effective. Be sure to check the ROI of the keywords you support (along with your ad copy and landing page) before you carry out your campaign in a large way.

Besides paid advertising tools, the Internet also offers the opportunity to carry out grassroots marketing campaigns at no-cost through forums, social networks, and bookmarking sites. But don't expect the kind of ROI you get from posters, e-mail, or search engine ads from Facebook or Twitter. Social media marketing, according to Weinstein, "is a fantastic medium for interacting with your clients, but it takes constant care and feeding and is not ideal for marketers looking for an immediate return." If you select a web, print, broadcast, or directory advertising platform for your next campaign, it pays to do the math before investing the hard-earned dollars of your business. A little preparation will now make sure you know which half of your advertising budget works — and which half you'd be better off spending elsewhere.

When it comes to an electronic marketing campaign, there is one aspect that matters more than any other: the return on investment (ROI). If you can optimize and maintain your ROI in the long term, your marketing strategy would be an overwhelming success, by definition.

So, which marketing campaigns online tend to have the highest ROI?

Initial Considerations

Before I can expect to address this question in any rational or substantive way, I have to explain a few initial points and lay the groundwork for my reasoning: ROI is a little difficult to pin down.

Investments are both time and resources.

Long-term ROI is distinct from short-term ROI.

Execution relies on marketing strategies.

Each enterprise is different.

With those worries out of the way, let's look at some of today's most common marketing tactics, and how they compare each other.

Paid Advertising

Most business owners who've tried it will tell you that paid advertising offers a successful ROI. There are nevertheless a few important factors that hinder paid ads, making it difficult to draw an unbiased conclusion on the strategy. The price for each click on a Google search ad, for example, will vary widely depending on which industry you're in, often up to $50 or more per click. Plus, with a paid advertisement campaign, you are not "building equity," no matter which platform you are; it is more about paying rent. When you cut support for paid ads, they turn off automatically, and the only lasting benefit you get from it is the profits you made when the ads were working.

Content Marketing and SEO

In comparison to paid advertising, it is theoretically feasible to get started in content marketing and SEO without any money investment. If you want to measure your strategy to a realistic level, however, it will take a substantial amount of time and/or money. When you start, the results will leave you wanting more, but the true power of content marketing and SEO is their ability to grow exponentially over time; instead of giving you linear results, as with paid ads, any new piece of content you create will carry an enduring, Semi-permanent interest in terms of web real estate, referral traffic and domain authority for your brand.

Social Media Marketing

Marketing social media social media marketing is another field where it is theoretically feasible to try with just a time estimate. Social media marketing can cost thousands of dollars for each month, depending on the size of your efforts. As for the value —- that's more difficult to calculate than outcomes you'll get from SEO or direct ads. You can calculate commitments, traffic, and conversions, but the prestige value your brand has created is hard to quantify accurately. Moreover, when it comes to social efficacy, there is a broad difference between sectors and the price of paid social media advertising.

Email marketing

Email marketing has been described as the highest online marketing technique for ROI, when properly applied, with 67 percent of companies citing this as the highest earner for them. Part of it is the low cost of making a list and sending out emails; time or money does not cost you much. There's also some growth factor because the importance of your email promotions increases with your list size. Nonetheless, email marketing relies on a variety of other interrelated approaches to be effective —

and actually have the email list built up first, which can be very expensive.

The Final Contender

Out of the major online marketing channels I have mentioned, it's hard to pick a clear winner, particularly after recognizing the considerations I outlined above. In the short-term, paid ads will produce a good return, and email marketing seems to work better for most companies once they've built up a large email list. Though, if I had to pick one "best" strategy when it comes to ROI, I would choose content marketing and SEO — thanks to its multifaceted range of effects, permanent value, and potential for compounding returns, there's just no better way to spend your marketing budget (though ideally, you'll pursue all of these strategies in one form or another).

How to Get the Best ROI

It's time to ask the most important question: "Is this strategy working?"

How do you measure your true return on investment (ROI)? When you're marketing your business, understanding how to interpret your campaign results is crucial.

When you truly know what's working and what's not, your advertising dollars will go toward the strategies that are moving the needle.

Get Specific with Your Goals

Without a clear goal in place, you won't know what to measure. Examples of specific campaign goals might be: increase store traffic by 25% during the holidays, boost traffic to the website by 15% in Q1, or build brand awareness over one fiscal year.

Discover What Works and What Doesn't

It is also crucial to pay close attention to your results during the campaign. For instance, which channels and programs are bringing your business the highest audience engagement? TV, digital, or both? Use A/B testing by running spots on the same channel to see what performs best.

Understanding Your ROI 101

Now that you've gotten the basics of what to expect, all that's left to do is download. Fill out this form to get a free copy of your guide.

Start getting the best return on your marketing investment.

In fact, it is no small feat to balance the twin demands of raising your client base while spending less on ads. Luckily, between the two, there is a success metric that resides somewhere: return on investment (hereinafter referred to as ROI).

PPC's Measurability

We've blogged about how to classify initial ad budgets in the past, but it's not productive to gage account results solely on spending. It can be a perfect strategy for less observable platforms, like bench advertising, places where attribution is grim. Inevitably, however, if a budget cap were the sole measure by which you measured the success of your Google Ads (formerly known as AdWords), you'd end up stunting development based on an arbitrary cap.

Conversion targets, on the other hand, can serve as something to aim for, but they are also an unreliable way to educate account structure and optimization. Sure, you can spend thousands on a handful of keywords for large matches and rake in sales, but that would be wasteful. AdWords is not ads spray and pray, nor does it have to function like direct mail.

Yeah, there could be budget and conversion targets in the back of your mind. Yet output on a regular basis calls for more precision. Here's where ROI enters.

Why Google Ads Is More ROI-Friendly than Conventional Advertising

Conversely when I post up at the Hynes Convention Center T stop on a Wednesday at 5:07 pm, I'm forced to gaze blankly at the collection of ads between tracks before the people-packed Slytherin-tone aluminum tubes — complemented with, you guessed: more ads — block them from view. The purpose of these ads is pretty straightforward: to be the only thing to look at in an aesthetically unattractive, poorly lit room. Thousands of people are walking by or standing before them, and those experiences are important in principle, right?

How can you say if tactics work?

Many elements of online advertisements, such as brand recognition, don't provide concrete statistics that we can calculate.

According to the new Benchmark State of Marketing Survey, 53 percent of companies are struggling to find a clear figure for ROI.

If you have trouble calculating or justifying your investment return (ROI), then you're not alone. Let's delve into how online ads can deliver a return on investment.

How to get your ROI from online ads

By 2021, there will be internet connectivity for an estimated 2.1 billion global customers. Fortunately, you may take several measures to ensure the highest ROI is reaped when you seek to hit them. Keep in mind those ideas.

Unless you don't limit your audience into single categories, the content you produce would be too broad for anyone to find interesting. Focus on small pieces, instead, and build content customers would love. You want traffic and leads to high quality, not just the traffic alone.

Focus on value

What adds value to your online advertising? Don't worry: You have many options to give your audience value — just make sure that every post has some form of trigger.

Pull at heartstrings Inform them about issues Make them laugh Educate them about what you know Help them save money Show them how to improve email marketing Focus on email marketing gives you a one-on-one way to communicate with your subscribers. You don't have to battle algorithms or search engine rankings with text.

Plus, you can split your subscription list into separate demographic and interest-based segments to offer the most important content possible. That's why email marketing provides some of the best Digital Marketing platforms ROI.

You should concentrate on creating lifelong relationships with your leads and customers through customer journeys.

Integrate your online marketing campaign across various channels Integrating your marketing strategy will ensure it reaches your target audience — regardless of which channel they use. The Campaign Dashboard easily combines hundreds of devices so you can hit your audience on different platforms.

You should concentrate on creating lifelong relationships with your leads and customers through customer journeys.

How to calculate your online ROI ads

At the campaign level, ROI is a more malleable (and valuable) benchmark for your optimization decisions than just allocating a daily budget and waiting to see what's going on: budget should be guided by the return you see, not the other way around.

A search campaign that targets keywords at the bottom of the funnel will almost always have a stronger ROI than a Show campaign that uses something specific (like keyword targeting). Remarketing to abandoners in carts provides a greater return than serving ads to all visitors to the platform. This degree of granularity is what makes PPC so special and helps ROI to be, not just an idea, an operating concept.

Your return includes several considerations for online marketing.

Yeah, certain things such as brand recognition sound almost impossible to quantify. You may also look at a wide variety of key indicators to get a detailed image of your total ROI.

Number of unique website users per week or month How your average order value has changed over time Your average cost per lead Your cost per click Domain location in search engines such as Google Number of new email subscribers per month Growth of your social media followers Contribution to social media (likes, shares, comments, etc.) Return On Investment can be calculated using the following formula: (Revenue-Costs). When you are selling a tangible product, don't forget to make a factor in the cost of production and distribution; consider the expense of your care programs for lead generation.

You can individually check out each platform (Google Analytics, Facebook, etc.) and put together a chart with your stats each month.

However, Campaign Monitor provides a wide variety of applications for analyzing the data across one simple interface, such as the integration tool Google Analytics.

Is it really important?

Completely. Totally. The main concern of any marketer or organization is to get the highest ROI possible. No one will want to waste money on something that doesn't work.

You will focus on achieving the highest ROI right from the start of your efforts by adopting best practices. To analyze your data and monitor your ROI, use the integration tools. From there, you can tailor your strategy and strategies to match your particular audience and produce top-notch results.

What is it right now?

Now that you understand how online marketing will offer your return on investment, you will concentrate on implementing your marketing strategy.

Create special audience persons to learn about the needs and desires of your customers. Check out where the online audience is going, and what kind of content they consume. Make an attempt to produce as useful material as possible, and the ROI will follow.

Need help narrowing your audience down? Through your scope, learn how to build a lookalike audience with Facebook and email.

Content That Hits The Right Target Audience

The effectiveness of content marketing starts with the awareness of how to find your target audience.

After all, how can you start content creation until you know who your audience is?

Good marketing material takes time—much of it. You can not afford to waste time with content that doesn't concentrate perfectly on your target market. You need to figure out who your folks are. But how do you?

By the time you're finished reading, you'll understand: how to identify your target audience and consider your target market to build a straightforward image of who you (and aren't) writing for exactly.

Take tips, techniques, and audience gathering approaches.

Using your enhanced public awareness to build content that interacts with their Why Define Your Target Audience?

Many content marketers apply the "Field of Dreams" approach to their work.

True, great content appears to attract an audience, obviously. Though, it doesn't guarantee that your brand will be the best audience. That means visitors who are likely to: Link to your product your content.

Buy your product on account of its content.

Defining who your target really is will help you concentrate not just on creating great content but also on creating the right content. This promotes content creation, which establishes you as an authority in your profession, rather than creating content for your own benefit.

How to understand your target market

Off with a few basic questions to ask yourself. This could include: What problems does the product or service of my business solve? You would have some understanding of why the product or service works if you've been in business for some amount of time. The content should also be linked to that intent (that is to avoid the temptation to post meaningless memes just because they're funny — if it's not connected to your project, it's not part of your content marketing).

Who are our customers?

If you are not sure who is buying your product or service, almost certainly someone in your company would. Consider asking for this information from the executives or sales teams at your company. Segmenting the types of customers can also be needed. You can, for example, categorize clients based on venue, budget, or needs. HubSpot has created a great introductory guide to this method.

Who is my Contest?

You're already aware of who your clear rivals are. However, some fast searches on Google and social media (particularly on Facebook and Twitter) may sometimes show that you might not have been aware of the upstart competition. Seek to check for a keyword or two specific to your industry. See, can projects are coming up. Browse their profiles and explanations of the apps on "About Us." This is an easy way to get a feel for who your competitor is and quickly.

What do consumers (instead of a competitor) stand to benefit by choosing us?

What features are you offering that nobody else does? Is there anything else that you can do than someone else?

You'll have developed an appreciation for each of the following by the time you address these questions: Why your content needs to exist.

Who will read it?

What is your competition (and how do you do it better)?

Why should your audience select your content (and product) rather than the competition?

This isn't supposed to be a deep, thorough process. Take that as a clear starting point.

Creating Your Target Audience Description

It helps to know your target audience (and who they are not) until you can build content that resonates. A definition of an audience should ideally relate these three things: Your product or service Your main audience demographic The purpose of your content Here's what a simple definition of the audience could look like once you've done evaluating your audience: "[INSERT YOUR BRAND] creates content to support and educate [INSERT DEMOGRAPHIC] so they can better [INSERT ACTION]." We're pretty eager to understand our audience, and we want to make sure we're doing what we can to support our writers.

We look at it in two ways: We want to make sure that we build features that our customers are already using as we build our product. That requires us to understand their problems and frustrations, particularly those that we can solve.

When we create content, we want to make sure we produce content that is genuinely useful to our audiences. We're not only searching for likes, shares, and page views. Rather we aspire to be able to rely on trusted resource readers.

We need to consider our target audience to achieve those goals. It is just as plain as this.

How are we going about it? Firstly, we find the center of our content.

Finding Your Content Core

The object of the core exercise of content is to understand the difference between what you are doing and what you need to address.

One of the big mistakes early content marketers make is thinking about themselves and their product, rather than the issues they really care about their customers. It is an utter misconception of what it means to meet the target market.

Your product is, of course, helpful to your customers, but that doesn't mean it's going to be helpful to your blog readers as well, the community of potential customers is possibly interested in a much greater variety of topics.

Visually, the heart of content looks like this: what you do is in the middle of your material. We make editorial calendar software at CoSchedule, so this is a mix of the topics of social media and programming content. We address problems like offering a single platform for the preparation and execution of content marketing activities for our customers.

Showing a forthcoming release schedule on a monthly calendar visualized.

Allowing users to reschedule content via a simple drag and drop operation.

To promote team coordination and productive workflow.

Providing an instrument that lets them save time and improve their blog traffic.

There are definitely stuff we should write about on our blog. It's not everything that we write about, though. We spend our time writing about the ideas surrounding these subjects, too. This is the main concept behind "expanding our core content." As we step away (ever so slightly) from our core content and concentrate on what our target audience actually wants to hear about, we are increasing the efficacy of our content marketing and concentrating more on the needs of our target audience.

This step woudl also allow us to keep the issues that we're writing about linked to our specific topical emphasis.

This takes us to the topics at CoSchedule on how to prepare, coordinate, and execute all content marketing material.

Such topics tackle the problems our company already tackles, but in a way explicitly tailored towards what our target audience cares about. The problem is: What does it really care about your readers? There are quite a few easy ways to find out.

13 Strategies To Reach Your Target Audience

We started trying to understand who our target audience was before CoSchedule ever launched. Here are a few of the methods and techniques we are still using to keep our understanding clear.

Build Reader Personas

In an early planning meeting; we came up with a couple of Lean UX-type users who were designed to help us solve problems that our CoSchedule users really needed to solve.

This has been done as a team exercise and has been extremely useful in our process. Looking back, we weren't quite correct about what our customers cared about, but building from it was a good spot.

Now, we often recommend your own blog for the creation of user personas.

Such writers are trying to capture the real motivations and curiosities your readers are inspiring. By identifying them, you will be able to help find your target group when the time comes.

The first move to visualizing the audience as you write is a public persona. You can tailor your content to them when you picture a person.

By following this form of the writing process, the person reading your content will often feel like you're talking to them directly.

Here's what you need to know: These details are protected by a great audience persona: Who What When Where Why Precise details are needed for what aspect. If possible, include things such as Gender Personality Family Life Job Title Job function Employer Location Income Needs Pain points Challenges

Main Takeaways: plan to develop people for your audience so you can picture your audience as you write to them. This need not be robust; it acts as a resource to help you concentrate your content on the correct messaging.

Take paper and write down the target audience's who, what, etc. Go to a stock picture website or Pinterest and find a picture of the person you write for. Getting a vision of who you write for will help you "sing" through your content as if you were talking to them directly.

You are more likely to turn readers into consumers when the audience feels like you're talking to them and their questions.

Conduct User Surveys Regularly

Periodically perform user surveys. We use a free tool called Survey.io to periodically conduct user surveys about our company.

To participate in the survey, anyone who establishes a CoSchedule account will be asked to. This was a great tool to help us keep a constant pulse over what our users are thinking. We should turn the input from that into a deeper understanding of our target audience.

Only as good a survey as the information you obtain from it. Below are a few ideas to make yours as useful as possible: learn from each problem what you want to know.

Make the questions short and answer them easily. It will help boost the chances people will be able to complete it.

Think hard about giving a giveaway to take a survey, or not. They can help improve participation. Some folks might just respond to get a prize, though.

Use Google Analytics

If you know how to find it, use Google Analytics Google Analytics has a ton of data about your audience.

With Facebook Insights, Find Your Target Audience On Facebook

Facebook offers a powerful set of insights (analytics) to every Page owner that are free to use whenever you want. From here, you can easily assess the most active user-profiles and decide the topics they have in common.

Visit your Facebook page to get started. Click the Insights tab: Next, select People: You can find what you need to understand your Facebook audience here.

By Connecting to Your Twitter Followers Dashboard, Find Your Target Audience On Twitter

Twitter also has a fantastic dashboard for followers that you can use when you sign up for a Twitter Advertising account.

The dashboard performs an excellent job of letting you know what affects your followers — specifically mentioning popular topics and other Twitter accounts that your followers have in popular. This knowledge is important and goes well beyond simple demographic data.

Run Annual Audience Survey

Blogger Michael Hyatt conducts his blog readers' survey each year as a way to keep track of who they are and what they want to hear about on his blog.

After the results of the survey are collected, Michael shares his observations with his readers, which often leads to a great discussion where both confirms and/or refutes his assumptions.

This is a very constructive way of getting the target market to understand. In fact, it is so strong we are taking a similar approach to our own annual Better Marketer Survey.

Track your social behavior

Which social networks are your readers sharing the most of your content?

Actually, this little tidbit of knowledge will tell you a lot about what they want and want to learn. Nevertheless, when we studied the CoSchedule system's nearly 1 million headlines, we found that the sound and subjects covered on each network varied wild. These basic hints offer clues as to who you write about, and will help you find your target audience.

This process can be as easy as day-to-day monitoring of your social media and taking note of who interacts with your content. Beware of their bios. This will tell you a lot about who you are meeting right now (and whether those folks are the right people to reach).

Track your best (and worst) content

Looking back at Google Analytics, finding your best and worst posts for a week or month should be easy.

At CoSchedule, at the end of the month, we compile a traffic report that does exactly that. As a way to assess the overall success of a blog post, we use both total shares and pageviews. By comparing the content that performed well to the content that did not perform well, we will gain a deeper insight into what our readers really want to hear.

Ask for Audience Reviews With An Automated Email

When users subscribe to one of our mailing lists, they are automatically added to an email queue that will ping them up about 30 days after they sign up to see if they're enjoying our content.

The aim of this email is to request an answer that usually generates substantive conversation if there is anything the reader can share. We often regularly use the strategy with our application's users.

You can build a friendship and an open forum for contact and feedback by communicating with your audience in person.

Here's how to set up such an email using some of the top email marketing platforms: MailChimp Campaign Track Aweber Constant Touch

Talk To Your Social Follower

You will learn a lot from being an active member of your own social media network. Follow these tips: Answer every comment and message you get. Any contact with the audience provides an opportunity to know more about it.

Find and participate in popular Facebook and LinkedIn communities. Involving yourself in conversations related to your niche or industry will provide valuable insight into what matters to your audience.

Occasionally create posts asking the audience what they are interested in. Which are their greatest problems? What is it they are doing outside the office? What items or features will they like to have? These are only a few topical ideas that you could easily turn into Twitter surveys.

Analyze the Twitter Followers for Your Competitions

This one is easy enough to use Followerwonk, Moz's fantastic freemium Twitter review tool.

This method enables the following: Find keyword-based Twitter bios.

Compare your followers to 2 other rivals.

Analyze who follows what account (and which follows).

Track the growth of Twitter followers for every profile.

Order followers on any given profile based on the number of tweets, followers, the length of time the profile was live, and social authority (a metric that measures the degree an account has).

Analyze Your User Information

It is likely that users of your latest content (social followers, forum readers, email subscribers, etc.)

might not be the same people who purchase your product or service.

This may be because of producing material that draws in the wrong audience. It is also likely that your product or service appeals to more groups of people than the goals of your current content.

That is where it can be useful to evaluate actual customer data (and not just marketing advertising data). The KISSmetrics team has put together an excellent guide on where to find the data and how to best analyze it. You may just be able to find a breakthrough that will help you create soaring material.

Using social listening software

Social listening is important for understanding what your audience on social media is thinking about. Our friends at Mention wrote this great post about social listening, which showed how and why to use these tools.

How to Find The Most Significant Issues, Interests, And Concerns

The demographic research is a challenging part of defining a target group.

Those insights also involve your target audience's age, sex, and place. Although these figures are useful, they are also very difficult to measure in terms of what to write about on your blog, or not to be.

Rather than dwelling on who they are, concentrating on what they are dealing with could be beneficial instead. For example: What want to do they do better?

Who motivates them really to be better?

What's keeping them up at night?

Content marketing is about exchanging the time and energy of your readers for useful and valuable knowledge.

When identifying your target market, make sure to take that approach instead of just following shallow demographics.

3 Strategies For Knowing What The Audience Needs To Read

Get Out Of The Building

One of the early lessons we learned here at CoSchedule was that it's just not enough to ask our readers a question or two via an interview. The approach can be abstract and too far away from what people really want to say, missing the deep emotional knowledge you need.

But besides all these other approaches, "getting out of the house" is also helpful (and necessary). In other words — talk face-to-face with your readers.

This could be harder than it sounds, depending on your venue. We performed most of our face-to-face interviews on a Google+ Hangout at

CoSchedule, but that didn't make them any less important.

As a content marketer, you can easily opt to interview a few regular readers in one-on-one environments.

You would be shocked by how welcoming and ready to chat are the majority of them. Once you get them to chat, you'll be shocked at how helpful they can be, too.

Don't just settle for the percentages and figures while trying to find your target audience. The target is not facts and numbers; they are human beings.

The beauty of the web is that with supportive and informative content directly aimed at them, you can understand them and touch them.

2. Using Ubersuggest And Google's Keyword Planner Tool

The first thing that people often do is turn to Google when they need to learn something. Here is a fast way to learn a great deal about your audience easily.

Type a subject in Ubersuggest, or keyword. Start with a keyword which is key to your business:

Check results from keywords Import the.csv file into the Keyword Planner for Google. To do this, sign in and select "Get search volume and trends." Then press "Upload File": you now have a lot of keyword choices, all of them seeded by words that people initially punched into searches via Google.

Then, export the data from the Keyword Planner and open the.csv file: Look for two items as you skim through this data: keywords related to problems, desires, and concerns you've learned about your audience using the strategies described in this post before.

Keywords that have a good search volume level as well.

This should leave you with a vague idea of which topics people are most keen to learn.

Analyze Your Competitors' Top Performing Content

Try to search for it with BuzzSumo before creating content around a given keyword or subject. Although it takes a paid account to get the most out of this device, it provides enough power to be used for free.

The video offers a great explanation of what it can do: Using data to avoid making assumptions about your audience is one of the worst things a content marketer can do. We end up creating content that will make our audience feel dumb.

4 Common audience assumptions

It is easy to make assumptions to avoid. They're shortcuts to critical thinking that make us feel like we can quickly and easily assess a person or circumstance.

But when you make an incorrect assumption about your audience, you run the risk of producing content that would alienate them. In a reader, when presented with a false belief, two responses happen: "You think I'm dumb. "Oh, this article is not for me. I'm just going." It's for those people who know things. "Either way, the outcome is the same. The reader bounces off the paper, discovering what they've been looking for elsewhere.

Every single piece of content begins somewhere. Furthermore, if that point of departure is off-base with your audience, then it does not matter how good this content may be. By avoiding these four assumptions, make sure that your research hits the mark.

Chris Marshal

Hypothesis # 1: Your audience is just like you. Your audience probably has many similarities with you. We may have common issues or interests, or fall into about the same category.

But they're not the same person that you are. They may care about the same things you do, or they may not. In reality, their personalities and interests may vary widely from yours.

This is mainly true if you're working in a field that you are not specifically passionate about (for example, you maybe passionate about producing content while serving an audience in an industry you're not familiar with).

Let data and experience guide your public perception.

Assumption # 2: They know you know your audience the same things, and you don't know the same things.

They also know something. They do know less at times. You both just know different things, sometimes.

They will come to your content in a lot of cases because they have a gap in their knowledge. To ensure that your writing doesn't go over their head, follow these two tips: Think like a journalist by writing in a way that everyone can understand. News organizations are also expected to write on a given subject for a large audience that may not be experts. We normally use plain, straightforward sentence structures and seek to avoid ambiguity. Using those principles will help you create simple and easy to read the content.

Err on the side of giving too much detail and not enough. Read a political news article, and you'll probably read a sentence describing the candidate of a political party as "[INSERT PARTY]'s presumptive presidential nominee [INSERT CANDIDATE'S NAME]." You could read that and wonder, "Doesn't everyone already know that an individual is running for office? "Maybe not the answer. When it comes to providing information, being thorough and clear means that the reader leaves with an accurate understanding of what you are attempting to convey.

Hypothesis # 3: They care about your brand. The rest of your audience is more concerned with their families, friends, and themselves.

No one is dying to have an evening of social media bonding with a company. A survey showed that, in their lives, 77 percent care about real people, not brands. Participants thought relationships were reserved for families, acquaintances, or colleagues.

If you're frank with yourself, then you'd probably agree.

You've already failed when you build content that assumes your audience starts by caring for your brand, and that it only gets better from there.

If you're going to make an assumption, you're better off thinking they don't care, and you have to win your way into their peripheral vision.

Using the material to cultivate your desire to care for people and support them in their lives.

Ask yourself: Does my content support the real issues and relationships with my audience in real life?

Hypothesis # 4: They know The Business Terminology The AP Style Guide has a strong tradition of thoroughly describing what is before referring to it in acronym form.

I'm guilty of losing out on this. I think everybody knows what CTA or SEO means because this blog audience certainly learned because.

However, we have both new readers and experts who are reading this article, and they can happen on a blog post (through search) out of the order in which we would have written them.

I must assume that this is the first time that the reader has seen the term, and Identify that call to action (CTA) and search engine optimization (SEO) is what I'm talking about when I first use it before I can use the acronym for the rest of the post.

Any of that ties to sound. Are you talking in your journal, or using the company's stiff buzz words? And if you're talkative, you're expecting less. You dive headfirst if you're all into jargon and start tossing acronyms around so you can get to the point quicker.

Ask yourself: Does my audience understand the terminology I am about to use in this industry?

Now, use this insight to create content that interacts with your audience. Now that you know who your audience is, you're able to create content that fits exactly what they're looking for.

By establishing a link, great content moves your audience along the path to conversion and can be invaluable to develop your business.

4 Tips For Creating Content That Can Reach Your Audience

Tip #1: Focus Your Content on the Needs of Your Audience

Before writing content, ask, "How does this content fulfill my followers' interests? "You are showing your audience you hear them, and you care for their needs by discussing a particular challenge, pressure point, or subject of interest. Communicating that well builds confidence with your audience. Confidence is absolutely essential to turn website visitors into new customers.

Key Takeaways: Concentrate on questions you frequently ask your audience. Set up a list of all those questions (these can be compiled from social media and email answers from readers and followers). Then, arrange them from newbie to inquiries on an expert level. Such questions can quickly become convincing ideas about the content (after all, if your audience has questions, it is your responsibility to address them).

Show that you care about the audience and its needs. Brainstorm any reason there is for your product or service. These may be the answers to the questions you've just put together.

Communicate to build confidence. Trust is important for the transformation of website visitors into new customers. Give advice freely to develop that trust.

Bonus: If your company has a sales funnel, map on this list your list of questions and answers from takeaways 1 and 2 to the customer travel your sales team has created. Find out the best ways to use it or repurpose it for sales enabling when making your content.

Tip # 2: Share Income, Not Features Some content creators equate features with advantages. Don't just slip into the pit.

Discussing the features can be a perfect way to differentiate between the product or service. The real benefit for your target audience in marketing, though, is why they need it. If you focus on their needs and points of pain, it's easy to lead with benefits or the value that you can give them.

People are not buying apps. They're buying into the belief that a product or service can change their lives.

Let's say you own a car dealer, and you want to sell more fuel-efficient vehicles. You could create a blog post about the features of modern hybrid motors. That may even be interesting for people interested in learning how to make engines more eco-friendly about the mechanics.

As a marketer, though, you will need to concentrate on the reasons why someone wants to buy a fuel-efficient vehicle. Others could include: saving gas money.

Environmental benefits.

Trips to the gas station less regular.

Stuff, like saving money and protecting the environment, are things that people personally relate to. Most likely, they worry more about their own benefits, rather than how those benefits are made possible.

Then, the true value proposition is the benefits that your apps offer. Lead with advantages, and back them up with information on the apps.

Key Takeaways: Concentrate on the needs of your audience before focussing on your sales needs. Content that makes your audience do something better — even without your help — focuses on the advantages your product or service might provide. If your readers actually converted into clients. Don't be afraid to give away too much information or business secrets — if you have found it out, someone else might. However, your advice will position you as an expert on the subject, and thus place your company as a powerful solution.

Identify the best questions to answer with Why 'posts in the list of questions that you built in phase 1. When you plan the content, bear in mind how you are going to deliver it and repurpose it to build it suitably for each platform to make the most of your hard work.

To build emotional interactions with your content and brand using emotional terms. Clearly connect with your audience so you can easily get your points across.

Tip # 3: Build Urgency

When you describe the benefits and create an emotional connection, a sense of urgency is needed.

We live in a world of hecticity. Priorities change regularly, and things are placed on the back burner. That is why it's so important to build urgency with your content.

You stop being lost in the chaos of daily life by generating a sense that something has to be done right now.

Limited time, now, today, and now all words or phrases linked to urgency are. By integrating these terms properly into your text, you will create an illusion that something needs to be done without pause.

Using this urgency to remind your target marketing audience that they are reading your blog to address a problem they face right now. Conclude the piece with how failing to find a solution today would affect the audience member's life or work.

Key Takeaways: Using the descriptive model to help you compose in a more urgent way.

Nevertheless, you don't have to be crazy like the advertisements trying to persuade you that you need yet another tool for your kitchen. Until an offer runs out, think of countdown timers on landing pages and develop hacks to improve the work you are already doing.

Using terms such as right now, right now, instantly, time-restricted, imperative, and necessary.

Conclude the piece with how failure to find a solution today would affect the consumer's target audience's life or work.

Tip # 4: Inform Them of What To Do (Make The Call To Action Clear)

"Pass the salt" vs. "I'd like this pasta to have more flavor." "Pass the salt" is a better choice than the latter as it's simple and definite, meaning there is no room for confusion.

That's how you need to think about your content ending.

Visitors to your blog, social media followers, and potential customers seeing your website for the first time want to learn what they should do next. A simple call for action (CTA) is expected to significantly boost conversions.

The greatest obstacle to conversions is always wishy-washy CTAs or a complete lack of CTAs. If you want your post to be shared, tell the readers to "Share This Post." If you want them to sign up for your e-newsletter, create a button that says "Sign Up For The Newsletters."

Another tip: Keep your call for action above the fold. According to Wishpond, you can persuade someone to convert over 50 percent of the time if they see your CTA right away.

Authoritative, descriptive, precise, immediate, and appropriate is an efficient call to action. Below are some examples of great CTAs, which effectively communicate what action is required.

"Call for a consultation today." "Contact us for a quote now." "Share with your network." "Register for email newsletters." "Follow us on social media." "Subscribe and stay up-to-date on the latest news." For comprehensive tips on how to write a transforming call to action

Actionable Tips For Outstanding Content

Going into the nuts and bolts of content production is outside the reach of this book (you're here to know more about reaching your audience after all).

We suggest beginning with these posts when you are ready to take the next step towards applying your understanding of your audience to the production of expert material.

Now Get Out There And Entertain Your Audience

A whole world of soon-to-be fans is waiting out there for your material. It is up to you to help solve their problems and to provide all the knowledge that they are seeking. Fortunately, you're up to the challenge after reading this article.

Go ahead, and do your best!

How To Add Value To The Goods And Services

The use of "added value" has been widely promoted as a tactic to gain a competitive advantage in an increasingly hostile market environment and advice on organizational processes involved in the development of consumer value has been given. Yet nothing about the sense of added value, its functions, and sustainability has been written down. This may be because the value identifying literature is fragmented, and few distinguish between "value" and "added value'.' Managers must grasp what the word means to know the supposed benefits of added value. Research has shown that administrators have varying definitions of the principles taken for granted. Given the lack of consensus on the definition of added value, there is unlikely to be any agreement between managers on added value. The aim of this paper is to provide a better understanding of the added value structure, roles, and sustainability. We open up by analyzing preceding literature. We conducted in-depth interviews with 20 leading-edge brand experts to gain more insight into the added value and discussed their perspectives on its purpose, positions, and sustainability. They conclude that added value is a multidimensional concept; different people view it differently. There are numerous roles that play added values, and the emotional values are the more sustainable added values.

There was the predominant use of the word "added value" in trade publications. Far less has been found in academic journals. So we reviewed the "value" literature and then considered the consequences of "added value'.' The value of scientific literature in relation to pricing, customer behavior, and policy is discussed. With an overview of the value meanings in these three areas, we open, then consider how these apply to value-added.

Quality Literature on Pricing.

Value pricing is characterized as the trade-off between the expectations of the benefits obtained by the consumers and the sacrifices made. Monroe and Gale cited price as the primary advantage for their customers. Monroe suggested that the aspect of the sacrifice exercises a greater influence on the perceptions of the value of buyers. Everyone noted that the position of the price is complex, and customers don't buy on low price alone. The context, access to information for customers, and past interactions often influence market perceptions and ultimately value determination for customers.

Many meanings of value have a broader meaning of sacrifice, which includes non-monetary factors such as time and effort. From the customer's perspective, sacrifice is again described, as illustrated by Doyle's value concept as 'not what the producer puts in, but what the user gets out.' Zeitham noted four types of customer meanings of value:

1) low price (focus on sacrifice);
2) whatever the customer desired in a good or service (focus on benefits);
3) the quality obtained for the price charged (trade-off between one sacrificial component and one gain component); and
4) total benefits obtained for the total sacrifice incurred (all the relevant components considered).

The literature on consumer behavior

Here, interest is described in terms of customer needs and what is desirable. Rokeach suggested that "value is a lifelong conviction that a particular mode of behavior or end-state of existence is individually or socially superior to an opposite mode of behavior or end-state of existence." Developing means-end theory helps the laddering techniques to evaluate consumer values.

There are several subtle variants to the concept of Rokeach. Others describe meaning in terms of the mental images or cognitive representations that underlie the desires and expectations of customers and eventually influence the responses of customers in specific circumstances. Sheth described five consumer values ± "functional,' "financial," "emotional,' "epistemic," and "conditional" ± that could affect consumer purchasing and choosing actions. Levitt concluded that a product reflected a "complex value satisfaction cluster" for consumers, who added value to the product according to their perceived ability to satisfy their requirements. A brand that meets the realistic needs of customers delivers functional value, while a brand that meets the needs of customers to express itself delivers symbolic value.

Others noted that values might consist of common ideals or community expectations of desirable items that influence individual attitudes and subsequent behavior.

The literature on the policy.

Porter has described value as "what buyers are prepared to pay." By either implementing a cost leadership or a differentiation approach, businesses are generating value for their consumers by either reducing their costs or increasing their efficiency. Others have built on that ever since.

Naumann defined value as meeting or exceeding the standards of the customers in terms of product quality, service quality, and price-based value. All three elements of this Customer Service Triad must be in alignment for providing value. Likewise, Band defined three consumer value characteristics: quality, cost (monetary and non-monetary), and schedule (delivery: time and place of delivery).

Normann and Ramõ Ârez, on the other hand, postulated that consumer needs should not be the primary concern of managers, but instead concentrate on complementing consumer competencies and activities. Normann and Ramõ Ârez also spoke about the willingness of customers to pay for access to services, which either decreased their costs or encouraged them to do things they would otherwise not be able to do. The value of both suppliers and buyers was stressed by Brandenburger and Stuart. The value generated by "a vertical chain of players" was equivalent to the buyer's "willingness-to-pay" minus the supplier's "opportunity cost'," both of which depended on manufacturers, firms, and buyers' characteristics.

Chris Marshal

Problems with value definition

Several writers have acknowledged the difficulties associated with value interpretation. These are the product of value subjectivity, differences among customers, inside customers, between cultures, in various circumstances, pre- and post-purchase, and tangible and intangible offers. This is exacerbated by the complex idea of the customer interest changing over time. Nevertheless, it has been reported that consumer value is fundamentally vague and that value may be considered "one of the most overused and misused words in marketing and pricing today"' In an effort to simplify the different meanings, Woodruff proposed: "Consumer value is the perceived desire of a consumer for an appraisal of certain product attributes, attribute performance and consequences. Although Woodruff's definition represents the richness and scope of the term, the various contexts, tasks, and parameters hinder its transformation into a concrete operational definition.

Added value

We now consider the meaning of the term `` added value''. In contrast to customer value, there is a noticeable paucity of definitions of added value, but many variations in terminology. While some speak of `` added value'', others talk about `` adding value'' or `` value-added''. Furthermore, the latter term already has a precise but different meaning in accounting.

Jones claimed that added value formed the most important part of a brand's definition and was the primary basis for distinguishing a brand from a product. Gro Ènroos, one of the few to distinguish between value and added value, defined an offering's core value as the core solution and its added value as additional services. By contrast, McCracken defined added value as brands' meanings for consumers in describing their actual and aspirational selves. Macrae proposed a typology of six prominent added value communicators: ritual, symbol, the heritage of good, legend, belonging, and aloof.

Nilson talked about ``value-added marketing'', whereby a product must achieve over-satisfaction to deliver superior products to competitors'. Over-satisfaction, exceeding the satisfaction of customers' needs, is similar to Levitt's ``augmentation'', adding things the customer had never thought about, and ``customer delight'', whereby customers' basic expectations are exceeded.

Gro Ènroos observed that added value could be negative if it subtracted from the basic core value. Not all customers perceive an added value, either because some cannot use the extra services, or because the augmentation reduces an offering's value. De Chernatony and McDonald consequently defined added values as attributes that are both relevant and welcomed by customers. Others talk about ``adding value'' by manipulating the components of customer value, for example, increasing benefits or reducing sacrifices. By contrast, Farquhar described ``adding value'' as surrounding the tangible features with distinctive benefits perceived by customers as adding value.

From a strategic perspective, Brandenburger and Stuart defined the added value of a player as a vertical chain minus the value created by all the players except the one in question''. This definition explicitly views value from the perspective of all players (buyers, firms, and suppliers) rather than just customers. Normann and Ramõ Ârez suggested ``added value'' be replaced by ``the co-production of value'', whereby customers and suppliers jointly create value through complementing each other's activities. This reflects their conceptualization of the value process as a ``value constellation'', contrary to Porter's (1985) ``value chain'' in which value was added sequentially.

The roles of added value

The nature and role of added value are inextricably linked: the way in which added value is defined effectively determines its role. Furthermore, just as the value perceived by customers evolved over time, so the roles of added value seem to have widened in the literature. The traditional role of added value was to distinguish brands from commodities. Later a more competitive framework emerged, stressing superior customer value through operational excellence, customer intimacy, or product leadership. The focus also shifted to the processes that enable organizations to deliver superior customer value. Therefore, added value shifted from being a means of separating an offer from the basis of choice by means of indicators that allow consumers to perceive superior value and to be more secure in their choice. More recently, the role of value-added has been advocated as ensuring competitive advantage and long-term performance.

Normann and Ramõ Ârez viewed their position as promoting the value-creating activities of their own customers, either by relieving or enabling them. Normann and Ramõrez emphasized the active participation of both consumers and vendors, as opposed to the passive role played by consumers in Porter's value chain.

Value Added Sustainability

Little has been published about value-added sustainability. McCracken suggested the characteristics of a product that change over time, but the brand and the value it brings would last. Park claimed that throughout the life of the brand, it was the brand idea that was maintained. Hall demonstrated how intangible added qualities were more durable, an argument that de Chernatony and McDonald reiterated about the dedication of employees to customer service. Similarly, Doyle argued that service could be the most enduring differential gain. In comparison, Ehrenberg and Scriven denied that brands had any "added qualities" sustainable. Rather, they've argued that brands have very different numbers of people they're outstanding too.

Ways You Could Add Value To Your Product Or Service

For several years, the idea of value-added sale has been popular. I still have lots of friends claiming to be the inventors of the idea, known as value-added sales. I guess it's sort of like tons of people claiming to have invented the internet!

The real problem, however, is that the ability to add value to your product or service is an absolute necessity in today's market place where so many goods and services are seen as a commodity. There is no question that practically every good or service can be pushed down to the most bottom line-price in the absence of value-added components. The Issue? If you're just selling quality, you're never going to be able to sell any degree of high-margin revenue, and that's where profitability, long-term growth, and sales performance are.

Let's look at ten ways you can add value to your product or service no matter what you're selling. Many times people argue with me that you don't understand that my product is different or that my service is something else. The fact is everything can have added value. So let's take a quick look at ten various ways you can do it.

1. Providing expert advice and extremely high professionalism.

Many consulting companies, accounting firms, and even medical practitioners are charged a clean amount for the degree of advice they receive. However, to be able to generate value for you as a sales specialist, what you need to do is to realize that you need to have a much higher, more advanced, and much more important level of advice than your competition. What this means is a greater degree of intelligence, knowledge, and awareness of what you are doing.

2. Packaging and Bundling.

I'm not only talking about how the product or service really looks, but I'm also thinking about being able to put together attractive bundles, purchasing rates and a range of additional benefits that are important in value and are, in themselves, much more valuable than just the product itself.

3. Level of Service.

You can differentiate yourself not only by offering a higher level of service but by adding different levels of service depending on someone's size, frequency, or purchase number. For example, you may want to offer service rates in gold or platinum or silver that customers qualify for, are willing to pay for, and obtain when they do business with you.

4. Frequent services to customers.

The more you're bought from, the more useful service, prices, rewards, and related products they get, this is connected to the definition. For an airline, it's almost like frequent flyer miles. I know people who travel thousands of miles out of their way only because they want to build up the miles!

5. Transition and preparation.

When new customers join the company, you may want to provide action or change teams to help them better use the goods or services you are offering them. On the same token, the more information they have in connection with these goods or services, the more they would be able to use them.

6. Niveaus of appreciation and compensation.

This is very different from regular buyer programs because, with this particular value-added model, you actually give consumers or consumers appreciation based on their willingness to use your product or service, leverage their capacity, purchase those rates from you, etc. What this means is they are known for being good customers themselves. We published a Hall of Fame in our newsletter many years ago, and we had a lot of customers really interested in appearing and being a member of our Hall of Fame. It's a smart way to leverage healthy relationships and healthy will.

7. Qualitative support.

Based on somebody's level of purchasing, participation or engagement, you have higher product quality, likely a more advanced level of service, dedicated personnel, dedicated telephone lines, fax lines, or the like, which allows them a greater opportunity to be handled differently than the customer does. You even might be able to use that as a value-added feature for introductory customers.

8. Dedicated employees.

This works particularly well when you have a technical product or service or one that requires help. It's not difficult to understand that the more someone knows about the account, goods, machinery, equipment, or way of doing business with another entity, the easier it is to do business with that company. In this case, you basically appoint dedicated account persons to directly manage the accounts of your customers.

9. The pace of delivery or of service.

One way of differentiating yourself is to guarantee some form of delivery on time or faster. It is very well recognized and acknowledged that a key component for complete or maximum price charging is delivery on time. This is also a variable in that it involves the provision of value-added services and goods.

10. Data to insiders.

It is very popular when people sell information about securities, shares, financial details, or anything related to details or time-specific data. Using this method, you will want to suggest a daily newsletter (electronic or printed) that periodically informs customers as it relates to the very specific and relevant information they need.

These ten ways of adding value can all be implemented in your everyday sales activities. There is little doubt that imagination, ingenuity, and the ability to outsource the competition are needed. But the main sad truth is that if you keep selling the way you always have, the price will continue to dominate and I guarantee that you will have a rival who will take one or more of these ten ideas and put them into action. Your defiance? Start it before they get it done! Nathan Bedford Forrest as the famous Confederate General, once said after a fight, "I won because with the most, I got there first!" You need to do the same.

Adding Value to Agricultural Goods Risk Management

Agriculture added value produces several billion dollars per year in economic effects for the state of Texas. In addition, adding value to agricultural products beyond the farm gate generally has the economic impact of just agricultural production on many occasions. Agricultural producers get a lot smaller portion of the consumer's dollar than food processors do, particularly processors that produce brand name products. Capturing those extra dollars by adding value to farm or ranch goods is a target that many producers have developed. This brochure describes value-added activities, outlines the economic forces that make value-added relevant, and provides guidance for starting your own value-added business.

What's "Added Value?

"Added value" means adding value to a raw commodity by moving it to the next manufacturing stage, at least. This can be as easy as keeping your calves in the possession and wintering them on wheat pasture or putting them in a feedlot. Value can be gained by membership in a cooperative that stores your goods, like a cotton gin cooperative. Or adding value may be as complex as making a "case-ready" food product heading all the way to the market. If you are contemplating a value-added company, you have to answer two main questions:

1) What is the interest of the customer? And
2) What makes a commodity with added value?

What is Good for Customers?

"Customer value" represents the relationship between the benefits which consumers receive from a product and the price they pay for it. The more advantages, the higher the value of the consumer, compared to the price. This does not automatically mean that a lower price results in a greater value. The price of a specific product may be high, but the consumers view the product as valuable because the associated benefits are also high. This interaction generates value for the consumer and, therefore, the potential to add value to the product. Creating value for the customer is critical in creating a successful and significant business. Nonetheless, you must bear in mind that the understanding of the value of the consumers is important, not of the producers. Find the case of calves prepackaging. Does the cattle buyer view preconditioning as a way of adding value? That is, will the buyer pay more for pre-conditioned calves (sufficient to cover the extra costs) than other calves? It's also important to remember that different consumers have different value-added expectations. Those perceptions correlate to their price, operation, convenience, and selection expectations.

What added value creates?

"Quality" is usually generated by concentrating on the advantages of the agribusiness product or service resulting from:

Quality — Does the product or service meet or exceed the standards of the customers?

Functionality — Is the product or service providing the function it needs?

Type — Is the product useful in some way?

Place — Is it the right place for a product?

Time — Is the product right at the right place?

Possession Facility — Is the product easy for the consumer to get?

To produce added value, a commodity must have one or more of those qualities. Remember, a product is simply a package of benefits, and the more advantages there are, the more consumers can see the product as good.

What is Value Added Driving?

Agribusiness, particularly the food sector, is consolidating rapidly and reacting increasingly to rising customer tastes and preferences. Consumers are having higher salaries than ever. They concentrate more on comfort, price, variety, service, health, and social awareness. They face the increasing value of (and demands on) their time, too. To put it briefly, customers are more aware of interest than ever. The increasing rate of disposable incomes of consumers and the market fragmentation caused by retail consolidation increase competition but, at the same time, leave it to exploit other niche markets. This provides incentives for producers to offer their goods added value.

Creating a Value-Added Product

To capture opportunities in this field, consumers must be identified and understood. What segments of consumers would want to see your product? What are the advantages these future customers wish for? When buying what conditions are they looking for? A significant first step in beginning a value-added company is to write these down as part of a business plan. Any enterprise can be viewed as a value chain. Every operation carried out should add value to the product. To do this, the activities at each phase in the value chain must be carefully controlled: acquisition of inputs, conversion of inputs into products; marketing and sales; supply chain logistics; and customer service activities. A new value-added enterprise should focus on the uniqueness of the product. What ultimately attracts consumers is the quality of your product or service (the value you add). This value-added approach is obviously very different from the commodity-oriented approach most farmers and ranchers are familiar with. A producer focuses on production costs in a commodity strategy with the goal of becoming a low-cost producer. Of fact, this is an emphasis on the "supply side." In comparison, the value-added approach includes an emphasis on the "demand-side "— determining who the consumers are and what they want. Then, after analyzing your capital and source of differentiation, you have a product or service that effectively curbs the costs of production while meeting future customer needs. A value-added business, unlike a commodity-driven company, can't erode benefits or lower product requirements just to reduce costs.

Steps to Success in a Value-Added Company

Developing a new company is challenging and requires hard work (for farmers and ranchers, nothing new). But there are ways to craft an effective company value-added approach with all the confusion.

Key considerations in a comprehensive business plan are:

- operating plan — market performance, quality and cost control
- Staff plan — requirements, expertise, and training
- Selling plan — providing daunting yet achievable targets
- Management plan — abilities, shortcomings and capital
- Expenditure and financial plan — cash flow planning

Examples of Agricultural Value-Added Items

Value can be applied in several ways to the grain of wheat. One way is for farmers to grow grain of wheat for use in food or feed products. The wheat straw, a waste product, can be harvested, processed, and then turned into building materials. Another way of adding value to wheat is to graze it with stocker cattle, which raises the wheat yield by inducing the plant's "artillery" and also generates income from cattle operations. Wheat grain can also be processed into natural organic foods and sold at health food stores. It might be hard to believe, but woody plants such as cedar and mesquite can be given added value. Cedar fiber can be used for making boards and extracting oil wells. Mesquite wood can be used to make shelves, boxes for jewelry, lawn furniture, and floor molding. Cedar and mesquite sawdust and fiber can be processed into fiber-board. Some that add value to mesquite wood by making furniture and lumber are South Texas Molding, Texas Kiln Products, and Uvalde Mesquite Company. In the fed beef industry, there are ways to add value too. A rancher may add value through a feed yard by conducting a cow-calf operation or maintaining ownership of his cattle. Another choice is to make special products such as sausage and tamales or turn tongue and some of the viscera into menudo or tripas. Booker Packing Company, Caviness Packing Company and J&B Foods are some of the companies that, despite the production costs, effectively add value to meat.

A recent study of these businesses showed an average of 63 percent of their return on investment. Of the companies in the study, 42% had less than five employees, 21% had sales ranging from $50,000 to $250,000, and 26% had sales of less than 50,000 pounds of meat per year. Many of the companies are based in rural areas, others are near to urban centers, and they care for the local population. When calculated by revenue dollars, market volume, or the number of staff, the smaller companies tend to be the most profitable.

Description Beyond strategic strategy and market analysis to get to know the consumer, the basic elements for success in a value-added sector can be boiled down to four main ingredients for business managers: Responding to changes in the market.

Be open to trying out new ideas.

Function as a project manager rather than a supplier.

Realize the importance of networking and the need to create alliances.

These are hard since they need a new farm or ranch vision. Managing capital and pursuing new ideas means looking inside the project for new profit centers. That may seem repetitive, but it is precisely this that adds value.

How To Build A Brand Persona That Is Relatable To Your Target Audience

Throughout my career, I was lucky to be working with a variety of different companies, all of which were at entirely different stages of their marketing maturity.

Whatever stage they are in, one of my first goals is to build in-depth individual marketing.

Marketing people are like the cornerstone on which to create your marketing house.

How do you know without persons what message would appeal to the needs of your target market?

Or where to get to the public to raise awareness and bring them to your website?

Or what do you write about in your marketing efforts on content?

Or how to converse on social media with your audience?

The problem is, much of the marketing persona literature takes you down the road toward: "John has a wife, three children, and a dog ... that has never proven all that helpful to me. How does a portrait of John's family help me write good copies or content? It really isn't.

That is why I decided to write this book, to share with other businesses over the years my insights and learnings from designing marketing personas. Let's plunge in the data.

What are marketing personnels?

My favorite description of a marketing person came from Ardath Albee, who, when it comes to B2B personas, I think is possibly the definitive source. The meaning is: A marketing persona is a composite depiction of the main audience segment.

Let's break that down a bit:

Composite sketch – A marketing person is not expected to describe a particular person and should never be focused on a single individual. Rather, it is a composite drawing that is meant to be representative of the majority of people it reflects.

Your main customer segment – A brand persona is supposed to reflect a portion of your target market, not the entire thing. If your target audience is 'Marketers,' having several people for the various types of marketers is perfectly appropriate as long as there is ample overlap between them to justify a separate individual. You may have several individuals split up by company size, sector, or something that makes sense to your company.

Here are a couple of other people I've met and used in various ways you may want to consider:

Detractors – Detractors are the other people in the purchasing loop who might possibly disrupt the transaction even if your main person is all for it. This is especially common in complex B2B transactions, with longer selling periods and involving multiple people.

Influencers – Influencers are individuals who, while they might not purchase the product directly, so great and on such a scale affect the actual consumer that it is worth spending time in those individuals. A good example of this is accountants advising small business owners to use which accounting software or web designers asking their customers which CMS to use.

Anti-personas- An anti-persona is a marketing person's complete opposite. It's a fictional character representing a group of people who aren't your actual clients. Just to clarify, creating an anti-person doesn't mean you're going to be deliberately stopping these people from using your product or service, it's just meaning you're not going to concentrate your marketing efforts on attracting certain customers. Here are a few situations where it makes sense to have an anti-person:

price > budget – Perhaps the number of reasons that you would want to build anti-personnel is when there is a specific consumer that you know is actually unable to afford the product. If you sell a piece of software for $1,000 a month, then it is highly unlikely that the average small business owner won't be able to afford it (unless it's vital to the mission). Therefore, by developing an anti-person for this person and recognizing factors such as where they are hanging online, you can understand how not to waste your marketing resources by attracting customers who can never afford your product.

Positioning-There are often occasions when a positioning or product differentiation strategy does not suit a specific form of customer. At Campaign Control, we actively picked experienced marketers as our Marketing Persona at 50 + employee companies and had an anti-person of the small business owner as a way of positioning ourselves against MailChimp and Constant Touch, who concentrated heavily on the small business market.

Four steps to building customer personas

So now that you understand what the various types of customers you may be able to create are, it's time to start making them.

After doing this a number of times, I found that usually there are four steps: Quantitative Analysis Qualitative Analysis Drafting the Persona Socializing Let's dive into each one in more detail.

Step 1: Quantitative Analysis If you have a horizontal product or service that isn't used solely by a single consumer segment (i.e., buffer is used by people from several different sectors, work positions, etc.) then this is a crucial stage of understanding what the main customer segments are.

On the other hand, if you've a specialist product, such as an order management app for surfboard shapers, then you probably already know who your target segments are (surfboard shapers), so this stage may not be as relevant.

Regardless, below are the steps I take to finish a quantitative analysis to figure out who our target segments are: Compile a list of clients Analyze the list at the company level Analyze the list at the person level More on each point.

Collect a list of customers Start by compiling a list of all paying customers, with as much detail as possible on each customer.

What details you provide will depend on a number of factors, like serviced industries, the selling process, etc.

This includes basic demographic details about the company, including items like Business

Name Industry Sector Revenue Number of Employees Nation City Revenue Details. This includes statistics about how much money you receive from each customer, including items like Annual Contract Va.

My favorite tool for this is Tableau because you can simply drag and drop your customers' Excel sheet into it and create an amazing collection of charts and graphs all just drag and drop.

Some of the analyzes that I find useful in the past include Number of customers by industry

Average revenue by Sector Number of customers by Country

Avg Employee Size Number of customers. Employee market Size What you're trying to do here is to find patterns that give you some insight into which segments of your best customers are.

For example, in a quantitative study at a previous company, I broke down our customers by revenue band (i.e., how much they paid us) and found that while 83 percent of our customers paid us between $0-$100 a month, those 84 percent of customers actually accounted for 34 percent of our revenue.

On the other hand, the segment that paid us between $100-$1000 a month made up just 13% of our customer base but accounted for nearly half of our sales.

Based on this intuition, we started to look more closely at who these 'sweet spot' customers were (i.e., those who paid us between $100 and $1000 a month) and found that they were mainly from a few key industries: Based on this insight, we started to target Construction, Food & Beverage & Manufacturing as our main segments (Professional Services, though big on the above graph, is actually a mixture).

Analyze the list at the individual level

Now that you know who the best consumer segments are at the level of the business (i.e., creating businesses with 100-1000 employees); it's time to figure out who the perfect consumer segment is at the individual level (i.e., who you need to target within these businesses).

For this, the cycle is in large measure the same as above. Download a list of all buyers at your sweet spot (i.e., construction firms with 100-1000 employees) and then provide information about your product's primary buyer/user in that list.

This may include details such as Job title Department Gender Seniority (VP, Manager, etc.) Once you have this together, load it into your preferred analytics tool and start making some charts and graphs to see what you can find.

Continuing the above example, we noticed that it was mainly the Project Manager inside Construction Firms who used and purchased the product, so they became our marketing persona.

Step 2: Qualitative Research

Now that you have a clear idea of who your target audiences are, it's time to start learning more about these individuals, at both the company and individual level.

In my experience, good old-fashioned customer interviews are the most successful way to do this.

Here's the phase I normally go through: Step 1: Outreach The first step is to create interviews with your current customers (phone or in-person if you can do so).

To do this, I usually take the names and email addresses of anyone I want to reach out to a spreadsheet and upload it to a CRM / sales automation tool that can help send a series of emails to each of those customers and coordinate the efforts based on who responds or who needs more follow-up.

Here's a template for a series of emails I sent in the past: Email # 1 Hey John How are you doing?

My name is Aaron Beashel, and I'm the [position] at [company name] I'm reaching out as I'm interested in hearing more about how you're using our product, what benefits you're getting from it, what you used before, etc. My aim is to return this knowledge to our marketing, engineering & support departments so that [Product Name] can be better for you.

Would you like to talk to me over the phone for 30 minutes and tell me a little bit more about how you use [Product Name]? If so, you can just click here to pick a time that works best for you, or you can answer this email, and we're going to work out a date.

Have fun talking to you, John!

Aaron Email 2 – Sent three days after the initial one. Hey John, I just wanted to follow up on my previous email to see if you had 30 minutes to tell me how [Product Name] is being used?

As I said, the aim of this is to learn how the product is being used by customers like you, so that we can eventually enhance it.

If you're up for a fast talk, you can just click here to select a time that works best for you, and then I'll send you a call.

Have fun talking to you, John!

Aaron Email 3 – Sent six days after the initial email Hey John, I know you're really busy, so just wanted to send you one more email and see if you've had 30 minutes to talk with me about your [Product Name] use?

If so, just click here to pick a time that works for you, and then I'll give you a call.

If you can't spare your time, then that's fine too. I really enjoy using [Product Name], and I hope you're all going well. If there is something that we can ever do to help, please feel free to contact our support team at [Support Email].

The best of it all!

Aaron These emails include, as you can see, links to a page where people can book a time they want. I use Calendly generally for that.

The reason why using such connections is vital is that it prevents you from having to exchange ten emails back and forth with each customer trying to coordinate times, which is a big time-saver for everyone. I've also found that it raises the number of interviews that you actually have booked (as it makes scheduling easier for people).

Step 2: Perform the interview. It's time to start getting on the phone and hearing from your clients until you have those interviews booked in.

After having done more than 100 of these interviews, I built a little outline for what questions to ask and included my favorite questions below, along with some explanation as to why I ask them and what I expect to learn from each.

Q: Can you explain your affair briefly? I want to understand the scale, the primary expertise, the venue, etc.

I suggest that you start each interview on this topic. It gets people talking and it gives you a lot of details that you can use to segment the responses to later questions (i.e., looking at how big vs. small businesses respond) Q: What is your position within the organization? What department does it fall into? How many people are there inside your team?

This question gives you a good insight into who is using your product (especially for horizontal products that any organization might use, such as project management software, for example). It can also help segment the answers to later questions (i.e., what marketing teams are using the product for departments vs. finance).

Q: What are your principal targets and KPIs?

By knowing your target audience's key goals and KPIs, you will build content that reveals how your company helps potential customers accomplish the items they are paying for attaining.

Q: What are the principal frustrations and points of pain in your role?

By knowing the greatest pain points & grievances, you can build messages about how your product can overcome these pain points and help them achieve their role's goals and KPIs (as learned in the previous question) Q: What are you using our product to accomplish?

People 'employ' the product at its heart to do what they need to do. By knowing what work people need to do with your product, you can create powerful marketing that demonstrates how your product will help accomplish the job.

Q: Please explain briefly how you accomplished this before you found out about our product? What were the related problems to this method?

By knowing what people used to do to accomplish everything your product helps them accomplish (and the previous method's pain points), you will generate successful marketing that can persuade them to change their process and use your product.

Q: What's the key advantage of using our product that you get?

By knowing the main benefit that people get, you can start building a messaging hierarchy that focuses on the main benefits that people get, rather than any other benefits that you might think are important but are not really important. Such responses are also useful when segmented by position, sector, company size, etc. as they allow you to see the benefit that different types of users get from the product (i.e., a CRM makes it easier for Sales Reps to remember to follow up prospects, but a Manager mostly gets benefit from the reporting and forecasting features).

Q: What motivated you in trying to find a solution like ours?

This question, best asked for new customers, helps you understand what internal business occurrences prompt people to find a solution like yours, and can help you build sales and marketing strategies to identify these people while they are in an active buying state, or even cause the buying prompt to happen.

Q: What are the three top things you want in a product like ours?

Understanding people's expectations while looking for and reviewing a resource like yours will help you build powerful marketing & content that shows how well your product suits your needs.

Q: What's the purchasing process like for a company like ours? And who is engaged?

This question would give you valuable insight into (or lack of) the purchasing committee that will be interested in buying your product and can tell anything from the design of your website to the selling process that you are creating. For example, if you know someone from the IT individual also gets involved in the transaction and takes care of issues like security and data management, you can plan content that answers their concerns and accelerates the purchasing cycle).

Q: What was your greatest fear or concern about using our product? Is there something nearly stopping you from logging in?

Learning the various factors that deter potential buyers from signing up for your product allows you to concentrate your time and energy on removing such barriers and through conversion levels. A clear example of this is LogMeIn, which surveyed people who downloaded their software but did not go on using it. They noticed that people weren't sure the company would stay around, so they weren't sure how the business was making money. By optimizing pricing in the app and on the website, sales increased by 300 percent.

Q: Which newspapers, news websites, trade shows, forums, etc. do you read to obtain professional information?

If you have a clear understanding of where those people get their knowledge from, then you can schedule top-funnel activities to get to them. For example, if you know they're all attending a single event, you can intend to go there, or if they're actively involved in LinkedIn groups, you can try to promote your content there.

Step 3: Write the answers Although it takes a bit of extra work, I found it incredibly useful to compose a review of each interview in a spreadsheet (usually immediately after the interview is complete).

Doing this gives you a number of upsides: All the answers in one place – If you only have your rough notes in individual documents from each interview, you can not see all the answers to a particular question in one place, which makes it very difficult to recognize the patterns. However, by summarizing all the responses in a spreadsheet, you can simply look down on a particular column and see the answers of everybody to a specific question in one go, making it easy to identify trends.

Segmentation – By summarizing all the answers in a spreadsheet and including some relevant data on each client, such as sector, job title, company size, etc., you can then begin segmenting the answers and see how individuals in particular industries respond to a query or in companies of certain sizes.

Sharing – Every time I did this exercise, and created Marketing Personas, someone wanted to see behind them the raw qualitative data. You can very easily send it to them by getting all the interviews compiled in a spreadsheet.

Here is a snapshot of the table I'm using to describe the reactions of people. You will see the columns for summarizing the answers in line with my question template above, but feel free to copy them and add or remove anything to make them your own!

Step 3: Drafting Individuals Now that you have a good understanding of who your target groups are and have done a bunch of interviews with them, you should be given all the details you need to start drafting your Personas.

It should include key information such as: About them – A description of their information, including their position, industry, size of the business, etc. Essentially all pertinent demographic information.

Use Case – A description of how our commodity is used, what they are attempting to achieve with it, etc.

Previous Solution & Pain Points-A description of how things were done before your product and what were the pain points of the previous approach.

Advantages – A list of the benefits of using the product that they get.

Buying Trigger – A description of what leads them to search for a product like your Buying process – An overview of the usual process people go through to buy your product Preference factors – An overview of the kinds of things they are searching for in a product like yours Again, all parts in this Persona are directly correlated with the questions I ask during the interview, so feel free to add or remind yourself.

Step 4: Socializing the Personas

Now you've developed your Buyer Personas, it's time to get the details into the hands of the people who are going to use it.

How you do this will probably depend on your organization's structure, who will use them, etc., but here are some ideas from the ways I've done this in the past: introduce them to your company Put together a presentation that highlights the buyer's people you created, along with details about what buyer's people are, how they are to be used in your organization, your innovative methodology That could be at an all-company meeting, or maybe just to a few main teams.

Build products

We had one of our designers at SafetyCulture to come up with some custom drawings for each of our customers.

In the various offices and meeting rooms around the world, we then place each of these characters on posters to keep the customer and their needs at the front and center while employees make decisions.

Remember, a Persona is actually a fictional depiction of a real-life set of people, so why not get some of those real-life people to come and tell their stories?

Qwilr, a software tool to build ideas and quotes as beautiful web pages, frequently invites clients to their office for team events such as drinks on Friday afternoons.

Generally speaking, the customer will do a little talk or answer some questions about how they use the product, and then stick around to hang with the team.

Even after the initial presentations and anticipation are over, it's a great way to keep the Personas and the customers they serve top of mind.

Marketing Personas are the basis on which you can build your marketing feature. Without them, it is almost impossible to know how to communicate your product to appeal to the pain points and desires of consumers, or how to approach them in order to build awareness and push them to your website.

It is crucial to get them right, considering how much they influence almost everything else in your marketing process. So take the time to do quantitative and qualitative research and develop people based on the real experience of the consumer as it will pay off in the long run.

How to Create a Buyer Persona

A well-crafted buyer persona (or consumer persona, audience persona, or marketing persona) allows you to personalize your marketing to a large extent by humanizing your customer base's core target groups.

By creating the right message for the right users to successfully targeting your social ads, automation is clearly a must in the world of social media.

Even more importantly, customers expect targeted marketing. A survey carried out in April, 2018 found that more than half of customers expect the deals from businesses to be customized at all times. That is how over two-thirds of millennials sound. Two-thirds of advertisers, however, find it hard to conduct personalization.

But that effective strategy does not need to be thrown into the towel. Keep reading to find out in your social media marketing how to design and use buyer men.

What is a persona buyer?

A buyer persona is a model based on extensive audience research that defines your typical or target customer.

The idea is to create your ideal customer's profile as if he or she were a real person, so you can attract them with targeted marketing messages. Such communications should use the right voice tone, answering the customer's unique needs and wishes.

Because different groups of people that buy your products for different reasons, it is likely that you will need to build more than one customer. That person should include basic demographic data, behaviors, priorities, points of pain and patterns of purchasing.

You can't get to know each particular customer or prospect. But you can build a consumer persona to represent your customer base at every general category.

This makes it much easier to think about your customers as real people and consider their needs and wishes while you build your marketing strategy.

How your company should use customer or viewer Advertising personas allows you to create effective, tailored communications that speak directly to each group of clients.

You express important messages differently in your personal life, depending on who you want to meet.

Say you've got important news to share with parents, friends, and colleagues. You'd probably use various words and methods to enter each of those classes. You can call your mom on the phone, post on Workplace to warn your coworkers, or use a chat with your friends in the WhatsApp group.

Understanding your consumer personas allows you to consider the best ways to reach each of your multiple customer groups, just as you intuitively know how to better access and talk to different groups of people in your personal life.

Your marketing people can also become the shorthand for making business decisions across the organization. Is a new feature of the company better suited to your buyer's needs? If not, you have good reason to rethink your strategy, no matter how exciting it is for your marketing team, or for your IT department, or even for your CEO.

How to build people buyer in 5 simple steps To be useful, people buyer needs to be based on real-world facts, not on intuition.

Defines the people who actually want to buy from you, not the ones that you want to buy from you.

Which means starting with some in-depth research. Gather knowledge through these steps while you are working. Use it to fill in the template for the buyer persona when you get to stage 5.

Do comprehensive audience research

Here's a simple overview of your audience learning information. Know who you're buying from. Collect all the details you can about your current customer base. Age, location, language, income, buying behavior, interests, and activities, and stage of life (such as new parenthood or retirement) are some of the key data points you'll want to gather. Using email surveys, online surveys, focus groups, or even customer interviews to collect what you can from your customer records and consider verifying and supplementing the information.

Move into your social analytics and web site. Social media analytics tools can provide incredible amounts of information about the people who connect online with your brand, even if they are not clients yet. Facebook Audience Insights provides particularly valuable and comprehensive information.

See which is up to the challenge. Once you have collected information about your own clients and supporters, you can test who is engaging with your competition. Do they hit the same target groups that you are? Are they reaching out to communities that you have not yet reached but should? What can you benefit from their efforts to help you set the brand apart?

Even if the aims of your people do not directly apply to the features of your product, they may form the basis of a campaign, or they may simply tell the tone or approach that you are taking in your marketing.

Even social listening can be a good way to collect this information. And just as a good source of feedback for pain points was your customer support team, the sales team can be a good source of feedback into consumer objectives.

Your salespeople are talking to real people who are thinking about buying your company, and they have a clear understanding of what their clients are trying to do through the use of their goods and services. Ask them to collect real quotes that embody the experience of the customer. You may also ask them about the key tactics they use to resolve consumer concerns when selling your goods or services, which leads us to. Understand how your brand may benefit. Now that you understand the pain points and aspirations of your customers, it's time to get a very good image of how your products and services can benefit. As part of this move, you will have to stop thinking about your brand in terms of features and dig deeper to examine the benefits that you are providing to clients.

Marketers will find it hard to get out of the mentality feature — which is one of the reasons why buyer people are so essential. We help you to change your mind and look at your goods and services from a buyer's viewpoint.

Remember: What your product is or does is one feature. One advantage is how your product or service makes life simpler or better for your customers.

For every of the pain points and goals you've gathered, ask yourself one question: How can we help? The answers to this question will form the basis for the main marketing messages that you will be developing in the next step.

5. Turn your research into customer personas.

Gather all of your research and begin to look for specific features. You will have the foundation of your unique customer identity when you put those characteristics together.

Here's how that, in reality, feels. Let's say you recognize a core community of female customers in their 30s who live in big cities, enjoy biking, and own small dogs. Great — now it's time to take this abstract set of features and make them an individual you can connect with and relate to.

Give a name, a working title, a home, and other distinguishing features to your buyer persona. You want your persona to look like a real person without being too explicit and removing features that should reasonably be considered a part of this community of customers.

Goal on how much detail you'd like to see on a dating site, or what you'd know from a short airplane or bus stop conversation. Don't forget to include the goals and pressure points.

For example, the person you call Jogging Jane may be representing your community of dog-owning urban women runners. Rather than thinking about city life and dog ownership in general, you'll give Jane symbolic features that make her a real person: she's 35 years old She's lived in New York City She's employed at a software company She has a two-year-old Chihuahua called Sam She enjoys playing in Central Park And so on.

Note, a list of features doesn't equal an individual. A persona is a practical representation of an entity that represents one section of your client base. Of course, not all people in this category of customers exactly suit your person's characteristics. Yet this persona reflects this community of consumers to you and helps you to think of them in a human way rather than as data point collection.

Speaking to Jane is much simpler than talking to "people" or even "35-year-old women who own dogs." When you draw out your buyer-persons, be sure to explain who each person is now and who they want to be. This gives you the opportunity to start thinking about how your goods and services will help them achieve the position of ambition.

Thinking of your customer personas as real people helps you to build marketing messages that connect to real people. Marketers too frequently use corporate-speak that contains a lot of buzzwords, but it doesn't mean anything. If you craft a marketing strategy specifically for Jogging Jane, it's harder to slip into the pit.

What questions does she have that they can answer your marketing message? What social networks is it using? What kind of language does it use when communicating online with its friends? Thinking about Jane as a real person means you are considering her interests rather than your own.

That is where the suggestions come into the exercise of "how can we improve." Create one main marketing message for each buyer persona that addresses the question. How does your brand help the specific individual solve their problems and attain their goals? Capture it in one simple sentence and add it to the prototype for your persona.

Each time you make a decision about your company and your marketing plan, think about your buyer personas. Do those people right, and you're going to build a relationship with the real consumers they serve, improving sales and increasing brand loyalty and confidence.

Study on social media and reach your target audience. In addition to digging into the demographics of the audience, you can also write, schedule, and publish the messages you have created specifically for your ideal customer.

How to Build a Personal Brand

Creating a personal brand was never more important for freelancers and entrepreneurs than it is now. Anyone with internet and social media access can create an audience, position themselves as an expert and begin to draw customers for their company. And that is exactly what manypeople do.

A new Upwork report has shown that the freelance workforce is rising at a pace 3x higher than the total U.S. workforce. Freelance workers are projected to form the majority of the U.S. workforce by 2027.

While it's awesome to see that so many people embrace their entrepreneurial spirit, this also means that any professional self-employed, independent contractor and entrepreneur will soon face more competition than they already do. Creating a personal mark is the secret to differentiating yourself from your competition.

Why every entrepreneur should create a personal brand: when you build a company in your area of expertise (as an author, speaker, coach, consultant, freelancer, etc.), you actually get the idea of creating a personal branding. When you're the face of your company, it makes complete sense to create your personal brand.

Your brand separates you from your rivals, helping to create a lasting impression in your audience and client's mind. You may find yourself struggling to develop a successful and sustainable company without a compelling personal brand that draws your target market.

Yet even though you are building a corporation that has its own name (for example, a software or physical product business), building a personal brand also has its advantages.

A people are more interested in following other people than in the following business information. Hence creating an audience for your personal brand will potentially help increase your company's visibility.

For, e.g., Elon Musk has more followers on Twitter than three of his companies (Tesla, SpaceX, and SolarCity) combined. The same holds true for Richard Branson (Virgin), Arianna Huffington (Thrive Global), Gary Vaynerchuck (VaynerMedia), and several other highly successful entrepreneurs. All of them have good personal brands they leverage to raise visibility and draw more consumers to their businesses.

You don't need to choose between creating a personal brand and branding a business. Each can be installed simultaneously. # Personalbranding "It is crucial for an entrepreneur to have a personal brand because it is now more crucial than ever for CEOs and owners of companies/brands to come out in the forefront and communicate with their audiences. People connect with people. "Benefits from building a personal brand: trust and authority: having a personal brand helps build trust with your audience, and positioning you as a leading authority and thinker in your business.

Have a personal brand making it easier for you to sell and reach media (online newspapers, magazines, TV, radio, podcasts, etc.). The media are continually searching for experts who can share their knowledge with their viewers.

Create your network: When you have a personal brand that clearly articulates who you are, what you are doing, and how you are helping others, it makes it easier for other people and business people to see value in interacting with you. You can leverage your personal brand to quickly and efficiently create your network, both online and offline.

Attract more customers: Creating a personal brand that will place you as the go-to expert in a specific industry or niche will help you attract more of your ideal clients. Also, when you are positioned as an expert, it's easier for people to refer you to clients.

Premium pricing: Having a clear personal identity helps justify selling your goods and services at higher rates. You become a product that competes on price without a brand. And always there will be competitors who can beat your price.

Build a stable platform: The company will grow over time. During the course of your career, you can also start several businesses in different industries. As you move from one company to the next, your personal brand remains with you.

"With so much content, and a lot of small businesses emerging online, it's much easier to trust a brand that connects to a person's face quicker. 7 Steps to develop a compelling and profitable personal brand After reaching out to thousands of entrepreneurs and branding experts, we have outlined seven concrete steps to help you build a compelling (and profitable!) personal brand that attracts your ideal customers.

We have also developed a fillable Personal Branding Workbook, which you can use as you read through these steps to help improve your personal brand strategy.

Building Your Foundation

The first step to creating your personal brand is to lay a foundation you can build on with trust and authenticity. The main concept here is genuineness.

There is a misunderstanding that creating a personal brand requires having a persona. Yet by definition a identity is a mask. It's not a true representation of who you are and it's unauthentic, therefore.

You should not be an inauthentic person with your personal brand. Branding doesn't consist of portraying yourself as someone you're not. It's about consciously and strategically demonstrating your true self to your audience and clients. Your personal brand should really represent your talents, interests, values and beliefs.

"You want to find the unique thing that's YOU and then make your brand all about that. You can not make it up; it has to be true (although it can and should possibly be a little exaggerated)." Take stock of your current brand assets: to create a strong brand base, start by taking stock of the brand assets you already have. The intersection of those assets is where your personal brand should be created.

Your skills & credentials: What qualities have you gained during your entire lifetime? Which training, certificates, certifications, or awards did you get?

Your interests & passions: What sectors and subjects are you most interested in? What are you crazy?

Core values & beliefs: What are some of the most important core values you hold? What do you think? Who are you for? Which is it you are against?

Major elements of your personal branding foundation: once you have established your current brand properties, the next step is to start building up your personal brand's core elements together. This will help direct your choices as you develop your personal brand: Your brand vision: for what do you want to know? If you are known as the go-to expert of the world on the topic of XYZ, what would that be?

Your mission to the brand: Why do you want to create a personal brand? What does it mean to you? Who is it that you want to influence? What is it that you want to achieve?

Your message to the brand: What's the key message you want to get across? What message do you want to convey regularly in your content and your marketing? If only you could give your listeners one piece of advice, what would it be?

Your brand personality: What are some of the personal attributes and characteristics that you can weave into your company? Want to be viewed as highly polished and competent, or maybe more eccentric and adventurous?

"By understanding who you are, what you stand for, knowing your audience, and knowing your positioning, a great brand begins. What is the image you need to build to draw the target market you're trying to cater to? "One of the largest mistakes you can make when you create a personal brand is trying to appeal to everyone. In reality, not everybody is your perfect customer.

To retain the dream clients, you must be prepared to repel any you don't want to deal with. This means finding a common target market and creating an enticing brand for them.

It might seem counterintuitive, but you won't attract anyone if you want to be accepted by everybody. To stand out, you have to be polarizing. Not everyone who is introduced to you or who sees your message will agree with you or support you, and that is perfectly fine. You don't have to reach out to everyone to build a successful company. Only meeting dream customers.

"To have a good personal brand, you've got to advocate for something, believe in some way of doing stuff, and express those values from your platform with pride. Brands that don't accomplish this get a lukewarm response from the audience and wonder why their actions don't call their audiences to action. "– Amanda Bond A beneficial exercise we suggest to do is to build the ideal customer profile (sometimes called an avatar client). The more you understand the potential customer, including their expectations and challenges, the more prepared you are to build the products and services they really want and need.

Here are some questions to help you build your ideal customer profile: Demographics: what is their age, gender, employment, relationship status, income, occupation, etc.?

Desires and aspirations: what is a desirable future for them? What are their hopes, their ambitions, and their aspirations?

Pressure points and challenges: what's up against them? What is it that keeps them from achieving their objectives?

To learn more about building your ideal customer profile, check out Hubspot's manual for developing a comprehensive buyer persona.

"A strong personal brand is based on how well you understand your audience and the problems they face. Then you can determine why you matter and how to address those problems, for which you will be remembered. "Create a compelling offer To build a competitive personal brand; you need to have something to sell to your target audience. You need an enticing deal that will help your audience solve a particular problem or achieve a particular outcome.

Many entrepreneurs make the mistake of creating a product or service they want, only to find that nobody else wants it, or is willing to pay for it.

That is why it's so important to identify your ideal customer before you create a product or service. When you know just who you want to help, you can build an offer for them, which is the perfect solution.

How to build an offer your clients will love:

Your customers would know how to make an offer: the first step in making an enticing offer is to put yourself as a professional rather than a generalist. Promise a very particular outcome for your customers and develop a customized deal to help them achieve this outcome. Unquestionably, a standardized bid with a vague promise is not irresistible.

Second, consider the connection between what you do, what you do best, and what you expect most from your ideal clients. Then build an offer that sits at the crossroads of these requirements. We call this the Secret of The Irresistible Bid.

Irresistible Offer Formula: What you love doing+ What you do best + What your audience really desires = Irresistible Offer Once you have an irresistible offer, you need to be able to clearly express it to your audience. You ought to be able to answer two questions simply and succinctly: What are you doing? Your answer to that question is a proposition of your interest. What is the interest you owe your customers in return for charging them?

What are you? Offer one specific name to your operation, product, or service. When you give it a special name, it stands out automatically from any rival deals offering the same outcome.

For example, Nicholas Kusmich, a Facebook advertising strategist, helps companies rapidly scale revenue by using Facebook Advertising to get more clients. That's what He's doing. He built a proprietary method to help him stand out from thousands of other Facebook Advertisement experts doing the same thing, and gave it a special name: "Contextual Congruence."

"In the easiest way possible, people need to know who you are and what you are doing. Keep it quick. You should be able to market yourself in 5 words or less. "Design your personal website An essential aspect of creating a personal brand is to have a personal website. It'ss also crucial to have a strong presence on social media, but you don't own or manage any of the social networks on which you set up a presence. Your website is a network you own and manage, and visiting your website in many situations would be one of the moves your target audience takes towards being your customer.

First experiences are completely important. When you visit your personal website, your target audience will be able to easily understand who you are and how you can help them. They will feel as if they have come to the right place. If that is not the case with a couple of seconds, most new visitors will abandon your website.

Perhaps more importantly, you can customize your website to turn casual tourists into paying customers. There are many main elements that are required to make this happen, and most of them are right on your homepage.

Your website homepage main elements: A professional logo: get a designer to transform your name into a professional logo. If you are looking for a graphic design company, we recommend a few in our list of top business resources online here.

Your value proposition: make sure that your value proposition (whom you support and how you support them) is prominently displayed on your homepage, preferably close to the top.

Professional photography: get a photographer to take many pictures of you. Using these images all over your website and for your social media accounts as well.

Social evidence (media, testimonials): add the logos of any newspapers or media outlets that you have appeared in, as well as client/customer testimonials.

A simple call-to-action: offer a clear next move to your website users, whether they enter your email list, register for a free webinar, or apply for a free consultation.

Our friend Jeanine Blackwell comes as one of the best examples of a personal brand website. Here's a screenshot of the homepage of her website, which includes all the elements mentioned above: other important pages for a personal brand website: besides your homepage, here are the other important pages which your personal brand website will contain: about page: share your personal story. How did you get interested in your industry? What qualifications and expertise do you have? Whom are you helping? Why are you helping them? What are you doing? What are they doing?

We recommend checking out the Chris Ducker website here to see an example of a well-written About Article. Here is a screenshot of only one section of his About Page, where he shares his personal story Products / Services: make it easy for visitors to your website to become customers/clients. List any goods, programs, services that you have for sale, along with links to learn more about them or purchase them (depending on your selling process).

For example, on the "Work With Me" page of Sunny Lenarduzzi, she has many drop-down menus that include additional information on her various offerings, including free resources, coaching programs and online courses: content and/or free resources: blog posts, podcast episodes, helpful videos or resource lists that you have created or recommended.

Contact page: give the visitors to your website a clear way to contact you. Send them different ways to reach you (e-mail, social media, etc.), depending on why they're in reach with you.

Lewis Howes has one of the best communication pages we've seen. In order to help coordinate incoming inquiry requests, he has various modes of interaction generated for different types of inquiries: "When you develop a brand that is 100% focused on you, you lay the groundwork for capitalizing on your own blue ocean – an environment where you can function in an uncontested marketplace, free of conventional competitive forces – because none of your rivals can duplicate or copy anything Instead than attempting to show your audience that you can support them, you are producing content that actually benefits them. This creates trust and helps put you in your industry as an expert and authority.

It is no surprise that today's most popular personal brands (Grant Cardone, Marie Forleo, Gary Vaynerchuck, to name only a few) publish vast quantities of content online to help create and grow their audiences.

Develop a content strategy for your personal brand: To develop a content strategy for your personal brand, start by making a list of all the possible topics that your target audience will find helpful. Google's Keyword Planner, BuzzSumo, and Address The Public are all fantastic resources for keyword analysis and common topic discovery.

When you have a list of the topics on which to produce content, the next step is to decide which form of content to produce and where to publish the content.

Popular content types: text/articles Videos Podcasts Webinars Online courses PDF guides, checklists, worksheets Infographics slideshows case studies Popular content outlets: your own blog/website Podcast directories (iTunes, Stitcher, etc.) YouTube Other blogs and online social networking publications (LinkedIn, Facebook, etc.) Don't publish content that would negatively reflect on your brand, and be consistent with how frequently you publish new content to your audience. Content marketing is a long-term strategy, but, when done correctly, it pays enormous dividends.

Creating and promoting content often takes more time and is more expensive than most people know. For this reason, we suggest beginning with 1-2 forms of primary content (such as blog posts or videos) along with 1-2 primary content platforms (such as YouTube - for more information on Youtube Marketing Guide or Facebook). When you start to get good results for your primary content types and media, go ahead and broaden into other content types and media for more people to touch.

"A good personal brand is coherent, simple, consistent, and designed to represent a particular audience. For an entrepreneur, a personal brand is critical because it's the best way to share your authentic message and attract Your specific tribe! "Have a visibility strategy. It is a perfect way to develop your audience to publish content on your own sites, but it also takes a lot of time. A simpler way of building up your audience is by access to audiences of other people.

Here are some common ways to improve your visibility: Interviews & PR: get interviewed as a guest expert on podcasts, virtual summits, and mainstream media like television, radio, and print magazines.

Guest blogging: write articles that your target audience reads for other blogs and online publications.

Public speaking: refer to live events, local Meetup groups, and conferences attended by your target audience.

Collaborations & Joint Ventures: Creating mutually beneficial relationships with other individuals and companies will lead to a variety of opportunities, including guest blogging, interviews, joint ventures, collaborations, and customer referrals.

"The single greatest hack for development is having you published on major publications. If you want to build in your niche authority and reputation, what better way to do that than to get one of the most popular brands to mention you? This gives you a reputation instantly.'

Create a Community Instead of attempting to construct a broad and diverse audience, change the attention of being a group leader in a specific niche. Defines your target market and creates a forum for them to connect, exchange ideas, help each other, and reach out directly to you.

Here are a few ways to develop a community around your brand and business: Create a private Facebook group for your audience and/or customers. It will give you the chance to connect with your audience in meaningful conversations on a daily basis, and just as importantly, provide them with an atmosphere in which they can communicate and encourage each other.

Live Events: Organize live events so you can spend time with your viewers and/or clients in person. Casual gatherings, private meals, seminars, retreats, and strategist groups are all perfect ways to improve the audience's long-term relationships.

Membership Sites: build a membership portal where your customers can access exclusive content, live calls and/or webinars with you on a regular basis, in exchange for a small monthly charge, and the opportunity to communicate with each other through a membership forum or community only.

"A good personal brand is one with a high impact rating, which then contributes to success among the people who follow you. The trick is to use social media and other social networks and environments to construct meaningful and important dialogs between you and the people you want to affect. "Start building up your personal brand. There has never been time better to be a businessman. The obstacles to joining entrepreneurship are practically non-existent, thanks to the internet and technology. Anyone can build online a brand and audience, and create goods and services to sell to their market.

You have rivals as a freelancer or as an entrepreneur. However, you don't, as a personal brand. There's no real rivalry when you are creating a personal brand. Yeah, other people and businesses may be offering similar goods and services as you are, but they're not you. There is absolutely no other person in the world who is exactly like you. You are 100 percent special as an individual.

That is why it's so important to create a personal label. You automatically distinguish yourself from your competitors when you create a personal brand because you are different from your competitors.

How To To Engage With Your Audience To Gain More Insights Into Their Needs, Wants, And Pain Points

Marketers always seem to be thinking about pain points.

Unlike a bum hip exacerbated by the environment, however, the kind of pain points advertisers usually experience can be a little more complicated.

Today we're going to dive into the customer pain points area – specifically, what are pain points and how you can place your company as a potential solution. We will take a look at some real-world examples to see how marketers overcome some of the most common consumer pain points, as well as general guidance on how to make yourself invaluable to your consumers in the right place at the right moment.

But before we get to the cases, let's continue with the fundamentals.

Where Are Sources of Customer Pain?

A pain point is a particular problem faced by prospective customers in your business. In other words, pain points can be thought of as problems, pure and simple.

As with any problem, consumer pain points are as varied and complex as the prospective customers themselves. And, not all prospects will be aware of the point of pain they're talking about, which can make selling to these customers difficult because you have to help your prospects realize that they have a problem and persuade them that your product or service will help fix it.

While pain points may be regarded as simple issues, they are also grouped into several broader categories. Here are the four key forms of pain points:

Financial Pain Points: Your prospects are spending too much money on their current provider / solution / products and want to reduce their spending

Efficiency Pain Points: Your prospects are wasting too much time using their current provider / solution / products or trying to make more effective use of their time

Cycle Pain Points: Your prospects want to boost int. For example, if the pain points of your prospects are primarily financial, you might highlight the benefits of your product in the sense of a lower monthly payment plan, or emphasize the enhanced ROI of the experience of your satisfied customers after becoming a client.

However, while this form of categorization is a good start, it's not as easy as defining price as a pain point before pointing out that your product or service is cheaper than the competition. Most prospective customers' concerns are complicated and nuanced and may incorporate issues from several of our categories above. That's why you need to look at the pain points of your customers in a holistic way and view your business as a solution not only to one especially difficult pain point but as a trusted partner who can help solve a variety of problems.

How can I define Pain Points for My Customers?

They need to find out how to actually identify them now that we know what pain points are.

Although many of your clients would undoubtedly experience the same or similar points of pain, the root cause of these points of pain may be as diverse as your clientele. For this reason, qualitative research is a vital part of finding points of customer pain.

In comparison to quantitative research (which prefers structured questions and representative, statistically relevant sample sizes), the reason you need to perform qualitative research (which focuses on comprehensive, individualized answers to open-ended questions) is that the pain points of your customers are highly subjective. Even if two customers had exactly the same problem, the underlying causes of that problem would differ considerably from one customer to another.

There are two key sources of knowledge you need to recognize the pain points of your clients-your own clients and your sales and support staff. Let take a look at how to get your customers the details you need first.

Conducting Qualitative Consumer Research

One of the best ways to learn about the greatest issues that the clients have is to really listen to them.

We recently held our first Customer Feedback Round Table session, where we invited 11 WordStream customers to spend some time in our Boston offices to share their experiences-good and bad-openly and honestly with us.

As part of this process, we invited participants to engage in a workshop on Ideation & Design, a collaborative, hands-on session in which our clients described some of their greatest challenges as online advertisers. This helped the participants stay focused on the issues they discussed as advertisers, rather than as individual entrepreneurs and business owners, and also enabled us to concentrate on solving problems that were within our control.

We learned things about the challenges of our customers that even the most detailed questionnaire would never be able to unravel, and it gave us the opportunity to address those issues in the light of the broader problems our customers face. This gave us a surprisingly detailed view of the pain points of our clients, as well as a broader view of how the current economic climate and other factors affect real business.

As a company, that kind of event is invaluable to you. It not only helps you to converse freely with the people who actually use your goods, but it also creates an environment where problem-solving is a collaborative process.

Doing Qualitative Market Analysis

The sales team is another research tool at your fingertips. Your sales representatives work on the frontlines of your prospective customers' fight for their hearts and minds every single day, making them an invaluable source of insight on the pain points of your prospects.

However, as useful as the input from your sales team can be, it is important to distinguish the pain points of your sales reps from the pain points of your prospects; the concerns of your sales reps may be very real, but you are not developing a product or providing a service to make life easier for your sales reps.

Separating business issues from real client pain points is key. Let's say your reps are experiencing a sluggish quarter, for example, and sales targets have been missed for two consecutive months. Could things get complicated here? Faced with the prospect of missing another sales target, the reps may be tempted to lament a lack of eligible leads or the quality of the leads they are given. While this may be a legitimate complaint, it has absolutely nothing to do with the suffering of your customers, so you have to filter out the noise to get to the real issue.

Now let's say your reps tell you they've had several potential deals falling through because the prospect told them that PPC was "too hard," which is a real point of pain for the client. This speaks to various potential pain points, including lack of experience or training, poor understanding of PPC best practices, poorly allocated ad budget, a fundamental misunderstanding about your product and what it does, and dozens of other potential problems.

Whatever triggers the pain, now you have a point of pain that you can count in your marketing. Remember our pain points list in this article from earlier on? Let ujs take a look at the pain points we found to see if we could fix them in our marketing: financial: highlighting the lower price point (if applicable), highlighting the average savings of your consumer base, using terminology that reiterates better ROI productivity: highlighting time-wasting reductions encountered by current customers, highlighting user-friendly functionality (such as at-a-glance overviews or overviews).

It's important to remember that you can't "prove" that you can ease the pain of your prospects, and that what works for one client might not work for another. That's what makes social feedback so important when using consumer pain points in your marketing; word-of-mouth endorsements and user reviews become far more convincing when a prospect already trusts that your product or service will improve their lives.

That's why in your marketing, you should use consumer testimonials and other social validation resources – a great review or glowing testimonial will sell your product far more effectively than even the most silver-tongued salesperson.

Mini Case Study: WordStream for Organizations Faced with many unique challenges when it comes to PPC. Life is far from simple for Agency PPC practitioners, from juggling account management with sourcing new customers to improving performance and demonstrating ROI.

We set out to learn in May last year what makes the average internet marketing agency tick – with particular emphasis on the challenges facing agencies – by conducting a survey of more than 200 internet marketing agencies specialized in paid search from around the world.

The findings have been interesting if, in some cases, a little predictable.

During our survey data review, we consider time management to be the single biggest problem facing organizations today. It was perhaps the least surprising outcome of the study – it's no secret that companies are under tremendous pressure if they want to succeed in today's world of online advertising. Even the most trained PPC professional still has to spend time actually working in the accounts of their clients, making time management even more important for PPC managers of the organization.

When we created WordStream Advisor for Agencies, we already knew that time management was a major pain point for agencies, but when we introduced the tool, we also wanted to talk to the pain points of our agency clients.

While we also highlight the range of tools provided by WordStream Advisor for Agencies and the ease of use offered by the application, time savings take center stage throughout this page specifically because time management is a top priority for agencies.

Nearly all of the copy on this page reiterates how much time PPC professionals can save using our software, and this benefit-driven approach forms the entire page's style, sound, and language.

We know time management is the biggest pain point for our agency prospects, but this alone isn't worried about all of our agency prospects.

Remember how we said that many companies faced another pain point in juggling the time between account management and finding new clients? The screenshot above demonstrates how we addressed this specific pain point directly within the framework of time management and efficiency – both Productivity and Process pain points, which logically follow from the initial definition of time management as the main pain point of agencies.

Know – it's not only about finding the pressure points for your prospects, but it's also about stressing what makes your prospects do to relieve this pressure. The simpler in your copy and ads you can make this, the more likely your prospects will be to react positively.

Leveraging Consumer Pain Points in Online Advertising

Now that we have a little more thorough understanding of the idea of pain points, let's start with our examples of how to exploit this pain in your online ad campaigns.

You have done qualitative research on what pain points your customers are feeling, and now you are able to use this information in your quest campaigns. What looks like this?

Payroll is one of the greatest financial challenges facing rising businesses. Paychex says payroll will cost between $20 and $100 a month, in addition to a fee of up to $5 per employee per payroll run, anywhere. This can make recruiting new employees a major expense for some firms (particularly when you're factoring in benefits and other costs), especially young, smaller ones. This ad promises us two months of free payroll services from the get-go, but that's not what we're interested in-we want to take a closer look at the copy of the ad.

The first copy line-" Let ADP Take The Weight Off Your Business With Quick, Simple & Reliable Payroll-hits all the right notes. For one, the use of the term "Let ADP Take The Weight Off Your Company" implicitly addresses the strain of payroll and uses language that evokes relief, suggesting that the prospects for relief will feel when they let ADP handle its payroll.

The use of "Quick, Simple, & Reliable" is also very smart, as these common adjectives all tackle pain points themselves, namely that payroll is a complicated, time-consuming pain in the ass that can't be delegated to other businesses – not bad for three copy terms. Finally, you can note the inclusion of several extensions that provide the critical social validation we mentioned earlier, as well as offerings for a free quote, a demo of ADP's payroll program, and the two-month-free offer highlighted in the title.

Addressing customer pain points in social advertising Social ads maybe even more effective than search ads when addressing consumer pain points. Why? For what? Because many people are aspirationally surfing social media sites like

Twitter and Facebook, we are posting updates that represent the people we want to be, not necessarily the people we are right now.

As such, a well-designed social ad that discusses pain points directly from a prospect might be strongly convincing.

If you know a lot about software development or are buddies with any of your office's engineers, you may already know that the option of a developer's text editor – the software programs where developers actually write their code – is a Very Big Deal, and this ad leverages it to great effect.

Firstly, the ad makes a bold, potentially controversial argument that developers who use Vim and Emacs, two of the oldest and most common text editors out there, are twice as likely as users of Eclipse, another text editor, to pass a technical interview with Triplebyte. While this argument is based on actual evidence, it is a clever emotional cause as well. Developers using

Vim or Emacs feel a smug sense of self-satisfaction while reading this ad, but it may also elevate developers' hackles that prefer other text editors. It makes the ad very enticing for Triplebyte consumers, irrespective of their chosen text editor.

Second, the ad tackles a very specific pain point among techies looking for a new gig — the fear of passing a technical interview successfully. Companies such as Google are renowned (or notorious, depending on your perspective) for the deviance of their technological interviews, and Triplebyte's ad infers that by using Vim or Emacs, prospective candidates will bring themselves ahead of the (ferocious) competition for top technical roles.

This may not be the most common use in social media to exploit pain points, but it is an excellent example of how well-crafted social ads can incorporate emotional triggers to tackle very specific pain points.

Addressing Consumer Pain Points in Landing Pages As our final example of how to exploit customer pain points in your marketing, we come to the humble landing page, one of the most effective – and leakiest – sections of the conversion funnel.

Landing pages are very crucial to the success of a lot of marketing campaigns, particularly PPC campaigns. Aligning your landing pages with your advertisement copy is a well-established PPC best practice, but your landing pages can also serve as another opportunity to reinforce why your product or service can ease the pain of prospects.

Let's discuss how that works.

No Pain, No Benefit

By now, ideally, you have a better sense of what your clients really are trying to do when they're looking for businesses or goods like yours. While several client pain points are identical, there is no one-size-fits-all approach for addressing the pain of your clients. Fortunately, no one knows your customers as you do, so immerse yourself in your research and start helping your customers achieve what they really want.

Any other ideas do you have to help consumers surmount pressure points?

7 Directions to Reach Your True Target Audience

Think quickly: Do you know your target audience?

Many marketers would love to respond with a resounding "Yes!" or of course! "Sadly, when it comes to determining just who they're trying to target, many brands are struggling.

The Outcome? A marketing plan that is on the entire spot and an audience that is not necessarily interested.

Here is some food for thought in the form of followers or sales for those looking to expand their online presence. The population is engaged on social media around a third of the world. Meanwhile, by 2020, eCommerce revenues are expected to reach $500 billion and are on the rise year after year.

Although these figures demonstrate just how many incentives modern brands have to draw followers and customers, they also fill us in on how stiff marketer rivalry is. That's precisely why brands should prioritize honing their target audience in search of a genuinely successful marketing strategy.

Why The Target Audience Matters

Companies live and die depending on how well the audience learns. The marketing mission is exponentially simpler when you have a good focus on your target audience and their needs.

Arby's is a good example of a brand that, despite being in a competitive market, has managed to find their voice and build loyal following. The contents get lots of love from their three million-plus followers on Facebook, and constant reviews about how their marketing team destroys it.

If you're looking for clients or "likes," it's important to know how to speak the language of your audience. For example, the following aspects of your company are shaped by a well-defined audience: the types of content you produce and where you deliver it The voice of your brand and the tone of your marketing messages The places you spend most time prospecting for new leads The biggest mistake marketers make when seeking to attract new leads and followers cast too large a net. No-one wins when you try to appeal to everybody. Your marketing ads and videos tend to be generic, and you're just another crowded face.

Instead, advertisers will strive to narrow down their target markets, carving out unique consumer niches and subsets rather than adopting a one-size-fits-all approach. Those advertisers who are reluctant to become too specific to their target audience should remember how obviously off-the-wall products and brands can still build massive customer bases and counts of followers.

Brands like oVertone, for example, have done a masterful job of carving out their niche. Targeting millennials with bold, follower-submitted images and playful posts, their followers are enthusiastic and engaged despite being a "smaller" player in the beauty industry: Also think about how brands like Barkbox have accrued well over 1.4 million Instagram followers and 2.7 million Facebook fans despite selling an incredible niche product. Definitely heavy. A dog subscription box may sound ludicrous on paper, but it doesn't lie the devotion of its followers.

It is a smart way to attract new clients to improve customer experience. It is one of the easiest ways to cultivate consumer loyalty, too.

Just 41 percent of marketing managers use customer engagement data to inform their marketing plan, according to Teradata.

Despite this, both advertisers and other corporate leaders ignore the consumer both before and after the sale. The biggest obstacle to even beginning is generally, first of all, the lack of a clear understanding of the consumer.

A thorough understanding of the customers is important to achieving the key business objectives. If you are attempting to create (or optimize) the consumer experience, producing more engaging content or through sales, it's important to understand your clients better than they do.

Apply Intelligent Customer Engagement Sales and retention are important for improved customer experience. That can be a source of consumer knowledge if you have it right.

Real-time interaction with the customers has become easier to get to thanks to new technologies. Messenger is becoming an increasingly popular customer service platform, while tools such as Drift allow you to speak to your customers while they visit your website: these channels are a way to gather consumer insight. No matter the platform, the proprietary data from communicating with your customers will help you better understand them. Work with the customer service staff to find trends and respond to the feedback you are creating.

Nothing beats consumer growth on top of that. Having your customers frequently on the phone will help you dive deeper into their problems, desires, and challenges.

That is precisely what Alex Turnbull, Groove's CEO, does to get his customers to learn more. He schedules daily calls to better understand what they enjoy about his company, or hate it.

As a consequence, he has helped develop his onboarding process, transforming dissatisfied customers into satisfied customers and developing more complex buyer personas.

Think of your budding partnership as a two-way street when you strive to keep your customers satisfied throughout the first phases of the customer journey. Encourage consumers to express their thoughts and views by integrating a survey of customer satisfaction into their email drip.

SurveyGizmo proposes these three main concepts when creating a survey: eradicate bias: Ask the consumer for their opinion without imposing your own. Get their unbiased, uninfluenced opinions. You want observations that are real, even if they are negative. One example of this could be something as easy as "What better do you think we should do? "Be concrete: use clear language on a particular subject that asks for input. For example, "How did you use our software to increase marketing effectiveness? "It will help decide the interest you get from your customers.

Focus: There is one aspect of customer service that your surveys will tackle. The goal is to get insights you can then act on.

Keep those things in mind when you personalize your consumer survey with brand and product questions.

Most marketers make the mistake of using generic demographics such as age, occupation, and place to build their customer personas. Such data points actually don't provide adequate details to generate content that resonates on an emotional level with your audience.

One way to delve deeper into consumer tastes is by using Google Analytics' Acquisitions tab to see from which social media channels, business blogs, and technical forums your site traffic originates. To apply this knowledge to your customers so that you can figure out where and when to more efficiently meet them.

Additionally, the collection of keyword data is a valuable way to discover the words and phrases used by other customers to describe the services.

For example, to segment clients based on keyword searches, use Google Webmaster Tools to build a list of popular keywords that drive people to your site. Then organize the keywords into common themes, and allocate them to specific individuals based on the data that you have.

This Bryan Harris video will help you find ways to get around "keyword not given" and help you recognize keywords that people use to get to your website.

Incorporate these keywords into your website text, content marketing campaigns, and other online interactions to put this vocabulary into effect. Using the same language as your clients is a discreet way of making the present audience feel more comfortable.

Customer Analytics Produce Data

From clicking a link to reading through a web page, through consumer behavior, offers useful insight into consumer behavior.

You should use a consumer behavior analysis device to assess how consumers communicate with your Website. Tools such as Google Analytics and Inspectlet are useful ways to gain information like time on page and bounce rate. Inspectlet can also provide user's short videos in real-time on your website.

The behavioral data you gather will bring you to conclusions about what your audience doesn't understand what they do and don't like and how you can construct a better website experience.

For example, if people were having trouble navigating to the sales page, change the interface to allow for a more user-friendly experience.

When there is one page on which people spend more time than others, then examine the content of that page and see what keeps the interest of people. Most importantly, if there is a high bounce rate link, then seek to see what makes people leave.

It is just as necessary to foresee, forecast, and prepare for the future To develop a plan for potential consumer interaction to create a plan for the present. It puts customer service teams in the right state of mind to respond to customers in conditions of stress or challenge.

Predictive modeling software mines current consumer data in order to detect cyclical patterns and trends which may guide decision making. Two great tools are customer analytics from RapidMiner and Angoss, both of which deliver future practical models.

Imagine you are working with a SaaS business that wants to change its product roadmap to foresee consumer desires and see how predictive modeling informs consumer strategy.

Looking at historical data on actions will show you which features consumers have found most useful over time, and which features they have not used. Understanding your most common and viewed pages will also inform your content strategy, concentrating on subjects and formats that best answer issues for your audiences.

Draw patterns across the apps most frequently used to assess why the clients enjoyed them. Therefore, looking at industry trends and research will give you a clear understanding of what other businesses have already done in your space, so you can formulate new features to expand those areas.

B2B International's Julia Cupman stresses the value of market research: "Most businesses are turning to focused market research as a form of insurance, that is, as a means of mitigating business risk. The next section discusses how market research is used in product creation – not just as compensation, but also as a method for recognizing needs and obtaining potential consumer knowledge. "The picture above illustrates how market research supports all phases of the product lifecycle. Continuous market analysis, as you can see, inevitably contributes to greater sales in the product roadmap. The more you understand the market, the better fit you have for the product/market.

Traverse the direction of your customer

The best way to grasp the special and complex experience of buying a customer is to put yourself in the shoes of your customer.

This is made possible by an innovative technique called customer journey mapping — a tool where businesses create a detailed, visual depiction of the consumer experience based on critical touch points — interactions between a consumer and the brand before, during, or after purchase.

Use Uber as an example to identify touchpoints and see how they relate to mapping customer travel. Minor touchpoints include things such as installing the software or following the social media program.

In comparison, the main touchpoints include items such as requesting a ride or completing driver training. Explore the circumstances affecting each touchpoint once contact points are established.

For example, an Uber marketer may ask: What prompted the rider to first download the app? Was Uber's customer retention system linked to that? Using these problems, engage the internal team to get a well-rounded perspective and encourage collective problem-solving.

If you find missed touchpoints, such as if a customer refuses to use the Uber app they have downloaded, set up a plan to reach these customers.

You will want to create benchmarks, such as when an app user has not signed into their account in three months or when the product is unexpectedly stopped by an enthusiastic consumer. It is better if the customer service team will call, write, or meet individually with customers to understand why they are disengaged.

If you don't have these tools, create an email marketing drip that focuses exclusively on re-engaging your customers based on some milestones.

An understanding of consumer behavior has become simpler than ever, thanks to sophisticated analytics, behavioral tracking software, and better customer touchpoints.

The strategies outlined in this article are standard practices aimed at educating and encouraging your customer engagement activities, but they should also be customized to your audience's needs.

How to entice and engage the audience at the knowledge stage According to the Content Marketing Center, the second biggest challenge faced by content marketers is creating engaging content – after the challenge of delivering enough content. It turns out that it may be a little more difficult to create content that drives traffic and keeps readers hooked than it seems.

A common misconception about content is you just need to build it to get all the world's attention. Okay, this is completely untrue. Derek Halpern claims that only 20 percent of the process is produced. The most critical aspect is bringing the material to the hands of people willing to buy what you're offering.

If you need to attract and engage people, and at the right time, you will need to offer the right content to the right audiences. People will engage with your content only if it responds to their particular pain points and needs. It doesn't care just how good the material is most of the time. If it does not appeal to the sensitivities of people, they are not going to consume it.

So think of the motivations and goals of your clients when writing your marketing plan. When you manage to grasp what they're searching for, you will produce information that can help them solve a problem. If you manage to hit their pain points and make their lives a little easier, you've succeeded.

Before completing a purchase, each prospect goes through a series of steps. Each of these phases, you need to consider their intents. In the marketing world, any buyer's cycle is the Buyer Journey, before the sale. So let's look at the purchaser process, and try to understand how customers at every stage think.

The Buyer Process Stages

Each prospective buyer goes through a series of stages before entering the buying point: The Perception Point (Top of the Funnel): At this stage, the buyer encounters signs of a problem. They can't normally call the problem yet because they're trying to learn more. At this point, prospects are seeking further information.

The Assessment Phase (Middle of the Funnel): here, the prospects grasp their dilemma and try solutions now. They have established the exact need and are beginning to explore their options.

The Decision Stage (Bottom of the Funnel):

The final stage is where the consumer has a good understanding of the different options on the market, more or less. We check their options in order to purchase one product or service.

The purchaser trip makes it clear that not every person who visits your site is there to buy your product. Various visitors have different motives and different intent.

Now you'll need to adapt your content to these various stages as a digital marketer. Otherwise, you will throw the content into a huge content of the ocean, hoping it would capture something. And believe me, this is not going to.

If you want to succeed in your marketing campaign, you'll have to give customers exactly what they want—every move on the journey.

"Content should answer the pressing concerns of consumers, regardless of which stage of purchase they are at" The process of producing the right content for the appropriate stage is called content mapping.

What Exactly Is Content Mapping

Mapping consists of creating a roadmap for the content based on the stages of the purchaser's journey? In other words, at each of the three levels, you'll need to build content that meets the needs of prospects.

Mapping your content is crucial in moving your prospects down the road. Adapting the content to your audience would help make visitors lead. In the final analysis, they will be able to make a purchase.

At first glance, the process of mapping content may seem simple and straightforward. Eighty-eight percent of marketers are producing custom content, according to TopRank Marketing. Sixty-five percent of advertisers still fail to grasp what works well and what does not. So much of the difficulty, according to Hubspot, is due to a failure to produce the best content for the right people and at the right time.

And you'll need to know how to chart your content if you expect to see your numbers skyrocketing.

In this article, we will concentrate on the first stage of the purchaser's path, the stage of understanding. At this point, we'll clarify what opportunities we're looking for. What kind of content you should sell them to fulfill your needs. At this point, we will help you understand your prospects, hopes, and motives. And make preparing your editorial calendar for them easier.

Why Is The Awareness Stage Important

Many people may argue that the awareness stage does not merit too much attention because, at this point, no sales are being made? Below are a few reasons to think about your funnel to the top.

The knowledge stage is your first point of touch with your client's ability. A prospect that first landed on your blog doesn't know your company, brand, or product. Typically, they are for details on your web. This stage is of critical importance as it creates the first impression. You only get one opportunity to keep customers, and this is the stage of recognition.

The second reason you need to convince people on this point is that building reputation and legitimacy in your field is your shot. When people read your content and find it interesting, they'd trust you in that niche as an expert. And if you manage to impress them, their friends may even recommend you.

And the last reason you should be worried about the stage of knowledge is that it defines the consistency and quantity of your leads. At this point, making the right content draws the most users to your website. At this point, the more focused and personalized your content is, the better leads you will get. And price leads to greater chances of sales and prospering.

In order to build the right content, what do prospects look for at The Knowledge Stage? Now it is important to understand what people are looking for at this stage. At this point, prospects are looking to better understand a problem. They are looking for details and know-how. At this level, they don't care about your brand or even less about your product. But don't even speak about your company yet!

For this stage, adequate material is solely educational. You need to add value to your prospects and help them understand their need. The quality and helpfulness of your content will decide your relationship with your clients. The better the article, the more likely they are to read other blogs, get back to share your article for more.

At this point, the purpose of the content is to get people to hang around and read more. Browsing the website will help them carry the purchaser's path forward.

Your Call to Action will provide other material for them to read at this point. Don't bring your article to a free offer at the top. Don't underestimate them. They are not eligible for purchase yet. And introducing them to a promotional deal would destroy the promotional chances.

Instead, encourage them to eat more of your food. Show them some other amazing video you wrote, or some beautiful guide you wrote. Getting the prospects exposed to more valuable material would keep them around.

It is important to remember that eligible opportunities for recognition typically come from these sources of traffic: Search Engines Results Social Media (Facebook, Twitter, Pinterest.) Forums and forums (Quora, Linkedin Forums, Reddit.) Backlinks, guest blogging Knowing where your traffic originates will help maximize your distribution strategy. For the three stages, most of these networks will be functioning. Focusing on optimizing certain delivery channels for the knowledge stage would be smarter, though. It's where most of your prospects look for details.

Remember, right in the right position for the stuff.

What Content For The Stage of Awareness

Now We get to the exciting stage.

Through now, you need to know what the audience wants. You know how to cultivate your curiosity and aspirations too. To win their hearts, you do need to do one thing right; choose the right topics for your content.

If you want to rate your content in your niche, you need to write about the right topics. Now you've definitely set up an editorial calendar for the remainder of the month. And perhaps this works great for you. However, if you want to deal with content mapping all the way through, you would still need to focus on your content topics.

And here are the three big steps that will help you find the right content topics for the stage of knowledge.

Identify the core problem/need that solves your product.

When people hear at this point that they need to provide information and knowledge, they typically fall into the pit. They still create very precious and informative content; it is often fragmented and too large. And that's a huge mistake. You will need to narrow your scope and be precise if you want people to look at you as a credible authority. You will focus your writings on the specific need(s)/problem(s) you address. That's going to help you put yourself in that niche as an expert. Also, for something relevant to that subject, your website will become the go-to library.

In addition, writing content about the need you address can help customers travel further on the purchaser's path. For example, Kyvio is a multi-service platform that provides the founders with several ways to build and sell their products online. One of the solutions they have is a tool for creating sales funnels. Kyvio's main need/problem is solving the Lead Conversion, in this case. So the focus of the Awareness stage will be about Lead Conversion. Sales funnels will come up as a solution after reading on lead conversion. And finally, consumers get to know Kyvio as a solution for their needs.

With their material, you can do the same. Think of one or a few key problems that you're tackling and design your calendar around them.

Research hot topics around this problem/need to use Google or resources like Buzzsumo Researching what's trending is the second step to writing appropriate and engaging content at the awareness level. This can give you an insight on what's fun for people and what's viral.

You will get an idea of the topics that will fit well from this search. Figure out what's going on and go beyond it. Look for the best performing content and build even better content around that subject. That will give you more authority in your niche and more reputation.

Using Google or software such as Moz keyword explorer to conduct a keyword search.

Finally, this is where a keyword search is important. It's very interesting to learn what the people are looking for. You can get to know the audience's pressure points and even the exact terms that they use to study them. Begin drafting titles for your content using the most searched keywords. Make sure you optimize your content around the chosen keyword. Including the keyword in the title doesn't suffice. More on how to improve keywords can be read here.

At this point, the ideal content styles are: Blog posts Youtube videos Podcasts Training Quora answers Medium Stories By now, you should be well aware that any content mapping begins with a good marketing strategy. Only getting the best material right there isn't enough. You need to bring it right in front of the right people. You have to offer what the people need. Otherwise, it would go unnoticed entirely. It is like giving a delicious meal to someone who is dying of thirst. They were not going to eat anything. They might even throw it over your nose.

Satisfying the needs of your customers should be your number one priority, and how you can do that is content mapping. This gives you the opportunity to take your prospects by hand and help them decide what they want. If they need information, then it makes it easy to find.

Your prospects are searching for answers on the knowledge level. They still don't want to buy your stuff. And don't feel obligated to press it up to them. Give them exactly what they want, and they'll want to buy your stuff one day. Be gentle with them, and maintain the friendship. Only believe me. It is paying off, literally.

When to develop a social media strategy

Phase 1. Set social media marketing goals that correspond with company goals

Set S.M.A.R.T. targets. The first step in building a winning strategy is setting the priorities and objectives. You have no means of calculating success or return on investment (ROI) without targets.

Each of your objectives should be: Specific Measurable Attainable Time-bound. This is the goal framework for S.M.A.R.T. This will direct your decisions and ensure that they lead to real results for the company.

Track realistic metrics Vanity metrics such as retweets and likes are easy to track but their real value is hard to prove. Instead, focus on targets like produced leads, site referrals, and conversion rate.

You may want to monitor different channel goals, or even different uses of each channel. For example, through its paid social ads, Benefit Cosmetics drives brand recognition but tests the acquisition and interaction with organic social posts.

Confirm that your social media targets match with your overall marketing plan. It would make it easier for you to explain the importance of your work and get a buy-in and commitment from executives.

Start designing your social media marketing strategy by writing down at least three social media objectives.

Stage two.

Learn all you can about your audience Create audience People Knowing who your audience — and the ideal customer — is, and what they want to see on social issues is key to creating content they want, commenting on, and sharing. If you want to convert your social media followers into customers for your company, it's also important.

Attempt to build market / buy customers. Those let you think of your future supporters, followers and clients as real people with real needs and desires. And that will give you the ability to think more deeply about what to offer them.

Don't make assumptions about gathering real-world data. Think Facebook is a stronger network for Baby Boomers to meet than Millennials? Okay, the figures show that the Millennials on the network actually outnumber Boomers.

Social marketing metrics Social media analytics will also include a lot of insightful information about who your followers are, where they live, which languages they speak and how they communicate socially with your brand. These insights let you refine your strategy and target your social ads better.

Jugnoo, an auto-rickshaws Uber-like service in India, used Facebook Analytics to find that 90 percent of its users who referred to other customers were between 18- and 34-year-olds, and 65 percent of that community used Android. They used the information to tailor their advertising, resulting in a cost per referral of 40 per cent lower.

Step 3. Proceed. Competition analysis Chances are, the rivals already use social media — and that means you can benefit about what they already do.

Conduct a competitive analysis

This analysis allows you to understand who is the competition, and what (and not so well) they are doing. You will get a clear understanding of what the company needs, which will help you set your own social media goals.

This research would also assist in finding opportunities. Perhaps one of your rivals is dominant on Facebook, for example, but has put no effort into either Twitter or Instagram. Instead of trying to win fans away from a dominant team, you may want to concentrate on the networks where your audience is underserved

Social listening activities

This is another way to keep an eye on the market. Here's how to use Hootsuite platforms for social listening and tracking competitors: You can note changes in the way these channels are used when you track competitor accounts and related industry keywords. Or, you may be spotting a specific post or advertisement that really hits the mark — or completely bombs. Keep an eye on this infO, and use it to determine your own goals and plans.

Phase four.

When you are not using social media devices, you need to take a step back and look at what you have actually achieved and accomplished. Ask yourself the following questions: What works, and what does not work?

Who has social relations with you?

What networks are your target population using?

How does your presence on social media compare to your competitors'?

When all of this knowledge is collected in one place, you'll have a strong starting point to prepare how to boost your performance.

Your audit will give you a clear picture of where each of your social accounts serves its function. If an account's intent isn't obvious, wonder whether it's worth holding.

Ask yourself the questions that follow to help you decide: Is my audience here?

If so, how do they use the platform?

Can I make use of this account to help achieve realistic business goals

Asking such tough questions will help keep track and concentrate on your plan.

Look for impostor accounts

You can identify fake accounts using your company name or product names during the audit.

Such imposters could be detrimental to your company, never mind catching your followers. Report them. You might want to check your Facebook and Twitter accounts to make sure that your fans and followers know they are dealing with the real you.

Step five.

Set up accounts and improve existing profiles Evaluate which networks to use (and how to use them) You will also need to identify your plan for each network as you decide which social media to use.

For example, social media manager for Profit Cosmetics, Angela Purcaro, told eMarketer: "We're all about Snapchat and Instagram Stories for our makeup tutorials. On the other hand, Twitter is reserved for customer service. "For example, here is how many small and medium-sized companies use social tools to communicate with clients. Notice that for this reason Facebook and Instagram outrank even email.

Social media marketing

It is a good exercise for every network to generate mission statements. These one-sentence statements will help you concentrate each social network on a very specific target for each account.

Example: "We're going to use Facebook ads to reach a specific audience to improve sales." One more: "We're going to use Instagram to promote and share our corporate culture to better attract and support employees." If you can't build a strong mission statement for a particular social network, you may want to rethink if that network is worth it.

Set up your accounts

Once you determine which networks to concentrate on, it's time to build your profiles — or enhance existing profiles so that they fit with your strategic strategy.

Using keywords to search for your company Using photos that are appropriately shaped for each network Here's a quick rundown of how to bring your social media profiles into tip-top shape: We do have step-by-step guides for each network to walk you through the process:

Creating a Facebook business page

Creating an Instagram bus. Know, using less channels well is better than stretching yourself thin trying to maintain a presence on every network.

Phase six. Find inspiration

While it's crucial for your brand to be exclusive, you can also draw inspiration from other socially superb businesses.

Social network success stories

Those can typically be found on the pages of the social network's business group. (This is Twitter, for example.) These case studies will provide useful lessons for each social network that you can apply to your own objectives.

Award-winning profiles and promotions

You will also be able to check out the Facebook Awards winners or The Shorty Awards for examples of brands at the top of their social media game.

Tell your friends Users can also add inspiration to social media. What do your target clients chat about online? How do you know about their desires and their wishes? If you have social media in place, you could even ask your current followers what they want from you. Only ensure you follow through and deliver what they're looking for.

Phase seven.

Creating a calendar of social media content Sharing great content is of course necessary, but it is equally important to have a schedule in place for when you're going to share content to get the full impact. Your calendar of social media material also has to compensate for the amount of time you spend engaging with the audience (although you need to allow some spontaneous interaction too).

Creating a posting schedule

Your calendar of social media content lists the dates and times when you will be publishing content styles on each site. It's the best place to schedule all your social media activities — from the exchange of photos and links to blog posts and videos. It includes both your day-to-day posting as well as social media campaign material. Your calendar ensures that your posts are well spread out and are released at optimum times.

Plot your content mix Make sure that your calendar reflects the mission statement you have assigned to each social profile to support your business goals. For example, you may decide that: 50% of the content will drive traffic back to your site, 25% of the content will be selected from other outlets, 20% of the content will support corporate goals (selling, lead generation, etc.) 5% of the content will be about HR and corporate culture. If you're starting from scratch and you're just not sure what kinds of content to publish, consider the 80-20 rule: 80% of your posts will inform, educate, or entertain your audience, 20% should promote your brand directly.

You might also try third party social media rule: One-third of your social content is promoting your business, attracting followers, and generating income.

One-third of the social content shares insights and stories from business experts or like-minded businesses.

Personal connections with your audience include one third of your social content.

Using scheduling software or bulk scheduling to schedule your correspondence in advance, once you have your calendar planned, rather than continuously updating during the day. It helps you to plan your posts' language and structure, instead of writing them on the fly whenever you have time.

Phase eight.

Test, review, and change your plan Your social media strategy is a very important document for your company, and you can't presume you're going to get it right on your first attempt. When you start executing your strategy and monitoring your progress, some tactics might not work as well as you'd hoped, while others work much better than planned.

Track your data In addition to analytics for each social network (see Step 2), you can use UTM parameters to monitor social visitors as they pass through your website, so you can see precisely what social posts drive your website's most traffic.

Re-evaluate, test, and do it all over again

Once this data begins to come in, use it to regularly re-evaluate your strategy. This knowledge can also be used to check different posts, promotions, and tactics against each other. Constant testing helps you to understand what works and what doesn't, and in real time you can refine your approach.

Surveys can also be a great way of finding out how well the plan performs. Ask your fans, email list, and visitors to the website if you fulfill their needs and desires, and what they want to see more of. Then ensure they deliver what they're telling you.

Things shift rapidly in the social sphere. New networks are emerging while others are going through important demographic shifts. Your company always goes through cycles of transition. All of this means your social media plan will be a living document that you constantly look at and change when appropriate. Refer to it regularly to keep track of yourself, but don't be afraid to make adjustments to better represent new goals, resources, or plans.

Be sure to let everyone on your team know when you are reviewing your social plan. This way they can all work together to help make the most of your social media accounts in your company.

Dos And Donts Of Social Media Marketing

Using social media for the purpose of marketing is a phenomenon which will not quickly go away. Indeed, global social ad advertising is growing year after year: Social media marketing spending nearly doubled from 2014 to 2016: from $16 billion in 2014 to $31 billion in 2016.

70 per cent of people in North America use social media on a regular basis and use social media more than they do watching television every day. All of this means using social media to market your business is really a worthwhile investment.

Using different social media accounts can help you develop deeper personal relations with your customers when done correctly. It can also spread the word about promotions, values and deals quickly, build a stronger brand persona and increase brand engagement. But what does it mean to "rightly do social media?" "It's different to use social media to support your company than using your personal Facebook account to post pictures of your children on the first day of school. It needs finesse, and an in-depth understanding of what the customers want. There are countless ways to communicate with your audience using social media; some better than others. Let's discuss some of the best (and worst) activities on social media.

Do Remember to Post the Best Times

Just the timing of your posting could be an art in itself. Think of the people you're following, or the people on your friends list posting everything they're doing, all day long.

Not always perfect, huh? You want to be careful on what, where, and how much you publish, so you don't have too many updates to inundate your followers. Also, make sure that you are posting when the majority of people actually see your content.

There are different suggestions as to when is the best time to post on the social media pages of your company. Hootsuite says this is a perfect time to post between 9:00 and 12:00 AM early in the week. Hubspot recommends posting to Facebook and Twitter around 9:00 AM, and to Instagram about 5:00 PM. There are plenty of data out there that shows when is the most successful time to write.

Do your study, and then see what are the best times for you. How are you having the very best performance from a post?

You don't have to stick to the rule hard and quick. When you have news that is breaking, you can share it immediately. And you can definitely post a "max" time during a time of day. Finally, you're going to start knowing the right time to connect with your audience and get a better understanding of when you're getting positive outcomes.

Don't Ignore Your Accounts One (or Any)

Have you started multiple accounts on various social media sites "to keep up with the times?" "If all you've done is launch an account, but you haven't done anything else with it, it's not only not representing your brand, it can potentially hurt your reputation.

For example, if a potential customer attempts to contact your company with a question via an overlooked social media account, you might leave them feeling lost and without a answer. Or, a visitor to your Instagram account that has been abandoned may feel like you are not available or present.

If cyber tumbleweeds roll through your account's main street, it does little to reflect your brand favorably, and can give your brand an impression of indifference, inattention, or negligence. Not right.

Instead: just sign up for as many accounts as you can handle reliably, and post something on all of your accounts when you post on one account. Apps and tools to automate will help you do that.

Too busy on Facebook, or not interested in uploading videos or updates to Snapchat regularly? This is perfectly perfect. If you have a strong understanding on only one or two sites on social media, that's perfect! Take on whatever you are willing to do well, and your fans and clients can see your social media pages as an easy way to connect with your brand and learn about it regularly.

Do Use Different Media Styles

Just like the way you don't post text-only blog posts (because it would be boring), you do want to vary the ways you provide your audience with details. You can make videos to post on your different social media sites using only a smartphone, a video editing app and a YouTube account.

Throughout the internet there are tools available to build your own shareable infographics and even more information on how to make a perfect one. You can also share pictures and short videos on Instagram, Snapchat, Pinterest, Twitter, and Facebook, or even "go live" to make an announcement, share sales or promotion details. In reality, 82 percent of people prefer a live stream to social posts from a company, and 80 percent prefer a live video to a blog post.

You can't ignore the fact video is highly successful, particularly live streaming.

Think of it as if you were creating a delicious tossed salad: the more ingredients you include, the more interesting and delicious your salad can be. The more your posts are varied, the more captivating they are for your customers.

Ignore Comments or Questions Social media should be just that:

Social. Your fans and customers would want to connect with you using the social media. In the hours, and even days, after a article, you will find an explosion of questions and comments and you have to learn how to manage them.

If you get an overwhelming response on one specific post from the group, it can be stressful. Do you need to answer every single comment? The response is "no." It is not only time consuming but wasteful to respond to every question. Yet there are times you certainly should be listening.

Often followers take advantage of the accounts to ask questions.

And you may even end up with a bad score. There are forums for feedback and comments and you can not neglect them. A negative review or message is a perfect way to communicate with a disgruntled consumer and turn their opinion of your brand around.

And answering questions includes members of the audience who are asking for help, and let them know that the organization is trying to support their clients.

Instead: Take a second to calm down before reacting to a negative comment – you're not ready to fight fire. Look for the true meaning or real anger behind the words in their message, and respond authentically in a compassionate way to try to help the situation get correct.

You may also call on a disgruntled customer to contact you directly. This is a perfect opportunity to mend your working relationship, and to model your outstanding customer service to any other followers who have seen the negative message.

Do Give Solutions

Help them overcome a current problem is one of the best ways to connect with your audience. When you've done your customer persona work, you probably already have a good understanding of the issues many of your clients are trying to solve. And how do you fix those problems?

Your posts on social media can be a great opportunity to present simple, clickable solutions to solve the problems that your audience is having.

Don't forget to include links

You need to include links to a landing page, a blog page, a shopping page, a contact us page – or something different to get your followers to your website. Your goal on social media is to communicate with your fans, but it's also to convert customers to fans!

The best way to help them get this done? Include links to your website in your posts so they know where to go and so getting there is easy.

When a customer has to loop back to your bio or find a connection, then you will lose them. One perfect way to make it easy to link?

Use the feature called "swipe up" on your Instagram post. Hubspot reports that the Instagram stories accounted for a 10-minute rise that people spend on the platform. Yet if they can't get to your website this doesn't mean anything! If you already have 10,000 or more fans, it should be easy to add a "swipe up"

Don't have as many fans as yet?

Here are a few ways to connect through Instagram if you've just not been given the magical "swipe up" feature yet.

Do Make It (Something) Personal

Your social media profiles are a perfect way to get your fans and customers to know your business better. That being said, you should consider your online voice sound, and how it fits in with the purpose of your brand.

Sparknotes is an outstanding example of that. Their social media posts contain a lot of fun and amusing memes to improve interaction as they care for students. A style of posting and sense of humor suit the audience's.

But why does this campaign focused on humour work for them? Since it suits their "buyer image," and Sparknotes and their followers are sincere about it. When the tone of voice in your company doesn't suit this theme, it won't sound true to your audience. Figure out what works for you: confidence posts, motivational posts, funny posts, news reports. Whatever your brand suits, that what you should do about it.

You may also use your social media pages to remind your team about your audience. Seek an Instagram takeover during a promotion from a charismatic employee, or show the outstanding work that a team member does on your accounts. Let your clients in, and let them meet you.

Social networking can be a great tool to further bind current customers to your brand, and help you find new customers in the process-if you're doing it right. Principal "Do? "Be real. We all spend a whole lot of time on social media that when a person or company tries too hard to build an online identity that is not true to who they are, we can tell you.

And if you use your social media pages to show off the "real self" of your brand, and you're smart about the type of content you share, you can't go wrong

Hands-On Advice On Developing, Implementing, And Measuring Social Media Marketing Campaigns

There are greater than two billion active users on Facebook each month, one billion on Instagram, and 365 million worldwide on Twitter.

Seventy-seven percent of the population of the U.S. alone has some sort of social media presence. If it's talking with friends, staying linked to people all over the world, or for company and networking purposes, users are on social media for several reasons — and advertisers know it.

Due to the sheer number of agile users on these sites, marketers quickly realize how important it is to reach their clients via social media. Indeed, investments in worldwide social media ads are expected to rise to around USD 48 billion by 2021.

When traveling, working, and even relaxing, with so many people monitoring their smartphone messages and social media notifications, what better way to advertise than on social media?

Social media marketing worrks

Audiences receive accessible, low-cost, impactful, and effective social media ads. Social media campaigns have become, exactly for this purpose, a key marketing tool for companies everywhere.

With billions of people on social networks — and continued growth in monthly users and influence — it's difficult to imagine how businesses will stay relevant without having a presence on social media.

Making use of social media would allow you to reach your target market, connect with current and potential customers, create brand loyalty, increase traffic on the website, and drive sales. Social marketing isn't just a phenomenon; it's a strong business tactic that's here to stay and help you reach out to more people around the world.

What's a Marketing strategy for social media?

A social media strategy is an organization's organized marketing program to boost the details (about a brand, product, or service) utilizing at least one social media channel. Such campaigns are strategically based, have observable effects, and are motivating followers of social media to feel or act in some way.

How to Set Campaign Goals for Social Media Marketing

When designing a social media marketing strategy, you should keep in mind clear SMART targets to ensure your research is as successful as possible. Here are some strategies and examples of organizations that have performed them well.

We've paired them with related examples of social media marketing campaigns to provide more context and help you get a better grasp of these campaign objectives. Let us take a look at this:

Social Media Campaign Examples

Coca-Cola's Share a Coke campaign to connect with their audience

ABC News website URL campaigns to boost traffic

Starbucks Unicorn Frappuccino campaign to drive sales

Snickers' #EatASnickers campaign to engage audience members with a unique hashtag

Work on Brand awareness

By sharing your ads on a number of sites; your company can increase brand awareness through social media. You may also use unique hashtags and provide opportunities for followers to share your content and add their mates.

Improving your brand image by social media doesn't need to take much time either. In reality, by spending just a few hours a week on social media, 91 percent of the marketers said they saw an improvement in their brand visibility. When you have a schedule for your campaign, you can map exactly where it should be posted, and when it should be posted to keep things effective.

The Apple Shot On iPhone campaign is a brilliant example of using social media ads to raise awareness about the brand. Apple's amazing iPhone cameras allow their 90 million+ users to take pictures with professional cameras that look like they've been made.

Over the years, taking beautiful pictures has also become more and more relevant to social media users, particularly with photo-focused platforms like Instagram. Apple has chosen to mesh these ideas and launch the Shot On iPhone campaign featuring customer-taken iPhone photos.

Users take photos with their iPhones, upload them on social (in this case usually on Instagram), and use the hashtag of the campaign, # shotoniphone, which has been tagged in over 4.3 million posts so far. Apple shares pick pictures from their 6.8 million followers on their Instagram account and offer participants a chance to get their pictures on a billboard.

Apple's strategy for social media marketing increases brand recognition through its Instagram account, hashtag, and encourage people to share their images with their own followers.

Apple launched the campaign, but the people doing the hard work are iPhone users. Through this campaign, the company is creating a stream of the most stunning and exclusive photos, which also serve as a way to increase brand awareness and promote the function of the iPhone camera.

Connect with your audience.

It is necessary to connect with your audience in any kind of marketing. Efficient marketing strategies are more important than ever in a world of growing distractions and diminishing patience. The nice news is that social media has made communicating with potential clients anywhere in the world simpler.

When you're working on a social media marketing campaign, you want to interact with your audience on both a surface level — through a follow-up, tweet, or "like"—and a deeper level — through a similar post that gives them a sense of your brand or goods in some way.

Coca-Cola's social media campaign Share a Coke successfully connects the company to a deeper level with its audience. By selling coke bottles with the names of people on them, Coca-Cola customizes the buying experience, which excites customers to buy and share the bottles.

If it's their name or a family member, relative, or co-worker 's name, consumers feel a connection to those Coke bottles. Some of the bottles are also fitted with stickers that customers can peel off and wear as a name tag or send someone else.

By developing labels with several different naming spellings and using less common names, Coca-Cola made the advertisement even more relatable. Customers can also customize their bottles for $5 on the firm's website. Through this initiative, the organization found a way to communicate with everyone.

Coca-Cola has also introduced a hashtag, # shareacoke so that users of social media can share their images and videos with friends and followers. Since the campaign went viral, the # (hashtag) has been used on millions of social media posts. For those who intend to share a coke, or post a photo of their own experience, Coca-Cola's social media bio section offers links to the campaign for more information.

The Share a Coke campaign gets customers excited about a personalized Coke bottle and makes consumers feel linked to the brand on a deeper level. Furthermore, millions of people have been encouraged to share photos, videos, and stories about their experiences of buying and sharing a coke on social media.

Increasing Website Traffic

Social media is a perfect way to improve traffic on websites. Simply inserting your website into your bio profile helps direct visitors to your site where they can learn more about your business or a particular product. Customers have no patience and easily lose interest. You can prevent any misunderstanding by including the URL in your bio and keep it easy for your future customers.

Your campaign team can also be able to reply to social followers with URLs to different landing pages on your site. Including links to your website as a part of a regular conversation or organic post is a perfect way to show them you are listening to and through the traffic on the website.

Finally, you can easily add a website or a landing page URL to your actual social message. By providing followers with links to the tools they need to address their questions and concerns on their own, you'll increase website traffic.

Lots of news stations around the world, for example, add URLs to their social media posts. Sometimes they are seen posting an eye-catching image, photo, quote, or comment along with a link to the story itself.

This works well, as it increases traffic on their website. If followers do not follow the link to the station's website, if they still want to connect, they can always select "Like," or "Share."

Drive Sales

Marketers are trying to excite consumers about their goods and brand. If a company can do this effectively, it will most definitely see a revenue boost. Social networking ads are a perfect way for people to get excited about new products as they have the opportunity to share, use photos, get the word out.

The Starbucks Unicorn Frappuccino campaign was one example of that. Starbucks has been known to create an exclusive "hidden menu" items, and photographing such drinks has become increasingly popular, as they often make Instagram and Twitter posts enjoyable. The company took advantage of it and began selling the Frappuccino Unicorn — a vivid, colorful drink that was only on sale for a short time.

Starbucks posted the Frappuccino pictures around social media and drummed up enthusiasm around the drink. They have developed a hashtag, # unicornfrappuccino, to inspire clients to share their beverage buying and drinking experiences.

The $5 drink was so popular with consumers that there were over 180,000 posts on social media that featured the drink during the single week it was available in April 2017. The drink also resulted in a 3 percent rise in the same-store sales for the second quarter, and the same-store sales in March 2017 rose by 4 percent.

Now that we've analyzed some of the most popular strategies for social media marketing let's dive into how you can kick off yours.

How To Build A Marketing Strategy On Social Media

Study your competition Build your strategy Appeal to your target audience Choose your content style and format Control the effects of your campaign strategy Promote one message during your campaign Balance your promotional and non-promotional content Ensure that your content is exclusive to your company Engage with your public regula Plans differ by sector, social media site, and type of campaign. Using the following tips – which concentrate on three major steps like studying the competition, creating the strategy, and promoting your content – to build your plan for social media marketing.

1. Study Your Competition

Find your competition at the planning phases of your social media marketing campaign.

What businesses are similar to yours and have already active social media accounts?

What companies have campaigns you think they've done well?

Do the companies that you usually review prizes, competitions, or live videos?

What is feedback on their social posts like?

You'll begin to understand what works well in your industry by taking a step back and asking yourself these questions. You'll also be able to find out how to make the campaign exclusive.

And look elsewhere for inspiration, too. If your competition is not on social, you are not a fan of their previous campaign style, or you have an incredibly unique company, then look for other campaigns that encourage you and decide how you can add elements like a similar theme, level of engagement, aesthetics, or a particular message to your campaign.

2. Craft your plan.

Next, form your plan for the campaign. Consider your target audience to determine your campaign goal.

Call upon your target audience.

Who is it you are trying to reach?

How can you figure out your target audience?

What do you think this campaign will achieve for your business and the public?

Why do you develop ongoing interaction with your followers during your campaign?

You should also prioritize, ensuring that your content and marketing appeals to your target audience. Note the crucial rule in your marketing strategy for social media. Do not lose sight of who you intend to link to and why.

Otherwise, your audience would simply scroll right past your social media or lose interest in your campaign within seconds.

Here are several ways to cater to your social media target audience: Find current trends. What is it that people want to see these days? Instagram stories, for example, and live streaming, became very popular. Can you integrate those patterns into your campaign and social routine?

Be aware. Make your public want to stop listening. Why'd they check out your post or campaign if you don't have details worth their time? Provide an invitation to your audience — create a giveaway that allows your audience to read your explanation from beginning to end. Also, tell them how to take part in the draw, and when to declare a winner.

Build exclusive visual content, which is convincing. Whether it's a Facebook video or an edited Instagram image, make sure that your visual content is persuasive and entertaining. Give something the audience didn't see before.

Keep in with your audience. Eighty-four percent of customers expect businesses to reply within 24 hours of posting on social media. If your followers leave questions, feedback, or complaints about your posts, then you can contact them back. You and your audience will form a personal bond that will make them more loyal to you and your brand. You'll also be more efficient in earning their trust.

Choose the format and type of content you want.

To decide the type of content you're building your campaign, think about why. Here are some instances where a company might build a social media marketing campaign: Holidays Special events or milestones Collaborations with other companies Competitions or rewards User-generated content promotions Consider what sort of content should be used on which platform. For instance, if your campaign makes use o a lot of still photography, then Instagram may be your forum. If you need live streaming and would like to share longer videos, Facebook could be a good option. And if you want to release shorter information bursts, then Twitter could be a good match. Think about what is best for each platform and go from there.

Manage your plan for campaign success.

No matter why you're designing your campaign, you're likely interested in knowing the level of success of your campaign. You'll need some sort of metrics to calculate and track during your campaign to draw some assumptions about your performance.

A common way to do this is via a metric tracker like Google Analytics, or the social monitoring and metric tracking tool from HubSpot. This type of quantitative data would show you details such as the amount of total campaign traffic, how many new followers you attract (as well as how many followers you lose), the level of interaction, website traffic changes, and any revenue changes.

3. Promote Your Content

Now, it's time to continue your campaign sharing and promotion of your content. Consider the strategies that follow on how to promote and distribute your content.

Promote one message over the program.

You will start by spreading one message through several different channels using content that suits the platform you have chosen. By constantly sharing the same message during your campaign, your followers will frequently hear the same content, which will encourage them to maintain your message.

In the past, marketing strategies have shown that when repeated, the messages are most successful. Repetition can lead to familiarity, promoting trust between your audience and your post, brand, and product. Keep on redundant posts.

Align your material, both promotional and non-promotional.

When you are actively forcing promotional material on them, your followers will notice. Through combining promotional and non-promotional, the followers will see you as helpful and want to communicate more with you.

It is about the followers not feeling stressed or obligated to become a client. When you provide your followers with promotional content that is matched with content that they find helpful and engaging, you'll be most successful.

Ensure your company has unique content.

Create an aesthetic that fits your label for your campaign. You want this to be special — anyone who lands on your page should know it's yours without reading your handle for profiles. Being special and genuine makes you stand out, it gives people a reason to want to follow you above your rivals as well.

Keep daily interaction with your audience.

You should set aside some time to answer questions, "like" comments, and respond to reviews, irrespective of how many followers you have. You'll give them a personal experience by taking the time to connect with your followers that they won't forget. These are the kinds of partnerships and interactions that keep the brand investing in followers.

Build a hashtag special to your campaign.

Both big social media campaigns have a hashtag for the social networks that should be the same. Hashtags (#) allow you to keep track of the interactions and make interacting with your campaign simple for your followers. Your hashtag should be unforgettable and special.

Snickers, for example, has a popular social media campaign called You Are Not You When You Are Hungry. They show characters who lash out, lose their minds and even turn into different people because they are "hangry" ... or hungry-angry. Such people go back to their usual selves after taking a bite from a Snickers bar and satisfying their hunger.

The campaign hashtag is # EatASnickers. It is straightforward, easy to recall, and action-oriented. In addition, "Eat a Snickers" is also one of their ad tag lines, which contributes to the campaign-wide uniformity.

Using planning tools to automate your content.

While it can be time-consuming to create engaging content and connect with your fans, there is a way to plan your campaign posts in advance to save you from having to do so in real-time.

Tools like Hootsuite, Crowdfire, and CoSchedule allow marketers to schedule posts that include text, images, videos, hashtags, and more. Any of these scheduling tools feature analytics to help users assess which scheduled posts are performing well, and which posts need to be updated.

Using live streams to your benefit.

By 2021, live streaming is expected to expand into an industry worth more than $70 billion. With live streaming, members of the audience can watch content from anywhere in the world in real-time, which creates a unique and engaging experience.

Facebook Live is one of the most common live content streaming methods, followed by other platforms, including Twitter, Instagram, and YouTube. You can use live streaming to update news folks as it happens, conduct gifts and contests, interview guests and influencers, or just make followers feel personally linked to your brand.

Your choice is the way you promote your content, but don't forget to check and evaluate your findings. This way, you'll know whether you should or should make any urgent changes while the campaign is still alive. The information can also be applied to potential campaigns.

Start Building Your Social Media Strategy has taken the world by storm. Although some patterns shift, social media is here to stay. Social media marketing strategies are a great choice for companies who want to remain relevant and effectively and efficiently promote their content.

With the potential for massive reach, the opportunity to connect directly with fans and clients, the convenience of sharing the content with thousands (or even millions) of people, and the work's budget-friendly nature, social media marketing campaigns cater to companies as well as consumers alike.

Start to create exclusive and entertaining content for your social followers, and make an impact that drives sales and pumps people around your brand.

The Latest Developments Of Facebook

After all, Facebook has launched some new apps and has also rolled out a new version of the Messenger mobile app, continuing as they always do.

This month, we've got new live streaming usability tools, the revamped Messenger app, a "quiet period," and a new download data tool that will improve both the consumer and marketer experience.

Let's look at all these recent developments and what they are doing for you.

New Live Streaming Accessibility Tools

Web content has had a huge drive in recent years for inclusiveness and transparency, and it's awesome to see this expanding into Facebook's live stream.

Facebook has had only live video stream options so far, where video material is shot and transmitted in real-time. While most users enjoyed it, this content created an immense entry barrier for those who are hard to understand and or who rely on screen readers.

Now, Facebook has announced they will release a live "audio-only" mode that will come with the automatic captions option. They have also announced that they will provide new ways to view live streams outside of Facebook itself, but we don't know much about it yet beyond the fact that even those who aren't logged in will see the content if they want.

Overall that's fantastic stuff. Automatic captions can have a strong propensity to be less than accurate (especially when there is mumbling/background noise / even the slightest accent involved), but they still enable hard listening users to follow along with the simple conversation. Brands will consider using and exploring this new format to see how well it fits for them. You can treat it as a short podcast when in doubt, and we all know how popular podcasts have been in recent years!

New Desktop Messenger App Rolls Out

Facebook's desktop messenger app is brand new, allowing users to engage in group chats and group videos from computers and laptops.

This is a new standalone Messaging app specifically built for your mobile. In the browser, you can still use Messenger, as you are currently doing; this is different.

This app was essentially rolled out because Facebook wanted to find new ways to help its users communicate with each other while potentially also weeding out details. The idea is that the more people are linked, the easier it will be for shelter-in-place orders, so why not keep them linked on Facebook and in Messenger

(Particularly since they can benefit from Messenger placements).

You can see what the latest app looks like here: This feature would be most useful for personal use, but it can be used by businesses if they want to communicate to small groups of customers on the web. They could likewise use the feature for internal communications, if necessary.

New "Quiet Mode" Rolled Out

Facebook has recently started to carry out "Quiet Mode," which allows users to literally mute all alerts. The aim is to get them to actually walk away from their devices (both phones and desktops).

This is a relief for many. When people are faced with shelter-in-place warnings at home, it is a little too much that they get pulled into Facebook and social networking sites. And while it doesn't sound that encouraging anyone to turn away is in the best interest of the network, in reality, it is a really positive thing. Inquiries have been made concerning the effect of social media on the mental health of users in general, and those concerns have been raised during periods of crisis. Facebook encouraging users to reduce their time on the website will lead to an increase in the user experience, which means that while on the web, they are able to engage with better content (such as your brand!).

As a company, be prepared for some users to take longer if they are using this feature to respond to you both publicly and in private.

For now, it's only rolling out on iOS, so it'll probably be available to Android devices beginning in early May.

Revised Data Download Tool

If you read the Instagram Updates article last week, this section should look a little familiar.

Facebook this month has worked to give users even more clarity as to why they see the advertisements that appear in their feeds. They released an updated version of their current data collection tool that allows users to access their own operation three new parts of information.

The latest reports show user experiences on both Facebook and Instagram, including updates to their own profiles, page material, post views, comments, and more.

Inferences about how Facebook combines different habits of the user with material that it finds important.

A list of categories given to Instagram accounts you are connecting to will specifically inform users what types of content Instagram feels they are interested in when deciding what to include in the Explore section of their app.

Again, companies don't actually benefit from this just as much as consumers do. That's all right;

building confidence with users to understand what they're seeing and why is crucial right now, particularly when so many users are distrustful of ad targeting capabilities in the midst of concerns about privacy. In reality, this may help create more trust between customers and advertisers by shedding some light on the process.

While not an officially approved usage, advertisers can review their own data to see if they are getting any new ideas about how to reach users based on their own network experiences. For example, many brands gladly view content relevant to their own business, so you could get some new ideas to consider for categories on Instagram.

Right now, it's not shocking to see a number of social media sites quickly shifting their attention to trying to find new ways to help users, brands, and advertisers during the time of the crisis, particularly because no one knows exactly how long it will last. It makes sense that in the immediate months, we will continue to see features that are geared towards this intent, particularly when many small businesses are struggling, misinformation is still circulating, and users are searching for more meaningful ways to remain linked.

Over the next few months, keeping up-to-date with what's happening on your primary social media sites might be more important than ever, particularly when these new features may be so useful. Facebook is a vital medium for businesses working hard to stay linked to their customers right now, so take the time to start engaging in your Facebook strategy and management. It'll be totally worth it.

As a result of the pandemic, Facebook has made a few improvements to their interface (which we'll look at first), but they've also worked hard on a variety of new features that will influence how users and brands communicate with the site.

Since we're all dealing with the coronavirus and its consequences, we would expect to see some improvements in best practices in marketing, a slight pause in the release of in-testing software, and some platform adjustments (especially ad campaigns) that could somehow be related to it.

Facebook Announces Improvements Related to COVID-19

This is one thing that we see people talking a lot about, so let's get it out of the way: How does the virus impact Facebook marketing?

There are a couple of ways COVID-19 could affect your campaigns right now.

Here are the basics: Facebook has confirmed that there will be delays and mistakes in ad reviews due to changes in the approval process and with employees out of town.

Make sure you design your advertisements and apply them for approval long before you actually need them, so you have time to change them, edit them, or appeal them if necessary.

Facebook has established a ban on any advertising and commercial listings aimed at capitalizing on the virus-related fears.

At this point, it is difficult to sell some potentially miracle remedies, hand sanitizer, disinfecting pads, and test kits. It's totally difficult to sell any face masks. This is just about stopping misuse, rather than anything that Facebook is actively testing new features on both WhatsApp and Messenger to reduce confusion about the virus.

Some of these disinformation campaigns (including "cures" and theories about government actions) have gained enormous popularity in messaging apps, so it can be useful to give users the opportunity to quickly investigate statements made in Messenger online until they believe it and reshare.

Here you can see what it will feel like:

Facebook Launches New "Mood" for Stories Frames

The new "Mood" mode of the Facebook Stories camera enables users to create a GIF-centric frame for their stories.

Users can look up a GIF, pick it, and underneath it will be framed with statements like "mood" or "LOL."

These are built to be fast and simple to make, and right now, they are using the popularity of GIFs in Stories.

We recommend that marketers use them to clarify their emotions or enthusiasm about the news that they have already covered in a story that leads to it instantly, such as an announcement of a new product or a consumer review post.

For Messenger, Facebook's Rolling Out

New Technology is having yet another update.

For Messenger, Facebook is rolling out a new update to simplify and concentrate your messaging experience.

Facebook is presently close to launching the next step, after first announcing its intention to simplify Messenger back in 2018.

According to TechCrunch, the biggest change is that the latest update will delete the segment on in-app Discover. All that's left for your key navigation options will be "Chats" and "Men."

Overall, this probably won't have too much effect on most brands, although some have benefited from the possible awareness boost of the Discover segment.

Stories seem to be incomplete, too.

Facebook Allows you to transform 2D images into 3D images.

Facebook's 3D photos app now has a new feature that other advertisers may want to take note of.

The device can now assess and simulate depth inside any image.

Static, flat, Rather 2D images may now have a 3D graphic appearance.

These pictures aren't really 3D, but they do make the feed more attention-grabbing and can look higher in price.

Users may also use their mouse to "tilt" the image, much like a 360-degree picture will.

Although you can use Facebook to build actual 3D posts (and these are going to be of superior quality), this is a good smart solution for brands who want to easily update their images.

Facebook Checking Instagram's ability to cross-post Facebook stories We now have the ability to create stories on Instagram and share them on Facebook as well. The only thing you've got to do is hit the little Facebook icon and boom, shared; on both interfaces, you don't need to recreate the story, so it's a great time saver.

The function has only worked one way until now.

Nonetheless, Facebook is now exploring the possibility of making Stories with them and then uploading it to Instagram by cross-posting. This was recently discovered by the incredible Jane Manchun Wong, who found the coding in the app's backend.

Although this may not actually be a massive game-changer, it will be a fantastic advantage for brands and advertisers and will improve future convenience.

This unity makes sense as more strong integration is needed between the messaging apps.

Marketing on Facebook is still fast-changing. Right now, the pandemic has us all on edge and taking precautions, and even if it slows down a little further progress, it's nice to see that Facebook takes its position and responsibility seriously here.

The organization recognizes that its platform has been used (intentionally and unintentionally) to disseminate false information and even take advantage of people, and they are doing their part to make sure that isn't happening anymore.

Remember to concentrate on important, empathetic Facebook ads as we pass over the next month and search for changes in customer behavior.

Your audience is likely to be more active, so now is not a time to slow down the post, but they might be more sensitive than others to other types of content now, so be on the watch out for that.

The one constant in social media marketing is that things constantly change, and this is especially true on Facebook, the world's largest social network.

Perhaps more fascinating these days is that there is a trickle-down impact on Instagram when

Facebook makes a move, which is particularly true with regard to ads.

Nice people at Facebook have announced some exciting changes that we should look forward to in the months ahead – changes that we should bear in mind when preparing our plans for 2019. To help keep you up-to-date, here are 11 new Facebook updates you need to hear about.

Facebook Ad Solutions and Features Updates

1. Shopping in Instagram Stories

Make shopping experiences more engaging and connect by adding product stickers to your Instagram stories.

Users reading your story will be able to get specifics of the product and other stuff, and they will also be able to move to your mobile app to make a purchase.

2. Augmented Reality Ads

With Augmented Reality Ads, advertisers would be able to create deeper connections with users by allowing them to engage with and imagine different Facebook products and experiences.

The ads, as you can see, will allow users to quickly access the Facebook camera to check your offers with a CTA 'Tap to try on.'

3. Facebook Stories Ads

Facebook Stories Ads will also allow brands to create new experiences through the Stories option on the platform.

Facebook stories haven't taken off the way Instagram stories do, but this kind of full-screen creative is really popular right now, and Facebook stories advertising will have more opportunities for reaching users across both platforms.

4. Playable Ads

Facebook has recently launched Playable Ads for Game Apps that allow users to "play before purchasing" – which will lead to higher-intention installs from users who have had the opportunity to sample the App before downloading it.

Updates for Facebook Accounts
5. You may have already seen this on

Facebook Page Recommendations, but Facebook Page Reviews have been updated to Recommendations.

The update aims to give Page users a clearer understanding of what they should expect based on the experiences of previous customers, which brings an extra degree of clarity to the reviews.

6. Updated Web Pages

Another change you're probably already aware of is that Facebook business pages have been updated on the smartphone, making them easier to access, which Facebook claims will drive more progress.

Facebook alerts on measurements
7. *Video Metrics Updates*

Facebook has recently updated its video ad analytics to help advertisers get a better perspective on true user interaction, and refine innovative content based on those behaviors.

8. Also, Self-Serve Brand Boost in Test and Learn

Facebook has launched new self-serve tools for testing and learning how your Facebook Ad campaigns affect your brand perception. This is a tool we can't wait to get to know each other better.

Creative Software updates
9. Video Production Kit

Is No? No problem-Facebook has recently released a new Video Creation Kit that helps you to turn your existing photo properties into mobile videos. These templates, which are simple to use, also provide text options.

Facebook Changes to Campaign Management

10. Value-Based Lookalike Audiences

Lookalike consumers are great value-based viewers, but how much better would they be if you could recognize and target people close to your customers based on their online and offline behaviors?

Now you can think of this as Lookalike Audiences 2.0.

Have articles about social media like this in your regular inbox Bottom of Form Top of Form Bottom of Form

11. Value Optimization with Minimum ROAS Bidding

Facebook also offers the power for marketers to monitor the value a campaign produces by allowing you to set the lowest appropriate return on ad spending. On that basis, the program from Facebook would bid to equal or surpass the value-another perfect way to automate campaigns.

And there you've got it, eleven cool updates Facebook has released into the wild – or will release soon. From adding product stickers to stories to enabling behavioral targeting online and offline, Facebook continues to expand its platform, offering new considerations for your campaigns.

The Latest Developments Of Youtube

YouTube views more than 4 billion videos daily. The user interface obviously does not scare tourists away.

YouTube is expected to unveil new YouTube apps and enhanced resources to make the experience of users and creators even more enjoyable and beneficial. Small businesses that use the video platform for marketing their goods or brands will welcome these changes — rolling out over the course of the rest of the year.

Here's a fast look at new features on YouTube:

1. Improved Comments

While comments are appreciated, junk comments are an annoyance for the majority of users when watching videos and interacting with like-minded people that not everyone wants to see. The new rating system is intended to reduce the exposure for a cleaner style of garbage comments.

According to Kiley McEvoy, YouTube's marketing manager, this has resulted in YouTube reducing the hate rate by over 36 percent.

2. Subscriber Notifications

Subscriber Updates Of billions of viewers watching videos every single day on YouTube, it's fair to say highly loyal followers enjoy their channels there. The new subscription notification function can be used by content creators to let their fans know they've posted a new video.

Every time a new video is released, fans will have access to opt-in and receive updates through their smartphone and email. Say FOMO (Fear of Losing Out) goodbyes.

3. New Card Styles

Supporting your content is one way to ensure that you retain your existing customers and that you increase the number of new viewers. The new types of cards would allow other material to be marketed, merchandise to be sold, money raised, and even more.

The first card is the Channel card that allows you to connect the videos you make to other platforms so that you can share them with people you work with. This interconnection will enhance your popularity by presenting your content to audiences you may not have considered in the past.

4. Easier access to the Subs Feeds

The subscription feeds allow creators to see who is making an effort to look at the content being created. The latest sub-feed will make stream and update the YouTube mobile app simpler and quicker to get to the subscriptions.

With so many metrics available to assess consumer engagement, customized service will be available to prioritized or loyal customers to ensure they continue to watch.

5. A Faster, More Powerful Creator Studio App

The company is focusing on enhancements to the Creator Studio app with mobile continuing to grow as the primary platform for accessing video content.

Creators would have more analytical tools to gain useful insight and make informed decisions about how to best communicate and maximize their platforms with their audiences. That includes new action notifications.

6. Go Video Management

Is the foundation of YouTube, and it's important to boost its quality. Data mobility management also has two new capabilities, focused on user requests. The first is the ability to update your mobile device's custom thumbnails, and the second is the option to allow or disable monetization on your images, wherever you happen to be.

7. 360-Degree Video recordings

This is one of the best features now available on YouTube. New video capture tools like GoPro and drone-based recording will add a new dimension to the content we view. The newly added 360-degree feature lets the audience see everything happening at a particular location. If that's not enough of an experience of immersion, YouTube is still working on adding 3D.

8. Better Live Streams

Good live streaming isn't all about video content. The distribution system covers entertainment, gaming, learning, and more. Whether it's video, software, or sports, content creators will now have an easier time setting up and handle their live streams.

The company has also revealed its new YouTube Gaming app that will offer gamers an opportunity to take advantage of the latest live stream technology for a trip.

9. New Creator Culture

As a social network, YouTube thrives on its built community of users. That is responsible for the success it enjoys at the moment. The new Creator Community will be a new online community to promote communication, knowledge sharing, and input from the company on how to develop products and services.

10. Updated Creator Academy

The way it has democratized education is an undeniable reality concerning the Internet. Users worldwide are now able to take free classes from Harvard to Stanford, and virtually all in between.

More than 50 lessons and features have been introduced to the Creator Academy designed to find the lessons you want to learn more quickly. It also allows customized instructions on what to expect next.

YouTube claims that some of these new features on YouTube will be available in a matter of weeks, while others will be published over the year after all the updates are finished.

When people speak about the most popular websites for social media today, YouTube is mostly left out of the discussion in favor of sites like Facebook and Twitter.

But don't be fooled: YouTube does have a lot to do. While Facebook may be the largest social networking platform, in terms of general use, YouTube has the second-largest reach after Twitter. It is also behind its parent company's second-largest search engine, Google.

And you can do a lot of fun stuff with YouTube that you might not know about, whether you're using YouTube to watch videos, share them, or both. Did you know, for example, that YouTube has its own virtual reality (VR) environment for watching any video in 360 °? And that you can build a connection to YouTube time that takes viewers to a specific moment in the video?

Mind-blowing stuff, guys. I have compiled 20 of the lesser-known hacks, tips, and features YouTube has to give to assist you make the most out of the still very popular website.

Tricks, hacks, and apps on YouTube

Convert any video into a GIF.

Creating a link to the YouTube time to start a video at certain stages.

See a video in the published text.

Have your own written transcript uploaded to the scan.

To make a written transcript using YouTube.

Using video playlists to build, share, and collaborate.

Save the videos for later viewing.

Creates your own custom YouTube URL. To promote similar content, add an end screen or cards.

Browse and download from the online music and video library at YouTube.

YouTube Enhancements incorporate artistic effects.

Play videos over mobile devices in the background.

Live stream YouTube videos.

Download and watch the 360-degree and VR videos.

Watch for a new algorithm for the YouTube ads.

For $10 / month, delete advertisements from YouTube videos.

Using Google Trends to explore common search words on YouTube.

Switch your kids' 'safer' YouTube on.

Clear your history as you watch.

Read about copyrights on YouTube in a different way.

20 YouTube Tricks, Hacks, and Apps That You Need to Learn

1. Using the URL, you can convert any YouTube video to a GIF.

Everyone loves GIFs, but it's not common knowledge to know how to make them. Oh, it should be, because all it takes is a little trick with a YouTube URL.

Pick a video to watch on YouTube and find the URL at the top of your screen to make a GIF from a YouTube video. Include the word "gif" right in front of the domain name, so it reads "www.gifyoutube.com/[your video tag]." It will take you to gifs.com, with your video already posted and ready to edit. Here you can find a left-hand menu of options with a timeline bar along the bottom of your screen. You may set the length of the GIF, crop the frame, add captions, etc.

Click the top-right button on "Build GIF," and it will ask you for a GIF title and tag collection. Then press "Next," and you've got a convenient landing page to share your newly minted GIF from. Keep in mind that simply by signing up with gifs.com, you can save this GIF to an offline device.

2. You can create a connection at a given time that will start a YouTube video.

Ever wanted to send a YouTube video to someone, but guide them to a specific moment? Let's presume you are trying to recruit your friends to learn the dance with you in the music video of Justin Bieber's "Sorry."

Rather than sending the general YouTube link to your friends and instructing them to hurry quickly to the minute mark, you could actually give them a different YouTube time connection beginning the video whenever you want. Click to see what I mean here.

To create a connection that starts a YouTube video at a certain time, open the video and click "Post" at the far right of the video title. Then, check the box next to "Start at:" in the options window that appears, and type in the time you want (in hours: minutes: seconds). Instead, when you want it to start, you can pause the video, and the field will auto-fill.

You'll see a tag attaching itself to the end of the generic YouTube link after a couple of moments (in this case,? t=50s). Only copy and paste the connect wherever you wish.

It's worth remembering that you can't embed a video because, at some point, it starts; you can't just relate to it.

3. The published transcripts of people's videos are easy to read.

Do you know that YouTube produces automatically a written transcript for every single video that is posted to its website? That's right — and everybody has access to the text unless the user hides it from viewers manually.

I can think of multiple scenarios where video transcripts can come in handy. You may want to write down a quote from a picture, for example, but the tedium of pausing-and-typing, pausing-and-typing would push you up a wall. Or maybe you need to locate a specific portion of a video, but you don't want to re-look the whole thing to find it. You will find details like this with a transcript in hand, without doing it all by hand.

To see the transcript of a video: Click on the video on YouTube and click the "More" tab under the video title. From the drop-down column, pick "Transcript."

(If you don't see that option, it's because the user has chosen to hide the transcript.) This transcript will appear in the same window as a new tab. In certain instances, the person who posted the video may not have gone back and edited the transcript manually, so it is not going to be flawless. But certainly, it will save you time and pain.

4. By editing or posting a transcript, you can help your video find itself in quest.

When ranking videos in the quest to decide what your video is about, both YouTube and its parent company Google look at a variety of things, and your transcript is one of those. (Your video description is an even bigger ranking factor, which is why Digital Marketing Strategist Ryan Stewart recommends you actually paste your transcript right into the description box as well.) To include a transcript to your video: open the video on YouTube, and you will see a series of icons just under the Play button. Tap the

"Subtitles / CC" button on the far right. (CC stands for "Closed Captions.") Set your language if you do not already. Then, you will be asked to choose between three different ways to add subtitles to your video or closed captions.

Attach a transcript of prewritten text or a collection with synchronized subtitles. (Learn more about the types of files that you can upload and more here.) Fill in a complete video transcript where subtitle timings are set automatically.

Watch the video to type them in.

YouTube people have done some amazing things to make the third option as painless as possible (typing while you watch it). For starters, if you check a box next to "Pause video while typing," this will make the entire process much smoother.

5. You can easily get free transcripts of your videos and audio files using YouTube.

I guarantee this is the last one about transcripts — but I'll bet you've never thought about them this way. YouTube will automatically add a transcript to each video, as you know from # 3. So if you're looking for a one-off transcription of an audio or video file, and don't want to pay for a subscription, the built-in captioning feature from YouTube isn't a bad starting point. You can still recover it later.

Simply post your video to YouTube, open it on YouTube's website, click the "More" tab under the video title, and pick "Transcript" from the drop-down menu. The Transcript appears in the same window as a new tab. For a user-friendly experience, follow the steps outlined in # 3 if you wish to clean it up.

To have an automatic transcription for an audio file: Using a service like TunesToTube, you will need to post your audio recording to YouTube, YouTube would need to post it somewhere from 2–30 minutes. Then follow the instructions outlined above to get an automated transcription for a photo.

6. Using video playlists to build, share, and collaborate.

Just like other favorite media sharing sites like Spotify and iTunes, on YouTube, you can create a "playlist" — which is just just a place to store and organize the videos (your own and others'). You can keep your playlists private, make them public, or even share them with others directly.

For several different types of users, playlists are useful, from a person compiling cooking tutorial videos for their dinner party to a brand segmenting their YouTube video content by topic.

To create a playlist on your desktop: go to your Playlists page by clicking here or by clicking on the 'your account' icon in the top right corner, select "Creator Studio," click "File Manager" on the left corner and select "Playlists." Then click on the top right corner of "New Playlist" and choose whether you want to keep it private or make it public.

To create a mobile playlist: Click here for instructions on how to create new playlists using your mobile devices, iOS, or Android.

To include a video to a playlist: If you add a video to a playlist when watching it, press the "Add to" button below the video title and check the box next to the playlist you want to add it to.

If you want to add a video directly from your Playlists tab to a playlist, simply click "Add Clip" and then paste it into a clip URL, pick a video from your posts, or search for a video on YouTube. When you find the video you want to add, pick from that video the "Add to" menu and add it to the playlist.

Your mates should also be adding to your playlists. Only switching on the ability to share on playlists is all you have to do. Once you turn it on, anyone with whom you share a connection to the playlist can add videos to that playlist. (Any videos they have added can also be removed.) To include friends to a playlist: go to your Playlists page again and open the playlist you want to work on. Click on the "Playlist Settings" button and pick the "Collaborate" tab. Toggle on the setting that allows partners to add videos to the playlist, and you can give them a link to add videos to the playlist from there.

When invited to a playlist, your friend will be able to add new videos to it and delete videos they've added in the past. We can just follow some on-screen directions first to confirm that they would like to be a contributor and save the playlist to their own account.

When you inc a video to a playlist on which you are collaborating, your name will appear in the playlist next to the video, and anyone invited to collaborate on that playlist will receive notice that a new video has been added.

(Read this YouTube Help article to learn more about how to handle users, avoid accepting contributions to a playlist, etc.)

7. You could save the videos for later viewing.

Have you ever seen YouTube videos for which you wish you could later bookmark? You might not be able to turn the sound on right now, or maybe you just have no time to watch it. Okay, YouTube has taken a page from Facebook's. Book. Book. By adding something very similar to the "Save for Later" feature on Facebook. You can save videos to a playlist called "Watch Later" on YouTube to access whenever you want.

The playlist "Watch Later" works just like a regular playlist, so the guidelines are similar to the previous stage (unless you can't allow anyone to work on your playlist "Watch Later").

To add a video to your playlist, "Watch Later": Open the video on YouTube and click the "Add to" icon below the video title and check the box next to the playlist to which you wish to add it, just as you did in the previous phase. The steps on mobile are very close, but if you want the full instructions from the Help page on YouTube, click here.

To access these videos, simply go to your homepage on YouTube and select "Watch Later" from the menu on your screen's top left-hand side.

You can replay the videos you saved from there, as well as quickly remove videos from the list you've already viewed.

8. You can make your own custom YouTube URL.

To get to your YouTube channel, do you want to give people an easy-to-remember Web address? In reality, you can create a custom URL based on things like your show name, your YouTube username, any current vanity URLs you have, or your linked website name. For example, HubSpot's is https:/www.youtube.com/hubspot.

Important Note: Make sure you're confident before you do this is the custom URL you want — because once it's accepted, you can't ask to change it or move it to anyone else. Keep in mind that both your YouTube channel and your Google+ profile will be linked to it too.

Sadly not everyone is eligible for a custom URL. You must have 100 or more subscribers to get one, be at least 30 days old, have a picture posted as your channel icon, and have posted the channel art if it sounds like you, read on.

To assert your custom URL: Open the settings of your YouTube account and click "Advanced" in the section on your name.

If you are registered for a custom URL, then by clicking a button, you will be prompted to claim yours.

Pick the box next to "I agree to the Terms of Service." Then click "Change URL" to make it final until you are completely confident it is the URL you want (because you can't ever change it).

9. To promote content, you can add an End screen or cards.

YouTube started allowing clickable YouTube links called "annotations" to be inserted into your videos in 2008. These annotations function like call-to-action buttons to get people to sign up for your website, see merchandise or fundraising campaign, visit another site to learn more, and so on.

YouTube has replaced annotations with end-screens to make them more normal parts of the user experience, where you can show more visually appealing call-to-action cards in the last 30 seconds of your video.

How to add an end screen

Is there a fancy closing screen for your favorite YouTube creators that allows you to keep watching their videos? You can also build a custom End Screen. By recommending other videos and places that they can check out, they help keep viewers on your page. Explore to your Video Manager, tap "Alter," and pick "End screen & Annotations" from the drop-down menu. From there, you are taken to the End screen creator room, where you can play with various models and context to decide how your end screen will look. Then click the "Connect Item" menu to decide where you want the viewers to be sent from your end screen.

Any YouTube maker can attach an end screen for their channels to be customized. Here's an article about the explainer with more information and inspiring ideas.

How to add a card

You can use cards to promote items that you want to sell on YouTube, used in your videos, or links to your website. If viewers tap the I in a video 's top-right hand corner, the cards will expand, as in the example below: To add a card to a YouTube video, head to your Video Manager, tap "Edit," and pick "Cards" from the drop-down menu.

Instead, pick where you want cards to appear in the video, and tap the drop-down menu "Attach card" to choose what you want the card to support. From there, when watching your video configure the content that will show to viewers when they tap the I

10. YouTube has a huge library where you can browse and download high-quality, royalty-free sound effects and music.

Want to add any cool sound effects or music (or any video) to your YouTube video? YouTube is for you. It has a full library of high-quality, 320 kbps audio tracks and sound effects that you can download and add to your videos with no royalties. (Or listen in your spare time. We're not going to judge.) To include music or sound effects to your video: Open the Audio Library of YouTube by clicking here or opening your Creator Studio, click "Create" in the left-hand menu, and pick "Audio Library." By default, the "Sound Effects" tab will start you. You can search for sounds using the search bar here, just as I did for motorcycle sounds in the screenshot below.

You can also turn by category (all from human voices to weather sounds) or swipe through favorites you've featured in the past. Pick the star to add the track to your Favorites to allow quick access in the future. The bars beside the songs show just how famous a track is.

When you turn to the "Art" tab, all of the royalty-free art can be browsed through. You 're not going to find the Beatles in here, but you're going to find some nice stuff — like suspenseful music, uplifting music, holiday music, jazz, etc. You may toggle by genre, mood, instrument, period, and so on, instead of toggling by category.

(NB: Some music files in there might have extra attribution criteria that you need to meet, but they're pretty clearly set out on a song-by-song basis. You can read more on YouTube's help page here.) Once you've found a track you want, click the arrow to access it and transfer it as an MP3 file directly to your device. And with that, you can do whatever you want.

If you want to source sounds outside of YouTube for your posts, you'll just need to make sure you follow all the guidelines for sourcing them. For best practices for audio sourcing, see this

YouTube Help page, and this one to know the music policies of YouTube.

11. The YouTube Enhancements add improvements and artistic effects.

YouTube has faded a range of features that it had experimented with at one time — including annotations and a not-so-popular slideshow builder — but Improvements is one editing method that remains very handy. Nine effects you can usually find on third-party video editing apps, you can now take advantage of native YouTube: auto-fix lighting and color Balance blurred camera movements Add slow motion Add time-lapse Trim sections of your video Rotate display filters Custom blurring blur faces To make changes to your current video: click on your File Manager to find a video. Click the drop-down icon next to "Delete" on the right side of the screen and click "Enhancements." If you are editing on a device, this button will open all nine tools on the right side of your screen, where you can apply different changes, filters, and blurring effects and see how they affect the final product in real-time.

Notice that not all developments on mobile devices are available. You can only cut, add music, and apply filters on Apple and Android smartphones and tablets. Read this post to learn more about improvements to YouTube.

12. Play YouTube videos on mobile devices in the background.

Your own music playlist also just doesn't cut it. Or maybe at an award show, you would like to listen to the success of your favorite artist.

Anyway, if you've tried listening to music through your mobile device on YouTube, you may have found one thing: you can't navigate out of the site. You have to keep YouTube accessible because to listen to anything on YouTube; you can't use your phone for something else. It's kind of stressful if you're trying to do multitasking on your home walk, yes?

Now there are hacks, so you could listen to background YouTube material while still using your mobile device. This is what you do:

Step by step instructions to see recordings out of sight:

iOS Open Safari on your cell phone, and explore to a video you'd like to watch on https:/www.youtube.com.

Start playing the video you'd like to listen to and then tap the Home button to close Safari. (I chose Katy Perry.) Then swipe up to open the Action Center on your home screen.

Then swipe left on your Action Center to show the second screen. The specifics of the video you picked will appear on YouTube, and simply tap Play to keep jamming from there.

How to stream YouTube videos in the background: Install Android Firefox or Chrome on your mobile device and navigate to a video that you want to play on https:/www.youtube.com. Then tap the "Settings" key in the upper right corner (the ellipses) and pick "Request Web App." Start playing the video on YouTube, then tap the Home button to get back to your home screen. The audio will continue to play in the background while other applications are used.

13. You can upload videos live to YouTube.

Live online video has been a big discussion subject for the last couple of years. Massive development has been seen particularly in recent years with the introduction of live videos from Twitter's Periscope, Facebook Live, and Instagram.

It's a bit more difficult (and confusing) to learn how to go live on YouTube than live streaming using similar platforms. There is no easy "start" button on YouTube's easier streaming option; instead, you will need to download and set up encoding software to use live streaming at all. YouTube has listed 13 + Live-Verified encoders.

So if you watch a live event, all you need is a webcam. We are going to get into that in a second.

Live Stream Login to YouTube from your desktop computer and press the "Upload" button at the top right of your screen. Here is where you will usually upload a pre-existing video — but then you'll want to find the "Live Streaming" tab on the right side of your computer. In that module, press "Get Started."

YouTube must first check that your channel is being checked, and you have no live stream limits for the last 90 days before you go live. When that's all set, you've got two streaming options:

"Stream Now" and "Live Events." Stream Now Stream

Now is the easier, quicker live streaming option, which is why live streaming is the default on YouTube. You will see a fancy dashboard like the one below when you pick "Live Streaming" from the Creator Studio menu on the left-hand side. Again, you will find there is no "start" button on the dashboard. That is where you will need to open your encoder and from there start and stop streaming. For more comprehensive details, see youTube's Live Streaming FAQ page.

Live Events

Live Events allows you much greater control of the live stream. Until it goes live, you can preview it, it will send you backup redundancy streams, and when you like, you can start and stop the stream.

After you have disabled it, select "Live Events" from your video streaming dashboard. Here's what the Overview of events looks like, and here you can read more.

When you stop streaming, we will upload your live stream archive to your channel automatically. Note that your concluded live stream videos are automatically made available by default on your channel as soon as the recording is over. In the "Upload Options" section of your live dashboard, you can pick "Make private archive when complete" to make them vanish from the public eye once you're done.

Streaming Live From Your Mobile Device

YouTube has now carried out live streaming for YouTube creators with 10,000 or more subscribers from mobile devices (as of this publishing date — it will soon be open to all creators, according to YouTube's blog post).

Live streaming from mobile devices is more intuitive than it is on desktops. Registered creators can simply open their mobile YouTube app, tap the camera icon at the top of the screen, and select "Go Live." From there, creators can enter details of the broadcast before broadcasting live to their subscribers immediately.

YouTube has released a Support article here for more guidance about how to go live through platforms about YouTube. Want to see what videos other people are sharing live on YouTube? By clicking here, you can search famous YouTube videos which are life right now.

14. You can upload and view 360-degree (live and pre-recorded) videos — and in VR.

Back in March 2015, YouTube first revealed its support for 360-degree content, and it was a complete novelty — not to mention a game-changer. Since then, some amazing 360-degree content has been produced by brands, athletes, and other users, such as this Samsung video: as you can see, the viewer experience is very, very good. On-screen, while the video is running, you can click around the frame to see all the different angles. It's even better on the mobile: To adjust the angle, you can switch your camera around. The trending 360-degree and VR videos can be browsed here.

How to make a 360-degree YouTube video

You'll need some serious equipment for this. YouTube-compatible 360-degree cameras are described here on the support page of YouTube, along with how to build and upload a 360-degree video file.

What about 360-degree Live Video? The announcement will come a year after the first one, in April 2016 — Facebook revealed its own concept for a 360-degree camera the very same week. Fortunately, it beats Facebook by endorsing both live streaming and 360-degree videos all at once for the people on YouTube.

How to view any YouTube video in VR

The Verge for YouTube named 360 live streaming videos "the gateway drug to virtual reality." You do not need any exceptional equipment other than the YouTube website or app to be able to watch a 360-degree live stream and feel like you're actually in it.

That doesn't mean that a headset isn't an option — and an excellent option at that, since YouTube released its carton function. Cardboard is present on any YouTube video you view or upload and works with Google Cardboard (Google's own VR headset) and several other VR headsets currently available.

Using Cardboard when watching a mobile YouTube video: pick any video in your mobile app from YouTube, then press the three dots in the video's top-right corner. Select "View in Cardboard" in the drop-down. You can already see this feature available in 360-degree videos in the bottom right.

This will make you connect your mobile to a VR device that is compatible. Prepare for a great experience once you do it, and just imagine what that will mean for the content you fill your own YouTube channel with.

15. YouTube ads target you based on Google and Facebook-like algorithms.

Why does the YouTube algorithm determine what advertisements you are watching play on the videos?

It turns out that it works a lot as Facebook and Google advertising do. The advertisers, as on other free pages, are helping to finance the YouTube experience in exchange for ad access. Owing to your age groups, your preferences (which is measured in part by what you are searching on Google and YouTube), and the content you've seen before, you'll see those advertisements over others, like whether or not you've connected with the videos, advertising, or YouTube channel of the advertiser.

YouTube's algorithms often seek to make sure viewers don't get overwhelmed with advertising when viewing videos — and often, it won't automatically display advertisements on monetizable videos, even though a demographic match is present.

Here are the five ad formats that you can expect on YouTube to see, and how they work: A. Show advertisements that appear next to the video, which only appears on desktop computers and laptops. Based on their range B, the advertiser gets charged when you see or click on the ad. Overlay advertisements that appear around the video window's bottom 20 percent, which currently only appear on desktop and laptop computers. Anytime, you can X out of the ad.

C. In-stream TrueView, skippable video advertisements, which are the most common commercials. Those are the ones you should miss after five seconds of viewing. Advertisers could put it prior to, during (yikes!), or after watching the video, and they will only get charged if you watch the clip for at least 30 seconds or until the video ad ends — whichever comes first.

C. Non-skippable video advertisements, which are the longer, 15-or-more-second advertisements you see before running and can't miss any time, no matter how much you're shooting on your phone.

E. Midroll ads, which are advertisements that are only available for videos longer than 15 minutes, spaced within the video, such as TV advertising. Before going through the video, you will watch the commercial. The way the advertiser gets his payment depends on the type of ad: Whether the midroll is a TrueView ad, you'll need to watch the end 30 seconds or the whole ad — whatever it's short. If this is a CPM-based ad, no matter how long it is, you have to watch the whole commercial.

F. Bumper ads, which are brief, non-skippable ads that play for up to six seconds until the user has selected the video. Bumper ads are designed for mobile devices and must be viewed in full before viewers can move to the video they want to watch.

16. For ten bucks a month, you can uninstall advertisements from YouTube videos (and view them offline).

Video ads are the reason you can view videos on YouTube for free. It's a fact that many of us came to recognize. But this doesn't really have to be so anymore with YouTube's subscription service YouTube Red.

You can watch YouTube videos for $9.99 a month. No ads. No advertising. And, in addition to ad-free content, you can save and replay content in the background and/or offline on your mobile device, and use YouTube's Music Feature (on iOS and Android) in the background, offline, and/or audio mode. It is no workout drill.

You'd think the ad-free video lure would have caused more controversy since its launch at the end of 2015, especially given the dominance of YouTube in the music room. Interestingly, I haven't heard too much of the noise. Yet YouTube hasn't released user numbers (the site currently has about 1.5 million subscribers), so it's hard to say how well it's doing. Either way, learning about it is good — particularly if you like to collect songs and music videos like I love to, but do not like it when advertisements break them up.

17. Google Trends helps you to explore and compare common search terms on YouTube over time.

You may already be using Google Trends to show the success over time of similar search words. (For example, it can be a great marketing tool for making smarter keyword choices.) But did you know you could make use of it in the comparison of the popularity of YouTube search queries, in particular?

All you've to do is open Google Trends and type a search term into the top search bar for "Explore Themes." Once the page opens, click on "Internet Search" to open a drop-down menu and choose "YouTube Search" to directly filter searches via YouTube.

You may find that the search patterns on Google are very different for certain search words than they are on YouTube.

18. For your children, there is a 'safer' version of YouTube online.

Any parent will tell you how frightening it is that their children have theoretical access to anything on the internet that is public. But there are ways to curb the exposure for your younger kids and have more say of what they're doing and finding — like a kids version of YouTube called YouTube Kids.

YouTube's people consider YouTube Kids "a better version of YouTube." It's not a wide-open catalog of online videos like YouTube is; rather, it uses algorithm-powered filters to find YouTube videos that are suitable for children to watch. Thanks to advertising (which are monitored as closely as possible), it's totally free too.

You could either turn on or turn off the search feature, depending on if you're cool with your kids looking for videos themselves — or if you'd rather restrict them to a certain selection of videos found by the user, along with those suggested by the app based on what they've already seen. You can set a timer to reduce the amount of time a child spends on the device, which is music to the ears of many parents.

The algorithm is darn fine — note, Google is the parent company of YouTube — but, as it warns in the guide to her parents, "no algorithm is flawless." Now, you can clear your past on YouTube.

Ultimately, you may want to remove things from your quest on YouTube or view history. YouTube helps you to clear your background entirely, avoid documenting what you're searching for and watching from that point, or via your archives and delete any images.

Navigate to the "Watch History" section to erase your history on your desktop or mobile device. Here's where it resides on your web browser homepage and in your smartphone device.

From then, you could "clear all watch history" (permanently erase recording of anything you've watched), "pause watch history" (stop tracking the videos you 're watching going forward), or individually disable videos from your history by clicking the X or ellipses next to images.

YouTube has released a Support article if you do need more help to remove things from your watch history on YouTube.

20. From a cast of crazy puppets, you will hear about the terms of copyrights on YouTube.

Has it gone so far? Here's a little reward: the "Copyrights Basics" FAQ page on YouTube, which is a YouTube video fittingly — and featuring a pretty fun cast of characters. It's very super insightful, and it looks like the video team from YouTube was having a lot of fun making it.

My favorite line is possibly, "You know there are links on this website, right? You don't have to watch this." Even though the gorilla puppet chorus was also pretty sweet.

The Latest Developments Of Instagram

I t is important to note to continue building relationships with your target market in order to keep your business going strong (even if you have to close your doors temporarily).

Instagram is, of course, an excellent forum for this, and they've just rolled out some amazing new features to help you engage your audience in fresh, relevant, and profitable ways.

In this post, we're going to take a closer look at all the updates from April's Instagram and note that if you fall back on a past month, keep reading; we still have this information below the update too!

New Select Partnerships Through Stories

Many companies are struggling through the pandemic right now, and Instagram has launched a few new features designed specifically to help with that.

One of these is the ability to set up with select partners to drive true, financial results using their own stories and interactive story stickers.

For items like gift cards, online shopping, or gifts, you can share links to buy choices. The aim is to inspire your followers to buy more, even if they may not be able to buy from you right now.

Customers are being encouraged to buy gift cards right now, for example, to help their favorite companies, particularly in service-based industries.

You can use the "Gift Card" and "Food Orders" stickers to push these acts, which you are already familiar with rolling out along with your regular interactive stickers.

As an added bonus, your fans and backers will be able to share in their own stories these stickers and your content to help spread the word and generate more results!

Businesses Can Add Support CTAs To Their Profile

In addition to including those new CTAs to your posts, you can also add CTAs for "Gift Cards," "Order Food," and "Donate" as clickable buttons on your profile.

Clicking on users will take them straight to your preferred site so they can complete their order.

Those CTAs will appear on your profile next to the current clickable options such as "Touch" and "Response."

Such apps will certainly be used by companies who offer gift cards, the opportunity to order food, or that qualify to receive donations.

It is a great way to remind consumers that there are different ways to help you, and the opportunity to order gift cards is appealing to many (especially because they can be sent digitally via email or text) not just for themselves but for someone else.

Using stories and in-feed posts to yell out these latest deals for better performance, and let users know how handy it is. And thanks to them for their nonstop support, as always.

Instagram Provides Access to Direct Messages Online

Instagram direct messages (or "DMs" as the hip children call them) are constantly being used by both consumers and brands alike.

Brands were anxiously awaiting access to the desktop because DMs were previously only available to read and react through the mobile app.

That is not the case anymore.

Instagram has confirmed that access to DMs is rolling out online via the site's mobile edition.

This is fantastic news; we've known that this app has been in beta testing since January 2020, but having access to the product is always exciting.

Brands and account managers also have better access to desktops when handling their social profiles.

Typing on mobile is quicker and simpler (and usually more error-proof), and it's simpler for individual users to take advantage of copying, pasting, and then customizing preset answers.

It would speed up customer relationship management, and greatly improve customer experience on Instagram.

New Access, Your Data App, Rolled Out

On March 30th, Facebook revealed that both Facebook and Instagram would have new applications for data access.

Download Your Data tool from Instagram is included in your app, which shows individuals how they used the site. These tools provide you with information about your interactions (including profile changes, post likes, and comments you left).

This will also inform you which subject categories you are interested in, giving you insight into why you see such subject in your Exploring tab.

The data is designed to show users what they are doing on the site and to clarify what information they are using to gather data that is used to deliver better advertising and organic content. This is emerging as a result of a drive for greater accountability.

Although companies are unlikely to make substantial use of this information, it is nice to know that this knowledge is out there and that it will be available to your audience.

Looking at your own data and seeing what Instagram has reported about your operation does not hurt to get a little more insight into how it all works; you can also get new ideas for targeting groups.

Even though the world has come to a standstill, it's been exciting to see Instagram rapidly introducing new features designed to help companies and brands in a difficult economic time.

Even if many people are low on finances, just as many would like to help their favorite companies so that once the pandemic is over, we are all in the best possible shape.

The latest CTAs are probably the most exciting updates we've got this month, but it's pretty cool to take advantage of the now-available on-desktop DMs too.

Instagram is constantly evolving, adding new features, updating their algorithms, and always keeping us on our toes all over! Because frequent changes can be overwhelming to keep on top of all the latest Instagram updates, so I have made a list of 24 latest Instagram properties you mayn't know of and how to use them!

Have in mind that IG is notorious for rolling out (and sometimes removing!) its features at random and without any clear order, so if you don't have any of the features I've mentioned, stay patient – they're coming your way!

Following Groups & Filtering Options

This recent Instagram update makes handling your following simpler and keeping track of who you most and least connect with! If you are navigating to the list of people you are following, you will find a few new additions now.

1. Two distinct categories: 'Most Interacted With' and 'Most Seen in Feed' 2. A tiny two-way arrow icon that helps you to filter your following by 'Earliest Followed' and 'Latest Followed' For those who are more interested in communicating with the people they are following, these resources can help you to decide who is worth

engaging. For instance, the people you've communicated with the least will probably appreciate some likes and comments, and the likelihood of your content appearing within their feed will increase!

Hidden Likes

You may've heard the news, or this update may already have happened to your account, but Instagram is testing to remove the amount your posts like to get!

The update is clear to all your feed users, so when you test your post insights, you'll always be able to see the like count personally.

Instagram said this move is intended to improve its users' overall mental health by taking away the value of vanity metrics.

I wrote a full blog post about this move and how it could affect you and your company.

The Arrow Pen in Instagram Stories

One of the nicest ways to get users to take action in your stories is to draw arrows to points of interest. For example, drawing an arrow pointing up from the bottom of your screen would allow users to swipe up and draw an arrow pointing to your profile picture can prompt them to visit your feed. Instagram agreed to add an official 'arrow pen' to your Instagram Stories drawing resources with many strategic uses, making it effortless to get the perfect pointer!

How to: easily open the camera for your Instagram stories (by swiping from your home feed right off). Take a screenshot, video, or upload a file, then tap on the top right of the pen device. You'll see a new addition from here, which looks like a tiny arrow. Click that, then draw a line-Instagram will automatically add an arrow to the end of the line.

Instagram Age Limits

Instagram also enable users to set an age limit for their accounts. I haven't seen a lot of people applying this new Instagram update to the degree that you usually don't want to restrict the number of people who can access your account. However, this function can be used by those posting content that is not appropriate for particular ages. (However, material that is not appropriate for all audiences will probably already be blocked by Instagram.) How to: add this setting to your account, go to your profile, click the hamburger icon in the top right corner, choose 'settings,' 'company,' then 'minimum age.' From here, you can decide that people must have a default age to access your account, or you can set age by the venue.

Creator Account

The Instagram creator account has added a third profile alternative to its current fleet. You can now choose between Private, Creator & Company. Significant difference? Okay, okay. Not too much. The creator account is targeted at creators of content and gives them a small advantage on their account growth by having a new insight feature. Other than that, the features are very similar to a business account.

Want to know the ins and outs in full? To read my Instagram Creator Page, click here – Is the move worth it? Write on site.

Dark Mode

If you woke up with a dark Instagram today- you're part of their new beta check! Users with iOS 13 and Android 10 operating systems will experience a darker version of our most sought after social media app.

But some people are flipping out because it's not completely obvious how we're used to transitioning to and from the Instagram, to the fresh, grungier, dark edition.

As mentioned, this is only available for users with different operating systems, but if you do, here's how to enable/disable dark mode: iPhone How to: Navigate to your phone Settings, select Display, and Brightness, Toggle the Dark feature.

Android How to: Navigate to Settings in your phone, select Show, select Theme, turn Dark Theme on.

Instagram Electronic mail Checker

Have you ever received an e-mail from Instagram saying you eligible for verification, your password has changed, or do you need to click this link as a matter of urgency to save your account from deletion?? I think at some point we all have, and some of us sadly clicked on the connection in those e-mails, and only moments later, realized their accounts were hacked.

It is the typical hoax on phishing. Unknown parties send e-mails that aim to trick you into entering your username and password somewhere, so they can steal it promptly, and take over your account.

Instagram recently recognized that this is a big problem and introduced a new feature that will help users decide whether or not the e-mail they received from "Instagram" is legitimate. This new feature can be found in your settings and will show any e-mails sent by Instagram during the last 14 days so you can know for sure whether or not the e-mail is genuine.

How to: go to the Instagram profile, click on the top-right hamburger icon, select Settings, select Protection, and finally, "Instagram e-mails."

I think this feature would be beneficial to everyone, but some simple tips for spam e-mails include: look at the sender name, if it ends in something other than instagram.com, then it's probably spam! Also, Instagram will never inform you by e-mail about verification or account breaches-you will ONLY get an in-app notification for these topics.

Keep healthy and still take for granted the worst when it comes to "Instagram" texts!

Anti-Bullying Profile Restrictions

Instagram just introduced a new feature called 'Restrict' which allows users to block user interactions that are likely to spread hatred, bully, or otherwise are unwanted.

This is different from blocking others because they don't know they 're being blocked. They could still leave their hate-filled comments on your page, but nobody other than them will be able to see it.

If they are interested, the account owner should be able to reveal the message, otherwise "limited message" will be in place, and you can move on without being influenced by the negativity of that person!

How to: if they have left a negative comment already, swipe left and pick the '! 'Pick button, then "restrict [username]." Instead, you can go to your profile, click the icon at the top right of the hamburger, select settings, select privacy, select 'limited accounts' from which you can add any known offenders.

Instagram Stories 'Build' Interface

One of Instagram's new updates includes an Instagram Stories facelift! Now, with a simple finger swipe, you can add Gifs, Countdown Timers, Quizzes, Polls, and Q&A boxes (because you go through the sticker button and select them manually before it was too hard. They also added two new fun Instagram story add-ons including: 'On This Day' which is something we've seen on Facebook for a while now, where you can relive the past by sharing things that happened You will be able to share posts that you posted years ago or mutual friendships that were created (i.e., @instawithalex and @latermedia started following each other three years ago) when you access this feature, the second new addition is "templates" that are pre-designed Instagram stories that leave empty spaces for you to fill in your answers. There's a template, for example, that says "top three accounts to follow," with three empty spaces to add your own favorites. Or "what do I listen to" with five spaces to add your favorite songs to it.

Such models add a fun twist to your daily Instagram stories so you can share your personality with your audience more!

How to: open your camera for Instagram stories by swiping right off your home page or by pressing the camera icon in the top right. From here, you can see text at the very bottom of your camera, and it should be "natural" by default. Slide the text to the right until you pick "Build." You could swipe left on the circles at the top of the text from here to switch between all the options, including the two new features listed above. When selecting certain options, you will note a dice icon at the top of the screen, tap that to see different variations of the selected feature.

Hashtag Insights

Instagram just added the ability to monitor exactly how many impressions individual hashtags give you! I think it's fair to say we've all been eagerly awaiting this update since we'd earlier get a large number of hashtag experiences that make it hard to assess what's going on and what's not. The latest Instagram update will make it infinitely easier to decide which hashtags function for us, and which ones have to go!

How to: navigate to a recent page, tap the button 'Show insights,' and scroll down to the section Impressions. Scroll down to the section before you see the 'Hashtag Experiences.' You can see the exact hashtag here, and how many impressions it brought!

Not seeing any of the hashtag impressions? Mightn't use the best ones! Check out The

Instagram Ivy League to learn how to pick the right hashtags for your unique account!

Removing Followers

Irrespective of what your posting or interaction strategy is, bots and fake accounts often manage to creep into your follower list and threaten it (they frequently come from poorly chosen hashtags or participate in the wrong accounts). These kinds of followers don't like or comment on your posts and are also called "ghost followers." You can bring down your average interaction rate after getting so many of these accounts, and Instagram doesn't like that. When our audience isn't engaged, they think our content isn't that interesting, so they're going to restrict the number of people seeing it!

You can use this new Instagram function to manually delete a follower and keep your engagement rate in top shape instead of installing a third-party app (which is possibly unapproved by Instagram and could further harm your account!).

How to: move to your followers' list and select the account you consider to be a ghost follower (often based on the profile image, user name or content on their page), click the three dots on the right side next to the follow/follow button and pick "delete." Have in mind that doing so will lower your follower count but will raise your interaction rate (in my opinion totally worth it!)

Instagram Stories Countdown Timer

This is definitely my first new Instagram update! You can now add a working count down timer inside your Instagram stories to help generate anticipation and excitement around whatever you need! Timers that countdown are a classic marketing strategy that inspires a person to act. So get people curious about what you're up so, I recommend using these regularly. Here are a few ways in which a countdown timer will come in handy:

- Announcing an upcoming event/promo/opening / etc.

- Encouraging your audience to sign up for a webinar

- Creating anticipation for a time-limited deal that expires Your audience will be able to login to the countdown timer, and they will receive an alert when the countdown is full!

How to: Create a fresh Instagram story and click at the top of the screen on the sticker icon (or swipe up from the bottom).

Select the sticker 'countdown' and insert a title. Then select the date and time your countdown is due to expire. The countdown can be personalized by tapping on the color wheel at the top of the page. This will go through a variety of colors allowing you to pick one that matches your account, vibe, or story!

Interested in getting more communication out of your Instagram stories and sales? Check out my Performance by Story course to learn how not only to build fantastic looking stories but also how to use them to improve your biz!

Post to Multiple Accounts

Have you ever spent a good number of time editing the perfect picture, writing a brilliant caption, and tagging a bunch of accounts only to find that you're on the wrong account?! Well, this new feature from Instagram helps solve the problem! Now it doesn't matter which account you are logged into because you can easily move to the account to which you want to publish your message.

This feature also allows you to concurrently publish several accounts, which can make it easier for companies to communicate the same message without the need to reinvent the wheel. Ideally, you want to build content unique to each account, but if you want to share a promotional picture or update, this might be helpful!

How to: make a post as usual, then you will see a section called 'post to other accounts' when you hit the details tab. Here you can turn to the account(s) to which you want to write.

Alt Text

The new alt text feature of Alt Text Instagram provides visually impaired users with an easier way to enjoy the platform! When allowing alt text on your pictures, anyone using a screen reader will be able to listen in depth to your explanation of the pictures. You could customize your alt text, or have the description created automatically by Instagram. Personally, I recommend that you modify your alt text to make sure you have as detailed a definition as possible. No matter how good this form of technology can be, it's not always the most reliable!

If you've ever researched 'search engine optimization,' you may be aware that the alt text you 're using on your website will help you rank similar keywords in search results. Instagram hasn't mentioned that their alt text would function the same way, but I personally think it's smart to add alt text to all your images just in the event they do! Imagine including "female photographer taking a picture of the landscape" in your alt text and the rating of your image in the hashtag # female photographer without even using it ..?! Now I may be dreaming but if it becomes a fact you better give me credit!

How to: Pick 'advanced settings' when uploading a new picture and under 'accessibility,' you will see the option of adding your alt text. If you'd like to add alt text to a photo that has already been released, go to the photo, click the three dots, press 'delete,' then tap the 'add alt text' button that appears in the photo's bottom right.

New Profile View & Shorter Bios

This latest Instagram update is updating the bios and profiles of Instagram that we have been so used to seeing over the past few years. While some users report a completely different look with less focus on the number of followers and more focus on the information (see the first picture below), others see their bios cut in half and adding a "more" button to hide the rest of the bio (second picture below). Because of the later update, we now need to prioritize details, so if anyone wants not to click the 'more' button, we still get our message across!

If you see the shorter description, you 're going to want to switch around some stuff and make sure that the first two lines of text describing who you are and have a convincing call to action.

Close Friends

Reward your loyal followers with the feature of Close Friends! This new feature of Instagram allows you to compile a list of people to whom you can submit exclusive stories, separately from your fans. You can create a list of your real, closest friends and start sending hidden stories to each other or you can do it with business in mind and place your most loyal followers or past clients on the list. From there, you can give them exclusive deals, sneak peeks on new items, or any other "insider" details you want them to know about your company!

How to: navigate to your profile and right-click the hamburger button. Select the 'close friends' option and select the people you want to add to your list. From there, navigate to your story camera on Instagram and create some exclusive content. Tap the 'close friends' icon in the bottom right when you're ready to post, to make sure your story goes only to those people! Note: At any time, you can make adjustments to your list, and other users (both within and outside the group) will not be able to access the list.

Top Posts (New Version!)

When looking at hashtags, I think most of us are familiar with section "Top Posts." It is usually where the best performing posts live within the hashtag. In the past, this section was done to every user based on the content that Instagram thought you would have an interest in. Due to a flaw in the algorithm, users often saw their own pictures in this section that was frequently unreliable and made it difficult to understand whether or not your picture was actually ranked.

The top posts segment is no longer limited to 10 posts with this recent Instagram update and shows the same images for everyone who views it. That means if your content shows up there, you know you're really in the ranking, and you might see a rise in interaction and followers!

Sharing posts to stories

This feature is one of my favorites and one that has a lot of usefulness. You can now upload any post to your Instagram story (yours or anybody else's!). Not only that, but the image itself is a clickable link that brings every consumer from your story straight to the picture that taps into it! This makes this a perfect way to send users from your story to your feed or send traffic to someone else (and maybe get some in return if they share your posts!) How to: navigate to the post you want to share, tap the aircraft icon below the picture and pick 'add post to your story.' This will open your camera for stories with an embedded message. You can alter your story to include text, gifs, locations, or any of the other typical material that you add. Only share it with your story then, and all your users can click through to the link!

Your Behavior

Following the regular efforts by Instagrams to keep you on the site for as long as possible, they have recently introduced a new feature that shows you the exact amount of time you spend on Instagram every day (down to the minute!) While this might be horrifying for others, it's a fantastic way to track whether the amount of time you're on the site actually results in something. Instagram also allows you to set up a regular reminder that will alert you when a pre-defined time limit is reached. You can also set your regular notification settings here so that any time anyone likes one of your images, you are not tempted to access the app. Thank you, IG.

How to: navigate to your profile, tap in the top right of the hamburger icon, and select 'your operation.' Notice that this latest Instagram update seems to be available exclusively for personal accounts (I think if you're a company, they want you on as long as possible!)

Posting Multiple Photos & Video to Stories

This is one more feature we've all been waiting for! You can now upload images and videos at the same time into your posts. You'd have to pick one picture previously, add all your customizations, post it, then go back to your phone, open your photo file, pick another picture and repeat it. Fortunately, this latest Instagram update allows you to pick up to 10 different pictures and photos to add to your stories and allows you to edit each and everyone before uploading as a community!

How to: move right from your home feed to your stories camera or press the camera icon in the top left corner. Swipe from your screen button to open your camera roll, then tap in the top right of the multiple posts icon. From here, you can tap and build a new post on the photos you want to use in your story (take note of the number applied to each as this reflects the exact order they will be posted to). Then tap next and, if necessary, edit each slide. Tap next once more when you're ready and share your story!

IGTV

Instagram TV. Maybe you've heard of it; maybe you have not. Instagram launched this feature sometime in 2018, but it was a complete flop from my view. IGTV is much more complex than the rest of the apps on this list because it's essentially its own Instagram app. You can usually add videos to your feed, but at 60 seconds, they cap out. IGTV allows you to upload long-form videos that range from 1 minute to an entire hour! For many reasons, this is cool, particularly of people who regularly create longer videos for platforms like YouTube, but there are many downsides you can read here in my blog post: IGTV What is it and How to Use it!

How to: View a step-by-step tutorial of my YouTube video.

Filtering Your DMs

This latest Instagram feature will come in handy if you receive loads of DMs like I am doing! Now you can easily filter your DMs with just the tap of a button so that you can regularly organize and respond to your messages.

How to: Go to your DMs by clicking the airplane icon on your home screen at the top right. You can see a tiny icon on the right-hand side of the search bar from there. When you tap on your whole inbox, unread messages or flagged messages can be displayed!

Tags Name

Recall QR codes? Well, with this latest Instagram update, Instagram is trying to get them interesting again. They are called Name Tags and allow you to share your account with others by creating a scannable image, similar to QR codes. Although some people see this as an important tool to use at networking events (instead of business cards), in my day-to-day life, I have not really seen or found useful use for it.

How to: Navigate to your profile, right in the top right click on the hamburger icon, and pick 'name tag.' From here, the name tag can be stylized and downloaded to your phone to share with others. This page can also be used to check the name tags. Alternatively, go to the search tab and select the name tag icon on the right-hand side of the search bar.

Apply for Verification

You know that you see a coveted blue check next to your favorite celebrities or usernames of super influencers? This is proof, and the average citizen does not apply for the same status in the past. Now Instagram has opened up the opportunity to request clarification, and you could even get a blue test on your feed if you fulfill the requirements!

How to: For the step-by-step guide, read my How to Get Checked blog post or check out my YouTube video here.

'About This Account' Details

Because after all of last year's Facebook privacy and data breaches, it appears that they are now taking action to ensure that companies remain open and accountable on their platforms. If you've ever wondered how someone's account grew so quickly or found an odd username in your feed, it could be because they bought someone else's account and added new content to it! Instagram (and it's users) see this as deceptive, so they've implemented the 'about this account' function that allows users to find out somebody's account history!

This feature lets you see the following details regarding any Instagram business profile:

- Date entered

- Nation

- Active ads

- Former usernames

- Mutual follower accounts

How to: go to the profile you wish to know more about. Click the three dots at the top right of the screen and select 'On this account.' You can see all the information on that particular account here. Pay special attention to the segment on 'old usernames' as this is where you can decide if an Instagram is authentic or misleading.

Shoppable Posts

This latest feature is a change of the game for all e-commerce firms! Have you seen that post on Instagram showing the price of a product when taped, and actually leading you directly to that item's checkout page?! Yes, it is real, it exists, and on your account, you can have it! This function is unique for people that sell physical items but doesn't need a certain amount of followers (unlike the swipe up function in ig stories!). This app will quickly boost sales, but don't forget that adding shoppable tags isn't the only aspect that will support. Make sure that you educate your viewers about your goods, and that's the benefit of your captioning. THEN (and only then), you should ask them to buy your photo by tapping on the link.

How to: Check my Instagram blog post for Shoppable and YouTube videos step by step!

Activity Status

Have you ever sent a message to someone for multiple days only not to get a response? Well, now you could catch them, ignoring you with the new function 'Activity Status!' Looking in your Instagram DM inbox, you will see text under every user name that shows how long ago on Instagram, they were last involved. Instead, next to their profile picture, you'll see a green dot that means they're actually on the web.

Now, apart from catching your mates, you can also use this feature to show your audience that you're engaged and at your disposal for chatting. As a company owner, you want to ensure that your audience has the chance to reach out to you. So, you create an incentive for contact by making your activity status available. You can turn it off if you choose not to have your activity status available.

How to: activity status is turned on for all users automatically, but if you want to turn it off, all you need is to go to your profile, tap the hamburger icon in the top right corner and pick 'settings' at the bottom of the screen. Then scroll until you find 'operation status' and click the on or off location button. Bear in mind that you will not be able to see the activity status of other accounts when you turn off your profile.

Data Download

If we have learned anything about Instagram, the site can often be totally unpredictable. That's why this is such a fantastic addition to Instagrams' latest "data download" functionality! If you'd like to back up your Instagram account to ensure you never lose any of the content on your website, you'll want to check this one out!

How to: Go to your profile, then click the top right of the hamburger icon. At the bottom of the screen, select 'settings,' then locate and tap 'download info.' Instagram enquires about your e-mail address, which is where your photos, comments, profile information, and more will be sent to.

Eventually, you will receive an Instagram e-mail with a link to download your info. This is only valid for four days, so make sure that in that time period, you access the files; otherwise, you'll have to ask for the data again.

Q&A Instagram Live

You might be familiar with Instagram live now, but did you know that there is a new feature that essentially combines the Instagram Stories question sticker AND Instagram live?! Yep, it just got so much easier to answer questions during your Instagram Live! Normally it can be frustrating or daunting when attempting to sift through a query in the comments during a live, but now a simple question box appears, and interested users can pop in their question, and it shows clearly and obviously so you never miss a question.

Your audience can always see clearly what question you are answering at the moment, so no matter when they enter the live they'll know exactly what's going on!

How-to: First, as you would usually do, you have to add a question to your story. Then you'll want to wait for some questions to come in for a few minutes, then start your Instagram live by navigating to your stories camera and scrolling over to the live tab. After you start your Instagram live, you will see an icon at the bottom left of the question mark. Tapping that will show all of the questions that you were asked. Just tap the answer you want and start talking!

The only odd thing about this feature is that users have to ask questions through your story and can't actually send any questions during the live (unless they type in the comments as normal). This is why waiting for questions to come in before starting the live, makes sense.

So, you got it there. A full and complete breakdown of all the new Instagram updates! As you know, the platform is always evolving, so as more Instagram features are added, I will be sure to put together another blog.

How To Use Social Media For Business

Would you love to use social media for your small business but are struggling to get traction?

Wondering how to jump but not knowing where to start?

It can be disappointing.

In reality, only 53 percent of small businesses claim they use social media actively. Anything else? They are saying they have no space, capital, time, money, or energy.

And I do get that. Running the day to day as a small business will leave you feeling stretched thin.

Add to that the relentless promotion of your company, and you have the meltdown makings.

But the upside here is. Using social media is not rocket science for your small company. In reality, once you learn a few insider secrets, it is pretty easy.

I have been opportuned to sit down with Peg Fitzpatrick during week 6 of our preparation.

Peg is assistant-author of the Art of Social Media and works with Guy Kawasaki on a regular basis. She maintains a whopping 13 million fans, between her thriving company and Guy's.

Holy cool, huh? Peg knows her stuff and was happy to share some of her top tips.

If you're able to get your small business going on social media, read on.

How to use Social Media [Infographic] for your small business

1. Creating a Reliable Reputation

Creating a credible profile on social media for your company is not as difficult as it sounds.

Will you want to know why?

Because you don't have to do it with a huge amount of following!

As a small company, you just need to connect with the RIGHT people instead of interacting with a lot of people —.

By creating brand awareness, you can start the cycle. The nicest way to do this is to build an online identity, which is a good representation of who you are online and offline.

Start by using visual marketing to traduce your brand. From your logo to website, blog, and graphics on social media-you need to create a look and feel that suits your persona.

Find someone to help build graphics that suit the essence. Create captivating and professional visuals representing you and your business.

There are so many professionals who will support you with this process — and you'll find someone whatever your budget is.

Or, if you have enough time than money — you can pick from a multitude (many of them free) resources and learn how to do it yourself.

If you want to fix these graphics yourself, then our ebook will show you how to do it. You can record that at How to Create Visual Content to Maximize Effect on Social Media.

Peg 's guide on learning from the big brands!

Get inspiration from very big marketing campaigns and turn it around in a way that's manageable for your own company.

2. Attract Future Clients

Peg narrated the story of her hairdresser, Betsy, during this preparation. In New Hampshire, Betsy owns B & B Style Salon.

Betsy wanted to know how to use social media for her small company — and Peg suggested using Facebook and Instagram to draw potential new customers.

Whether you do want to do this for your local company, the first step is to ensure the proper setup of the geotagging on your Facebook Business Page.

You want people who are at your company to be able to sign in while they are. It's free publicity for you any time anyone does that because all of their buddies can see their check-in.

The average Facebook user has 100 (and most are local) friends — so think of every check-in as advertising to 100 new potential customers!

Plus, that sort of post is better advertising than a boosted post because it's a genuine customer check-in (not a boosted post or ad).

Want to log in any more? Provide special opportunities for people to check-in at your service.

In Betsy's case, for example, she posted a small sign that those who check-in get $5 off their next haircut. You can offer whatever bonus you want!

Healthy advice from Peg.

Let it into the customers' pockets. That means getting into their mobile!

Betsy always decided to do a girl's evening out in her small town to promote herself as a hairdresser.

She changed her cover photo on Facebook — plus added a Blog message and an Instagram article.

By doing those three things, she was able to carry out her event with zero budget!

This is an excellent example of how a small business owner has been able to attract the right clients.

She focused on interacting with her target audience instead of attempting to spread a large net and attracting a lot of people who may or may not be interested in her services.

The takeaway — even slight improvements will affect your social media marketing enormously!

3. Connect with like-minded industry people

Partnerships are key in the world of social media.

If you're developing your professional network on LinkedIn or reacting to your tweets — it's important that you set aside some time to interact with like-minded professionals.

As the owner of a small business, you probably cringe at the prospect of wasting precious time engaged in social media with peers.

No problems with that! Peg has some excellent tips on how to get this to work.

She recommends you devote one chunk of time per week to the next week to focus on your material (she does this every Sunday). This means identifying and arranging the content you want or producing it.

How is it that helps you?

Now that your content is set up for the whole week — you can pop up 15 minutes in the morning and 15 minutes in the evening on social media to respond to feedback, answer questions and reach out to like-minded business professionals.

This will encourage you to make those important connections because, during the time you 're online, you'll be focusing on people!

4. Diversify Your Marketing Activities

We've all heard the saying, "Don't put all your eggs in one basket." Just as with your offline marketing, your online marketing activities will certainly be diversified.

Does this mean that you can build a profile on any social media site?

Definitely not.

What this means is that you can focus on who your target audience is, with a laser focus.

Instead of concentrating on the consumer numbers, you HAVE — try focusing on the customers you WANT.

That information will tell you what social networks to spend time on.

When you know more about how to use social media for your small company, you'll find the networking networks that you should be on almost obvious.

If you don't have a good idea of the social networks to be on, Peg suggests that you start with a presence on Facebook (keep sure to set up the geotargeting) Instagram (excellent for small businesses) LinkedIn (like an international Rotary Club!) Twitter (listening to Twitter conversations will provide useful insight) Once you determine the social networks you 're going to use — be sure to use them.

By diversifying your online marketing, you're going to extend your business' scope much further than you would imagine.

5. Repurpose Top Content

As you learn ways to use social media to generate new content for your small business — you can see very quickly how time-consuming it is.

Peg suggests you become a repurposing master for that reason!!

Let me just explain.

Let's say you're sending out a tweet on something you and your audience are excited about.

Knew you could repurpose the tweet into at least 13 other content pieces?

Yes, you can!

Have you ever seen anyone on social media who always seems to come up with new, original content? You start asking if he ever sleeps, right?

That's someone who knows how to reshape material. You might as well be that guy!

Peg has one word of warning here. Don't mistake material repurposing to replicate the posts on any social network.

If you do this — people do not have the incentive to follow you anywhere, because everywhere they will see the very same material from you.

Learn every platform's language instead.

Give people everywhere a reason to be following you! Don't exactly duplicate material.

For each social media, look at each piece of content in a different way.

For example, take a quote from an evergreen blog post that you've tweeted and made a quote graphic for Instagram to share.

Or take the helpful tip you've given someone on Facebook, and use it to build or scope a 2-minute tutorial on Facebook Live Video. Even in a blog post, you can embed the video.

And take your notes from a recent presentation and use the info to create an infographic. The redeployment choices are infinite!

To learn more, Peg should click on how to repurpose its material to this message.

6. Make Your Time and Resources Count

As an owner of small business — you know that time is money.

We all had those days when we got to work on Facebook, but then we see a friend's post, and all of a sudden 2 hours pass. Comfortable sound?

If you want to use social media in the most effective way possible for your small business, it is important to FOCUS every time you log in to social media.

Yeah, there's time to share those fun pictures and goof off — but when it's during the working day, be yeah to concentrate on the goals!

If you find yourself offline, first note why you are on social media.

Be responsible for yourself.

When it comes to money — only a few dollars will make an impact with Facebook Advertising (which is very do-able for small businesses).

You should stay within reach and keep it working for you!

7. Driving Traffic to Your Website / Blog

Your website/blog is the foundation of all your efforts in online marketing.

It's the location your future customers go when they decide whether to do business with you or not.

If they think about your company, it is what people should recall.

To get an idea of how to efficiently push traffic back to your website/blog you should read 15 Ways to Get Leads on Social Media (Marketer's Guide).

The best advice — do your homework!

We 're talking about "purpose" here at Post Planner. In other words, we 're asking ourselves, "What should people searching for our app search on Google?" Then we're optimizing our blog for those sentences. Our blog headlines address the question of intent.

Using any program that works best for you — but does the homework.

You can't focus your plan on guesswork if you want to push a large amount of traffic back to your website/blog.

As we always say on Post Planner here, be DATA-DRIVEN!!!

At Top Ways to Handle Social Media (and Prevent Burnout), you can learn all about that.

8. Using the Right Tool

As a small business owner — your best friends should be the right tools.

They will help you organize yourself and create a system for the chaos.

You could save time, cash, and a lot of anger by using the right resources.

Those methods used by Peg are

Trello

Evernote

Post Planner

Sprout Social

Relay

Canva.

How To Build Your Personal Brand

In many ways, Gresh explains, a personal mark is similar to a corporate brand. It is who you are, what you represent, the values you embrace, and how you express those values. Much as a company's brand helps to convey its importance to consumers and stand out from the competition, a personal brand does the same for people, helping to convey prospective employers or buyers with a specific identity and strong worth.

Or, as Gresh sums up: "Personal branding is the story of one." The story may play an important role in setting up or boosting your career. In fact, overwhelming 85 percent of hiring managers report that their hiring decisions are influenced by the personal brand of a job candidate. Your personal brand will highlight your strengths, develop a reputation, build trust, and convey the unique qualities you bring to your current (or desired) industry. Well-cultivated, your personal brand can signal to employers whether or not you will be the right choice for an open role. Tips for creating your personal brand. While establishing a personal brand can sound daunting; there are gradual steps you can take to create credibility in your field. Here are ten tips to assist you to create an authentic personal brand — and in that process, amplify your career.

Ten Tips to Develop a Personal Brand
1. Find out who you really are.

You first have to learn who you are to create a personal brand that accurately represents your personal and professional identity. Be introspective and make your personal strengths and weaknesses list. Ask yourself: What areas of work am I excelling in?

What gets me motivated?

What features did other people compliment me on?

What ventures have others to constantly support me with?

What functions do my resources appear to dry out?

I can spend hours on what tasks without feeling exhausted or tired?

If you're having issues answering these questions, ask peers, family, and colleagues how they'd characterize you. When you are more conscious of the different aspects of your personality, you will decide how to mark them the best.

Have in mind that a lot of people fail to pick a specific niche because they don't want to restrict themselves. Realize that as your career progresses, your personal logo, like other corporate brands, will change. The best approach is to pick a particular field that you would like to work on and let it evolve over time.

2. Determine the known for what you want.

Your personal brand is more than just a snapshot of who you are today; it's a guide to go from. As well as knowing your current talents and abilities, Gresh recommends identifying your strengths and weaknesses as they apply to the field or profession you want to break into next.

In doing so, you can reveal the strengths and characteristics that make you unique, as well as the areas where you need to develop or learn new information to progress. Predicting where you want to be in five or ten years — and the qualities for which you want to be known — can help you decide better what steps you need to take to get there.

3. Define the target.

You will need to decide who you are trying to meet before you start designing your personal brand. Is it leading thinkers in other industry? An individual at a given company? Hired Recruiters? The faster you identify the target, the easier it will be to craft your story, because you will better understand what kind of story you need to tell (and where you need to tell it). For example, if your aim is to meet hiring managers and recruiters, you could start by developing or updating your LinkedIn profile. Why? For what? Since 92 percent of recruiters use social media to identify candidates of high quality and 87 percent use LinkedIn.

At the other hand, if you are a graphic designer striving to please established clientele and draw new ones, you may want to tell your story through a personal website or portfolio, where you can better articulate your wide range of talents.

4. Study the industry you like and obey the experts.

Gresh suggests conducting research on experts in those fields when you start planning out the professions you want.

"So find out who the leaders of thought are in whatever area you are involved in, and not only imitate them," he says. "Go online to find out whether they have forums, or where they contribute to their thought. Look for people that are popular to analyze what they're doing. Emulate them, and then do one better." The aim of creating a personal brand is to stand out — but you can't get to the top without taking stock of who's there.

5. Request detailed interviews.

Consider reaching out to these experts to ask for an informative interview when you start building a list of businesses you want to work with and business leaders you respect.

"They take 20 minutes, but they are of great value," says Gresh. "Don't be afraid to ask someone you're interested in learning more from. You'd be shocked how honest and friendly people are." When you meet these people, ask questions that can help you gain new insights into your desired area, such as: How have you broken into the industry?

What steps would you take if the change were to be made all over again?

How do you see the sector evolve?

How do you keep updated with developments in the industry?

Are there any professional associations or trade associations I should be joining?

According to Gresh, insightful interviews come with an added benefit: "You 're talking about what it takes to get into the field, but you're also revealing a bit about yourself in the process of this conversation. What you're doing is developing your brand." While there may not be a work on the line in one of these interviews, one day there could be — and you want the employer to think about it.

6. Create an elevator presentation.

When you begin to conceptualize your personal brand, spend some time designing an elevator pitch — a tale about who you are 30- to 60-seconds. If you're attending a networking function or an informal gathering, getting an elevator pitch ready makes it easy to explain quickly what you're doing and where you're (or want to) going with your career.

"You have to come up with really simple, succinct things to say — stories to tell — that frame your qualities in the right light," says Frank Cutitta, founder of the Center for Global Branding and a graduate professor at the Northeastern University who teaches a personal branding course.

Keep brief about your elevator pitch by focusing on a few key points that you want to highlight. This may involve finding a new job, having strengths in a particular area, or having recently increased the value of your current department or company.

7. Take on networking.

As you develop your ideal personal brand, it's crucial to network to expand your professional circle regularly (and effectively). By going to formal and informal networking activities, interact with colleagues, and business think-leaders.

The more connections you make — and the more interest you can have in your interactions — the more likely it will be to remember your personal brand. And given that 85 percent of all jobs are filled by networking, attending such events on a regular basis can not only help you develop your brand but also potentially advance your career.

Do not be shy about asking fellow passengers to meet again for an informative interview or a quick coffee chat at these events. And note, if you don't get a chance to communicate at the case, reach out to spark a conversation through e-mail or LinkedIn.

8. Ask for feedback.

You're one of the easiest and most effective ways to define your personal brand by having a current and former colleagues and managers endorse you, allowing others to communicate your value to you. Just like a company could cultivate customer feedback and testimonials for use in collateral for sales and marketing, so too can you cultivate your own feedback like recommendations.

LinkedIn is an awesome place to ask for endorsements since these recommendations are likely to catch the eye of future hiring managers. But don't forget to ask the people who help you to serve as a real guide during your work hunt, making sure they're happy to talk to a prospective employer or write a bonafide recommendation letter if needed.

Not sure who would ask? Former managers who closely mentored you are ideal, but other associations may also formulate valuable guidelines, like professors and members of organizations to which you belong.

(Find out more about who to ask — and how — check out this comprehensive post on how to leverage professional references effectively.)

9. Grow your presence online.

One of the most crucial aspects of personal branding is to make sure that your online presence involves hiring managers, coworkers, and others — even if you're not hunting for a job.

With so many different platforms available today in social media, your online presence will certainly look different depending on the medium you use. Although your story will suit on all channels, you should redouble your efforts to tell your best story there once you know where your target market will most likely turn.

Alternatively, if you want one of your pages or accounts to be solely for friends and family, change your privacy settings to ensure that prospective employers will not trip over any details that could hurt your work chances. Below are some platform-specific tips to help you develop your personal brand effectively online.

LinkedIn

LinkedIn acts as a technical platform for social media and is the best place to describe the brand. The best way to make use of this network is to engage in groups, introduce people who are interested in you and ask for (and give) recommendations. Some other tips for telling your story effectively through LinkedIn include:

Focus on key industry skills: Recruiters will often search for keywords related to the role they 're trying to fill, so it's important to include terms from the industry in your profile — whether in your headline, summary, or job description — and explicitly state your abilities. For example, if you are seeking a career in communications, focus on your area of interest and key skills such as public relations, social media, or crisis management.

Quantify your achievements: Claiming that you are "performance-oriented" isn't as good as your actual results. Whenever possible, measure your successes, whether it be the number of papers you've written, the dollars you earned, or the deals you've closed.

Complete your profile: While this may sound obvious, leaving sections of your LinkedIn profile blank is not uncommon for users to. Recruiters want to see what job experience you have, your history in education, and a comprehensive list of achievements, so make sure you're presenting the picture in full. Convince them that you are the one they should be recruiting.

Using a professional photograph: LinkedIn users with a professional headshot earn profile views 14 times greater than those without it. Upload a real picture closely cropped to your face. Note, the focal point should be yours, so stop any noisy backgrounds — and smile. The more accomodating you look, the more likely recruiters are to contact this platform on Twitter Leverage to highlight and build on your expertise in the sector. Seek to integrate your personal brand into your Twitter bio by using hashtags to concentrate on your niche, following your market leaders, and retweeting top stories from the industry. Don't forget: what you're tweeting is still part of your identity online.

Personal website or portfolio It is especially important to have a personal website or portfolio that offers vital details about who you are and allows you to visually illustrate your work. You may use Squarespace, Wix, or WordPress, to build your own website, among others. Little brands and business owners could also take advantage of valuable design tools such as the logo templates from Canva and Venngage to start producing brand-specific content.

10. Remember, your brand is not just online.

Your brand is not just an online person; it's like taking you home, at the office, and even on your daily commute.

"It's just your name," Gresh emphasizes. "The more chances you have to partner with others, volunteer for ventures, and show yourself as a leader, take them. That's part of your brand." Leadership is not reserved for C-suite executives. There are strong leaders at every organization's level.

"Leadership comes from how you conduct yourself, how you act, and how you interact inherently with people," says Gresh. "That's real leadership." At the end of the day, this story you share, coupled with those everyday experiences, determines your personal brand.

Reinvent your personal brand as you expand

As the digital world evolves and your career continues to evolve, so will your personal brand. Adjust your personality accordingly as you meet different people, find new opportunities for networking, and grow in your career. Don't hesitate to build a brand that lets you shine, as long as it represents your professional life.

If you are searching for a better position, pursuing a promotion, considering changing professions, or growing your network, creating a personal brand will help you achieve your goals. We always market services and goods as marketers but forget that we need to market ourselves too! For example, follow these seven steps.

Step One: Decide and Prioritize Your Values and Passions

Values are important things you believe to be important in your way of living and working. They're at the core of who you as a person are, and they decide your goals. Some values include friends, family, honesty, community, ambition, and so on. Typically you rely on your deepest-held values when faced with difficult decisions.

Values are important to business, particularly when searching for jobs. When the principles of an applicant suit those of an organization, they are more likely to be recruited. Prioritizing your values will help you set your personal brand vision.

Passions are the ways to invest your time. These are usually separate from your principles, although they can often overlap. You must first define your interests-personal as well as technical-in order to create your personal brand. Technology, automation, and design may include professional passions, while personal passions may include kayaking, family, and golf.

Values and love help you determine where you want to be, including your desired career path, in two, five, or even twenty-five years. If a person were to be assigned the passions and values above, he would most likely perform well in an e-mail marketing position involving design and automation, although he would need to live in an area that provided him with plenty of opportunities for outdoor activities.

Step Two: Identifying Your Main Features

What will help you stand out from the crowd? These elements are your unique characteristics, and they help shape your identity.

The Big 5 Personality Traits are identified as Openness to Experience, Conscientiousness, Extraversion, Agreeableness and Neuroticism. Each of these traits is evaluated on a scale, and your unique personality is defined where you fall on a scale. To decide yours you can take a free check. This test should give you some insight into how pleasant, extroverted, open-minded, and so on you are, and help you cultivate your personal brand. Of course, these traits need not be permanent; if you don't like your results, you can take steps to move in one direction or another along the scale. Or, for instance, if you are closed-minded, you could try new things at work and in your personal lives. In comparison, you are unlikely to have a lot of luck adjusting main characteristics like extrovert and introvert characteristics.

Need more information on who you are today? Ask your family and friends for their truthful opinions. Start by asking them to provide three adjectives that they would use to describe you.

You can make your own personal brand statement once you have your key traits: Imagine your best self while making this.

Use this fill-in-the-blanks template from Dummies.com to help you get started writing your comment.

Note: Make use of this as a starting point but edit it to match your needs.

Step Three: Build Your Personal Identity

Once you know your beliefs, interests, and traits of personality, it's time to show them! Here are some ways to get started: take professional headshots and use them on Linkedin, in your company profile, and so on. Create a unique e-mail signature. (Use your personal e-mail when you can not edit your company's e-mail signature). Include all your contact details, signature, social media icons, company, and website.

Create content to establish a reputation. Use your personal blog, profile LinkedIn, or media-like publishing tools to get your message out on topics you know.

Dress up the part! Stay organized by holding a fresh blazer and pants or skirt polished and ready to go for networking events and large meetings.

Step Four: Identifying your target audience

It is impossible to make everyone like you, so why would you try to appeal to everyone when it comes to building your personal brand? It is important for organizations to define a target audience and for individuals as well. Think of when you were younger and when they were in a good mood, you made sure your parents accepted requests. This simple example illustrates a valuable lesson; the best way to spend your time and resources in an audience is to give you the desired outcome.

Includes

1. The target audience.

The Person Who Will Pay You: Usually, this person is a manager, creditor or customer. That person will be in charge of your next career move. Create a description of this person (whether actual or manufactured) and include as many details as you can about them. Then identify the personal and professional motivations that this person has. Once you understand his / her motives, it can help you understand more how she can help you achieve your own goals and even help her fulfill those!

Your boss may want to be the Chief Marketing Officer and spend more time with her family. By taking on additional tasks or streamlining processes, you can help free up some of her time. Then in exchange, she'll be happy to help you! Fix a meeting to outline your goals and discuss specific schedules and to-do items to accomplish them.

2. The One Who has Influences

The Individual Who Pays You: Make it easy for her superior or direct influencer for your boss/client etc. to put in a good word for you. Specify your current achievements and clearly describe your goals in a presentable format. Show how in your current position, you walked above and beyond.

3. Your Supporters:

For whom do your messages mean? Who will make the most of their use and provide you with what you are looking for? It is your supporters' target audience. If you're looking for a new job or promotion, your supporters might also be your colleagues who will help you get where you want to go by providing excellent recommendations.

Phase 5:

Create Your Online Presence

From Twitter to podcasts, blogs to Facebook, you have to get your voice out there to establish your personal brand. First, you have to secure URLs, social usernames, etc. that fits your brand best before someone else does! This includes your own website as well as any social networks you choose to join.

Tools such as awareness and NameChk will support you across hundreds of social networks to test availability. If you've already selected your preferred name, consider using dashes, underscores, or numbers to find one that suits your brand better.

Linkedin is one of the nicest places to start socially if you are interested in improving your job or searching for customers, then LinkedIn is the best place to start. The other major networks you want to take a look at are Twitter, Facebook, and Instagram. Here, secure your username and start building your profiles on the network(s) that will fit best and help your personal brand further.

Additionally, make sure your personal website displays your best attributes and/or work if you're a model or artist, set up a portfolio.

Begin a podcast or film yourself speaking at a conference, if you're a speaker.

Step Six: Commence blogging!

Many marketers view blogging as the best way to build a business, but when creating a personal brand, they can also be influential. Use The Complete Guide To Build Your Blog Audience to start blogging once you've got your website. You are well on your way to creating a lasting personal brand once you've got followers.

Some of the best strategies for attracting followers include: writing about influencers and getting them to share your articles Using social sharing buttons on your blog Joining the right online groups Syndicating your content Repurposing your content Once you have built up an audience, make sure you post regularly, follow best SEO practices and continue to provide best service to your audience.

Step 7: Follow an expert's footsteps.

Who admires you inside or outside the marketing industry?

Below are some examples of great personal branding you can borrow from the experts straight away. Take note of the way people present themselves and their jobs.

Mobile- And Location-Based Services Such As Foursquare And Gowalla

The geolocation and local social networks are buzzwords of the moment, especially in the social media circles. Whether you're a business owner, a marketer, or a consumer, you've noticed friends "checking in" with their latest tweets on Foursquare or associating locations. Small companies and big brands alike are trying to find out this new environment, which is constantly changing.

That's for a good reason: people use a variety of location-aware apps and online features, and some have been proven to offer a boost to social media-savvy businesses – especially businesses with a storefront or venue.

Go Deeper: How to Make Money on Foursquare

Using Location-Based Social Networks in Business: Learning the Basics

The demand for location-based services is on the rise, with check-in companies such as Foursquare, Gowalla, Yelp and Brightkite leading the way (Foursquare adds about 15,000 new users per day at the last check). The more established social players entered the market, more recently. Facebook has even made it clear, with the advent of Google Local and Twitter Places, that posting a current location – not exactly check-ins, but close – is a feature it intends to offer soon.

"If you look at the big picture, it's where social media was in 2005 or 2006," says Rob Reed, an industry writer and founder of MomentFeed.com, a company that helps companies use location-based marketing services. "Location is so much faster than social media has ever done. One year from now, we'll see location jumping the equivalent of three years of social media time." Business geolocation is not just about check-ins, which may sound a little empty and repetitive (say a customer comes into your bar. If they check-in, can they purchase more drinks? Very unlikely). The check-in act, though it's the first obvious relation, isn't where the interest lies in those networks. It is the data that the check-in and the behaviors revealed about the patterns and habits of a customer which really adds to the experience.

"If you are an organization that appreciates what Facebook and Twitter have done for you, the place would be ten times more important," Reed says.

Think like a customer to be a part of the advantages that your company will reap. By checking in, they 're, in a sense affirming that they "like" your business to a wide net of friends and online connections. It is a kind of endorsement. And, using customer and your business, this can deepen the connection between the geolocation. Unlike internet ads, it's all about reaching both current and future consumers in these networks.

Marshall Kirkpatrick, who co-alters the innovation blog ReadWriteWeb.com, as of late, composed a post titled "Why We Check-In." He says: "The Web itself has changed such huge numbers of ventures. Area and the physical area is significant for organizations and promoters. It changes everything. By sharing your coordinates, you're combining location and the Web, basically sharing where you're shopping, what you're eating, what you're doing, and what you're doing. These are some easy steps to take when you start out.

Hear, and know.

In case you're simply getting into area-based informal communities, it's truly simple to get included, regardless of how enormous your business is. Be that as it may, before you do that,

Reed prompts you, "look at what the significant brands are doing and follow their lead since they are doing all the testing and putting resources into this region." According to a report distributed in 2008 by innovation advertise examination firm ABI Analysis, area-based informal organizations will produce an incredible $3.3 billion in income by 2013. On June 30, Foursquare revealed it had raised $20 million in venture capital, taking the firm's valuation to an estimated $95 million. "If you're an independent coffee shop or just have a few places, you can learn a lot from more or less following Starbucks and their moves. They deserve a lot of credit to test the waters with Foursquare, but I really don't think they get the most benefit from location-based networks," says Reed.

Participate.

Start exploring your own room. Start by making sure you have a mobile phone, and then download some of the many applications that exist. A good starting point is with Yelp, the browser Layar, Foursquare, Twitter, Facebook, and Brightkite with an augmented reality layering. You could certainly explore additional apps, but these will be your simplest entry point into the location-based social networking game. Start using the tools as a person, track what your company is being told by consumers and users. Only then can you begin to use the services for your business, because you will have a much clearer understanding of what you need. "Another advantage is the data companies can obtain from those networks," wrote Todd McMurtrey of Amadeus Consulting, a Boulder, Colorado-based firm. "Foursquare, for example, has recently introduced an analytics tool that allows companies to track demographic data about who is checking in. This enables companies to access a variety of real-time consumer data, including male-to-female customer ratios, common daytime times, and other statistics. This and similar apps allow retailers to track and engage consumers at an individual level." To put it another way, give your business a digital footprint. Start with Google Local, and write a review, identify your Foursquare and Brightkite location, tweet your spot, check your Yep feedback, build a Facebook fan page if you haven't already done so. You want to make sure that the digital / mobile world suits the venue, name, and more of your real-world business. Synchronize your website, savvily spread your social media on your website, and just speak back.

Listen, watch, and commit.

Once you have activated your local social networks, location-based commitments become key (just as customer service and real-life experience do). Listening is the most important aspect of marketing that is also not being done properly by many companies. Monitor what customers say about your business and if necessary answer questions, complaints and compliments. The more proactive and attentive you are with customers, the more sophisticated the company can appear digitally.

Push Location-Contests and Interaction.

"This is where the real comes into the digital realm," Reed says. "You've interacted digitally with your customers, now you've got to impress them with the physical location they want to come back." So, while traditional business standards still apply (service, quality, etc.), it's also about incentives and engagement. Give people a reason to come along – give a voucher that appears when they check-in close by. Or use one of your networks and drive a promotional campaign (not unlike many traditional loyalty programs) to reward return visits. And once folks are there, consider using your physical location over the devices or networks with signage or targeted ads that can push participation. Foursquare and Yelp offer window stickers, but it can be as simple as as asking clients to follow you on Twitter to upgrade your engagement. Taking all these measures does not produce immediate monetary returns, but long-term customer retention, loyalty, and brand awareness can help. At the very least, the above initiatives will help potential customers find their company when they activate their location-based social networks, and this is the first real step.

How To Keep Track Of And Measure Results And Integrate That Information Into Your Overall Marketing Plan

What does it mean that your content marketing is "working?" Overall, that means it supports your marketing and business objectives.

In the seventh installment of our "Back to Basics" series, we explain how you can monitor your content marketing plan and, more importantly, how your team and management can communicate this.

How to track basic KPIs

Start by deciding how often you will collect your data when putting your measurement program in place. A good starting schedule is to measure marketing effectiveness on a monthly basis — we found that this worked well for CMI (although we can watch some metrics weekly just to make sure that monthly goals stay on track — especially for metrics we can quickly change). You'll then want to create a spreadsheet that will document and track the following: your marketing objectives. If you have several, placing them in order of priority may help. (You should have decided on targets with your management team on this point, but if you haven't, now is the time to go to the same page.) Key performance indicators (KPIs) will be used to evaluate your content 's marketing effectiveness.

Your plan to gather information about that performance.

Who will be responsible for the data collection and reporting?

Here's an easy table you can use, based on our CMI experience. If your metrics spreadsheet is something you intend to share with others in your organization (which we highly recommend), consider using Google spreadsheets or another sharing platform to allow anyone to access and make changes as needed.

Click on Enlarge Although everything in the above list is important, I can't stress enough that anyone who works on content marketing needs to know what the core KPIs are for measuring your content 's marketing effectiveness. Whether they are directly involved with your content analytics or not, it is critical that content creators understand how their work affects overarching company goals.

Here are some examples of KPIs that you may want to track: Getting the measurement started can be as simple or as complicated as you do. Don't actually calculate for the sake of having those numbers to present to the upper management. If you're not sure what you should be measuring, ask yourself these two questions:

Do these measurements support my key objectives?

Will I take action on these metrics (i.e., they can give me some perspective on how I can develop my program)?

If you are unable to respond "yes" to the above questions, you probably don't need to collect the data at least at first. This post from Andy Crestodina outlines certain critical data points that you can collect and put to good use immediately: 3 content optimization questions that Google Analytics can answer.

An example from CMI

One of our primary goals at CMI is to get new e-mail subscribers, as this objective is key to our business model. Where subscribers come from (e.g., SlideShare, our blog, webinars, etc.) Which subject brought them to CMI (e.g., content curation, content marketing plan, visual material, workflow, etc.) Opt-out percentages per month and opt-out sources Some tips from our experience: make measurement a priority. Our measurement processes are constantly changing, and it certainly takes time to monitor output, evaluate, and study. But over the years, we've learned how important this measurement and optimization process is to consistently be effective with content marketing.

Conversions to Chart.

Although certain vanity metrics are simple to monitor (e.g., Twitter followers, website traffic), they are seldom that informative independent of other data. We track our social growth, enabling us to look at trends and anecdotal information about where we get the most shares and social conversation. However, we found monitoring conversions to e-mail, and topics of interest is more relevant. This helps us to change our content marketing strategy appropriately so we can be sure that we can deliver on our readers' desires and expectations — actions that will definitely benefit our own end result.

Collect metrics that are actionable.

Just gather data you want to use and have the freedom to act on it. For example, we produced a KPI document in January 2013 that allowed us to track month-to-month growth in areas such as our e-mail program, website, and social media. The CMI team re-evaluated these metrics after a year of looking at these KPIs and made one major change: we are now only monitoring our most actionable metrics, such as e-mail subscribers, e-mail engagement rates, on-site time, and event registration.

Converse with and learn from colleagues in the industry.

We had looked at SlideShare subscriber growth every month early in our attempts to assess the success of our content — the only SlideShare metric we were collecting. But we found that this didn't take into account all that CMI was doing on SlideShare every month, nor the number of presentation downloads (and thus new leads) that we got from our platform efforts. Now, not only do we collect subscriber numbers from SlideShare, but we also collect monthly presentation uploads, and monthly subscriber downloads. This has helped us to decide the optimum number of presentations we will produce per month, the styles (long-form versus short) of presentations our audience likes, and whether what we publish on SlideShare should be open or gated. Another example would be our e-mail subscriptions: At one point, we monitored e-mail opt-ins by source, but with that knowledge we weren't doing anything. We had no concentrated efforts to look at deliverability of communications, opt-outs, and completed profiles — three areas where we would be well-positioned to act immediately. This has helped the CMI team fine-tune our procedures, boost the quality of our e-mails, and keep our priorities in mind.

Be able to adapt.

What you measure over time is likely to change, so review your metrics list regularly, bi-annually, or annually to ensure that you are gathering the data that best answers the main questions. We review our indicators annually to ensure that they continue to comply with CMI goals and priorities as they grow alongside our industry.

Automate selection of the data.

Consider how you can use reports to simplify data collection. With the help of our team, within Google Analytics, Salesforce, and our marketing automation system we were able to automate the dashboards. Every week we can look at these dashboards and then have a clear way of updating our KPI document every month. If automated data collection is not an option, however, consider additional resources and team members that you can access if you need help evaluating your performance of content. Since many team members at various points touch on our marketing processes, assigning oversight responsibilities for each KPI has improved ownership and accountabilities.

Take some time to analyze.

Just gathering data and adding it to a spreadsheet is not enough. The data needs to be analyzed in order to understand where the opportunities for improvement lie — and what the best way to achieve those improvements might be. For example, if data shows that our content marketing strategy blog posts all have large numbers of Facebook shares, LinkedIn updates, and tweets, a careful review of these data points will help us show the best ways to exploit these high-performance topics through our other content channels.

I can not hammer enough how important it is to monitor the effects of your content marketing efforts so that you can continually understand what your audience likes and use that knowledge to improve continuously. The Outcome? Happy results, happier customers, and better management.

What analytics tips and resources do you have that help you monitor and evaluate the success of your content?

Measuring the effectiveness of marketing communications
Why measure?

Measuring is a key aspect of marketing campaigns and other marketing activities. Measurement makes some people really nervous, as it makes marketing behavior accountable. Indeed this move can be one of the best friends of a marketer. If you don't calculate the impact of your marketing activities, you won't have a clue whether or not what you're doing is successful. On the other hand, if you calculate the effect, it will help you understand what works, and where and how your efforts can be strengthened. Marketing is, by definition a dynamic environment, as markets change and people change. What works fine this year could be a total flop next year, and vice versa.

Measurement – and the results or "metrics" that this process collects – are like a compass that helps marketers adjust course so they can accomplish their goals faster and better.

Deciding What to Measure

Measuring just to have numbers misses the entire point. Determining the right things to assess first, if you want to get a clear image of what's happening, is actually important. To do so, marketers usually go through a process of defining key measures of success (often called KPIs). A KPI is something measurable, which shows how much progress an organization is making towards its business goals. The KPI is different from the aim or purpose of the actual company; rather, it is something tangible that lets managers understand how well they are working towards the target.

Let's say you're a track coach who wants to capture data about the sprinters on your team to understand the importance of KPIs. You could measure all kinds of things about the athletes: their shoe size, how many cups of sweat they produce during a typical workout, how quickly their heartbeats during a race, etc. Will all of those measures be key indicators of performance? Possibly not. You might decide that their best running times and average running times (or something else) are the key performance indicators for sprinters.

KPIs can be determined in a company for many different levels of the organization. These are listed below: Business-level KPIs indicate the overall company output in terms of total sales, profitability, customer satisfaction rating, market share, or percentage of customer base growth.

Department level KPIs track department level results. It could be brand awareness, the number of qualified new leads generated, the cost per lead generated, or the conversion rate for the marketing department: the percentage of leads converted into customers.

The impact and effectiveness of team activities are tracked by team-level KPIs. For example, a team focused on digital marketing could track KPIs such as e-mail marketing click rates, the number of website visits, or SEO sales conversion rates: the percentage of individuals coming to the website through a search engine and resulting in a sale.

KPIs at the campaign level monitor the effectiveness of individual campaigns. By keeping track of similar metrics across multiple campaigns, it is easy to see which ones with target audiences are most effective, and then use this information to refine tactics and replicate successful approaches. Campaign-level KPIs are somewhat dependent on the design of the campaign; for example, campaigns typically track the "open" rate: that's how many people open an e-mail message once it's delivered. If a campaign is not using e-mail, then there is no open limit. There are however, some "common denominator" campaign indicators marketers can track the effect and success through IMC activities. For virtually any campaign, cost per impression, impressions per campaign, and conversion rate are metrics that can be tracked.

KPIs at tactical marketing level monitor the effectiveness of individual marketing tools and tactics. For example, KPIs for content-marketing track the effectiveness of individual pieces of content used on a website and in IMC campaigns. Such metrics, such as page views per article and number of social media shares, provide advertisers with insight into which content styles are most common with target clients and which content pieces get little attention.

Different firms choose different sets of KPIs, depending on what they are trying to accomplish and the strategies they are pursuing to achieve their objectives. It is necessary, at any given point, to restrict the total number of KPIs to those most critical and indicative of progress. If too many variables are calculated, managers have difficulty prioritizing what's most important, and homing in. An organization may also monitor a number of other metrics to inform its operations in addition to KPIs – which reflect important, strategic progress indicators–.

Alignment with Priorities and Objectives

Determining what to calculate begins with understanding the overall goals of the company, as well as the goals and objectives of the marketing department. The top-level KPIs will inform managers how well marketing performs in achieving their targets as a team, and how the team contributes to the overall success of the company. KPIs can represent absolute numbers, for example, total market share. Or they can track progress towards a target, such as progress towards 1,500 new customers over a year. KPIs should provide managers with the knowledge to guide their decision making on what works and when to change course.

Defining a standard collection of KPIs for assessing the efficacy of marketing campaigns and for the contributions made by different roles within the marketing organization is beneficial to a company: public relations, advertisement, social media marketing. Whenever marketers define S.M.A.R.T. goals at the outset of a campaign, these goals may include KPIs to confirm what the campaign is aiming for and how well it is doing to achieve these goals. For example, KPIs for awareness-building campaigns should focus on campaign reach, like a number of impressions or brand awareness after campaign.

Managers should be mindful of how many KPIs they track to ensure that measurement remains a useful activity rather than a burden that cuts into the broader team's productivity and effectiveness. Fortunately, as marketing becomes more data-rich and technology-driven, many KPI-type metrics are automatically measured by marketing-supporting systems, making them readily accessible. There are also tools that build dashboards for marketing managers and team leaders to help them track KPIs easily on a continuous basis.

Defining the Metric

Any marketing metric or KPI requires some measurement type, and it should be based on legitimate information. When determining a KPI, marketers can also specify which data will be used to measure the KPI, as well as the source of that data. Often different individuals or teams may have different ideas on how to measure the metric, so clarifying this during the definitional stage is wise.

It's not unusual for people to identify KPIs and then discover that they don't have ready access to the measurement information. This may be a good motivator to identify a method for obtaining that knowledge. Or it can be a hint that a particular KPI will be a better choice based on more readily available knowledge.

What to measure

Where to measure depends on what's readily available to track and sustain advertisers and managers. If it takes a lot of effort to generate a KPI report, or managers spend hours per day or week compiling and reporting metrics, it could significantly reduce to productive working hours — and it might be wise to investigate alternatives. Fortunately, CRM and other systems are readily available which creates KPI dashboard reports into their standard, daily functions. In these cases, systems calculate KPIs automatically, which makes them easy to track over time and change course as needed. Usually, managers will track KPIs at least once a quarter to gauge progress and learn what works and how to make changes.

Key Performance Metrics Examples

As mentioned above, different forms of KPIs concentrate on assessing success and efficacy in different marketing-related fields. There are actually hundreds of possible KPIs, so marketing managers should figure out which ones are most important for reaching their goals and focus attention accordingly.

Featured Case Studies, Step-By-Step Instructions, And Hands-On Tutorials

Marketers love to describe their collateral using the term "storytelling" If marketers are to be believed, then all is a story.

But most certainly the storytelling mark refers (or should) to case studies since stories are just what case studies are.

Case studies are self-contained examples about how a particular consumer uses the goods or services to solve their problems. Just like a novel, good case studies have a beginning, a middle, and an end, as well as a protagonist-your client-overcoming a challenge and achieving their target, much like a story's main character.

The reader will be able to imagine themselves as the hero in his own story by the end of a case study. They should be able to relate to your featured customer's problems and see themselves attaining their own aims by making use of your product or service.

What a case study is NOT.

Case studies aren't articles of the public. Although case studies may be used to accompany the launches of new products, they are not just vehicles to talk about new products.

Evidence studies aren't advertising. They can be used to promote new products or features, but that's not your business.

Good case studies are about the journey to the consumer, NOT your business.

Most case studies are bland, easily forgettable garbage because advertisers disregard the fact that, in the most literal sense, case studies are tales. They get worried about things like brand voice or messaging matrices and forget to take advantage of the narrative form, which makes stories so compelling. Or, worse yet, when it comes to case studies, they literally can not stop themselves from harping on how fantastic their business is, the gravest of sins.

Why build Case Studies for Marketing?

Case studies may not be as glamorous as a viral blog post, and as such, they are frequently ignored for other types of content. This raises the question-why at all construct marketing case studies?

The response is that they really do work.

B2B Marketing has asked a group of marketers in a new survey of how they feel about different content types like case studies. The findings were surprising: two-thirds (66 percent) of the 112 marketers surveyed in the study by B2B Marketing said case studies were "very successful" in driving leads and sales, and another 32 percent considered case studies to be "very efficient," making case studies the most effective content format included in that study.

In the 2016 B2B Content Marketing Study, more than half of the marketers surveyed (55 percent) said they considered case studies to be the most successful single content type.

Approximately 31 percent of respondents questioned in the 2015 B2B Technology Content Survey Report from Eccolo Media said that case studies were found to be the third most popular content type, only behind white papers (33 percent) and data sheets (39 percent).

How to Write an Excellent Case Study (with Examples) Now that we're clear about what is (and isn't) a marketing case study, and why you should create it, let us talk about how to write a case study worth reading.

Follow these seven tips to write a great case study that helps you close deals.

(Do you need help to get started? See my tips on how to write a persuasive introduction.)

1. Be realistic about the targets

I have been working on material for many years now for your case study and I have read hundreds – if not thousands – of marketing case studies. To date, I still remember and think of ONE case study as the "ideal" example of a great case study.

Most people aren't going to have a "favorite" case study, or can even remember one at all.

It is important to remember that case studies are not so important to your audience, before you sit down to create your magnum opus. Yeah, we want to create a valuable, beneficial tool for prospective customers, but let's be honest – for a case study, nobody wins a Pulitzer and it won't go viral on social media, no matter how well-written it might be.

Case studies are nothing more than methods that can be used either by the company's self-motivated prospects or by sales practitioners as tools to help persuade prospects to move-nothing more. They are targeted for audiences who are already considering being your clients, which is a smaller group of people but more knowledgeable than your general audience.

Be realistic about your aims as such. Don't be upset if a blog post about a case study does not perform as well as your best content. WordStream frequently publishes case studies but they never get as much traffic as our most famous blog posts, and that's all right. We don't have unrealistic expectations for our case studies and we know they are beneficial to both our sales staff and prospects.

2. Identify a Compelling Angle for Your Case Study

Last year, one of our product development managers asked me to write a case report for a company rehabilitating poorly treated and violent dogs. My first question was that any parallels existed between teaching tough dogs and coming to grips with AdWords as a new advertiser.

This thinking became the core of the entire case study.

The more aggressive the perspective is, the better the story. The better the plot, the more your case study will become engaging.

Seek to locate a customer of interest for your next case study. How is it that people use your products or services? Do any of your clients using your company to solve complicated or uncommon problems? If you are looking for someone to serve as the model for your next case study, get creative. That being said ...

3. But make your case study related to ALL of the prospects

Definitely, you want your case study to be interesting and have a compelling angle, but you also want to be able to identify with it the vast majority of your target market.

Using our earlier example of dog therapy we realized that it was fascinating to see the potential parallels between training challenging dogs and using AdWords as a newcomer to paid search. However, we also knew that given the persuasive angle we had chosen to pursue, the client in question had faced many of the typical problems with modest monthly AdWords spending in our core target market of small businesses.

Your angle is the "hook" that will attract your audience's attention, but it's important that ALL prospects can relate to and resonate with the issues faced by the "protagonist" in your case study . This means listening to your core audiences and target markets, and addressing the problems that your consumers most frequently experience.

4. In your case study follow the Classic Narrative Arc

Recall how we said that while not telling many tales, most advertisers are fascinated with the notion of "storytelling?" Okay, just like any good story has a start, middle, and end, so do the best case studies too.

At WordStream, case studies are usually organized in a similar way each time. We introduce the narrator of our story – the consumer – as well as the issues they try to overcome. Think of that as your case study Act I. While I never use strict rules when writing case studies, this section typically runs in length between 200 and 300 words; just enough to introduce our story's hero and tease the problems they face, but not too much to discourage more casual readers.

We introduce the solution in Act II, that is to say our software. I could include a brief explanation of what drove our protagonist to look for our products, before going deeper into how our software is used by the client. This segment will also include direct customer quotations, and is typically highly beneficially focused. This segment is where the story's main meat is, and is always the longest of the three stories.

Writers are frequently advised to "show, not say," and the final third of our case study – Act III, if you will – is where the use of hard data can be highly useful in your case study. If possible, I will try to provide as many statistical details as I can to explain why the use of our tools was so successful for the featured client (more about this momentarily).

You may distill this rough formula into the following structure: Question (Act I) > Solution (Act II) > Outcome (Act III) > Conclusion

5. Use Data in Your Case Study to illustrate key points

Your case study is a story, though that doesn't mean you should rely on anecdotes or whimsy to make your points. When writing a case study, cold, hard data is your best friend – more so than any other content ventures.

If possible, the data you add to your case study should reflect directly the challenges your protagonist faces in Act I. In our example, this could be an increase in the click-through rate, which can be easily shown by charts or other data.

That's why our sales teams love our case studies; they can listen to the concerns of a prospect on the phone, define a specific issue, and explain how the very same issue a customer just like them solved using our tools – yeah, and here's a handy chart showing exactly how they did it.

Not all businesses are as data-driven as WordStream, of course, and so 'data' may not be relevant to your business. In this case, it might be more accurate to use the word "proof" rather than "data" and this proof may include anything from time-lapse video to high-resolution images before and after.

Whatever you want to do, make sure to provide some details or facts to support your key points and explain how your featured customer solved their issue with your goods or services. Show, don't say.

6. In your case studies, picture your company as a support character

If your featured customer is the protagonist of your story, it is tempting to think of your company (or your products or services) as an equal participant in how the tale unfolds.

Instead, though, you should think of your company's role as a supporting character in the plot.

People are not purchasing items for the sake of purchasing them; people are buying items to solve specific problems. Likewise, nobody uses a product or service for their own sake, but because a product or service helps them solve a specific problem. Because of that, your business will always be portrayed as a helping hand that helped the story's main hero – your client – conquer their obstacle.

This method is so successful on two key reasons. Next, you want your audience to imagine themselves as the case study protagonist. That's even harder if you're not going to stop thinking about how amazing your business or product is. Secondly, adopting a more positive tone will help to improve the reader's credibility.

Remember, if in doubt, that your client is Batman – and your business is Robin (or Nightwing depending on where you are in the universe of Batman comics).

7. Let Your Clients say Their Stories in Case Studies

It is your duty to draw up a compelling tale about how your featured client triumphed over the forces of evil using your product or service, but that doesn't mean your protagonist doesn't have his own voice.

Making use of your client's direct quotes is a great way to let them tell their own story in their own words. This not only breaks down the case study's "expository" text but also offers more clarity and legitimacy by providing the client's viewpoint. This also permits you to draw the reader using techniques similar to those commonly found in feature journalism, gradually revealing more of your protagonist in an almost interview-style format, using their own words.

However, it does pose other risks as successful as this strategy can be, namely the possibility of repetition. If you intend to include a quote from your customer about, say, time savings, do not specifically mention time savings in the paragraph(s) immediately preceding the quote; let your customer do the talk. Set up the segue and build space to quote your client, and let them do the rest.

Being a quick case study may not be the most exciting content you produce but it may be among the most effective. There are no two companies alike and case studies vary widely in style, tone, and format. However, one thing that all marketing case studies share is their intent-to persuade prospects that it is a good idea to do business with you.

Marketing Best Practices Related To The Facebook, Youtube, Instagram, Platform

1. Learn all you can about your audience

First best practice with social media?

If you don't know who your target is, then what they want you can't give them. And then they will not give you what you (their business) want.

To whom do you try to connect?

Millennials, single-moms, canine kids? That is a start, but get as precise as you can to engage them in the best possible way. Do the research and have more reliance on data, less on your gut.

Keep the current customers open, too. So you can go and find the same traits and make new ones.

Example: Their ages Where they reside What languages they speak How much they earn How much they spend What they buy What they do in their spare time What stage of life they are in (student, parent, retired) Other tactics to know for learning about your audience are:

Analyze website and social media analytics

Be clear about the value of your products and services Creating a target market state of affairs We have an audience research guide that includes a template to help you build client / audience persona.

2. Because too many marketers spread too thinly across too many networks, choose which networks to use (and which to ignore)

How do you decide the networks on which to turn up and share?

Demographic studies. This will assist you in deciding which networks to use — and which ones to lose. These are the types of insights you should be searching for: Instagram demographics A billion users, 500 million of whom are active daily 71 percent of Americans between 18 and 24 use this network 43 percent African Americans, 38 percent Hispanic, 32 percent white for U.S. users Facebook Demographics More active monthly users than 1.4 billion regular users in any one country, and 2.13 bil. Regulation. Platform ...... platform. More so than everybody else.

330 million active monthly users I believe 45 percent of new users have college degrees.

Know all about your audience and who uses what social network to help sell your brand, and combine these two data points.

3. Have you built a social networking plan, summarizing what you want to do and achieve on social media?

Yeah? Good work.

Doesn't it? You ought to. Why? For what?

For every post to know if you're good or failing, share, like and comment.

This guide will direct you through every step of drawing up a winning strategy. But these are the highlights:

Set goals

If not, how do you know what is, what isn't, and what to change when content is produced and shared? And, follow through on useful metrics.

KPIs on social media are worth monitoring, too.

Conduct a Gather audit and review what works in one place, and what is not on social media. This will help you plan what more to do, what better to do and what to stop. Easily see: Who you're connected to Who's connected to you Which networks your target market uses to compare your brand to your rivals And ... ask yourself some (honest) questions about your social accounts: Is your market here?

If so, how do they use that platform?

Does this help you achieve your goals for the business?

Using the responses to assess which accounts are worth keeping, or canceling.

Need help with setting up an audit? We have a prototype that is for you.

4. Keep an eye on the competition because they can get the upper hand if you don't.

Often, to know about what they do, to help you decide what to (and should not) do. Why reinvent yourself when you can fix it?

You want to learn about your social media rivals ... Who are Where do they do what they did before How well do they do what they do? Any risks to your company find holes in your own strategy Do some research to question and respond ... What networks are they on?

How broad is its audience?

What frequency do they post?

How much (shares, likes, and comments) do they indulge in?

In what good are they?

And not so well?

What are those threats they pose?

To help with that, there are tools and techniques (and a template to organize your findings).

Competitors can inspire your social media activities to great degree.

Heck, I have contacted many copywriters and have friendships with them. We share stories of war about losses and victories as well as tools, approaches and ideas for doing better.

You may, too, (should).

5. Listen to brand mentions

And what people on the social media platforms are doing.

If you do — you can track those conversations, analyze them and respond. You're losing useful ideas for your company if you don't.

Social listening is a double-stage process.

1. Track channels to capture brand mentions, rivals, product, and keywords important to you.
2. Analyze those mentions to decide what to do next.

Like ... Respond to a happy client (or to a troll). Check one off against another program. Or change your voice and tone mark significantly.

Learn how people think of you in relation to the competition. Is a rival getting a beating in the press? Could that be a golden moment for sharing, showing or saying?

Beat the Discovery and Treatment of Pain Points rivalry. Is someone talking about a sucking feature of theirs? Can you easily add something new that doesn't work?

Identify defenders and influencers. Will anyone say anything excellent about you all out there? It's probably time to work with them.

Hear, know and receive.

These are some tools to help you listen to about social matters.

6. Track conversations related to your industry

Like social listening, it's about knowing what people think about your company.

There are resources to help you understand: who mentions your brand, which hashtags, and other developments in your industry.

Think of electronic monitoring as the base of social listening. Track Learning from the past. Hear creating your future.

On those tools? Here are some of the best social surveillance devices we've identified or used.

7. Establish your voice and tone on social media

I will obviously plagiarize the beginning of this piece — word by word.

It's all right, I just wrote it.

You're exercising your brand voice every time you talk, write, design, post, reply, launch, thank, and connect with others.

All. It's time.

If you are conscious or not.

People create an impression in their minds for all the ways in which you appear — online, on stage, on the phone or in person.

Do you not think it is best to be deliberate on all this?

For your continuing message to convey the voice and vibe?

But to 'get it' from your fans, followers, writers, listeners, leads, opportunities and customers?

Here are some ways to go.

Find your adjectives that will develop the voice and vibe for the personality of your brand. I have provided you with a list to start (and end) with.

Write, by avoiding jargon, as you write. Jargon requires that the readers convert brain calories. But they are not going to, they're just going to press somewhere.

Write from the perspective of the reader, to make them into the story, not you, the hero. Be straightforward so readers can know what they're going to get from what you're doing.

Fall over the drama. Evite headlines with sensation. Be over clever always clear. That forces you to understand the reader and to write to them more.

Full post has more tips and examples.

8. Employ the 'Thirds rule' social media for what?

Let us first think about what to say.

1/3 share posts to promote your business, convert readers and generate revenues 1/3 share posts of ideas from influencers in your industry (or like-minded enterprises) 1/3 share posts of personal stories to create your brand Now, back to the reason (for 2/3 share).

Sharing content shows your fans ... You know your industry You 're working together Where you're in the Easy business, right?

9. Respond to all comments and @mentions — promptly because it makes you look lazy, unwilling and all about you when you don't.

So get off your podium and enter the dinner party — by welcoming conversation, listening, and encouraging. Like a great host.

You orate — one-way contact while you are on a podium.

How you converse at a dinner party — two-way conversation.

Social media + comments + mentions + reply now = a relationship.

Here's a full guide to social media interaction for your social media accounts to shape healthy relationships.

10. Don't repost the same message across the networks

I get it, it seems efficient to post the same (exact) message across your social channels. Why recreate a piece (or rewrite it) several times versus once?

But reposting, like tip number nine above, is another way of appearing lazy and messy.

Instead, create a new message for every network and post.

Yeah, it takes longer, and more effort. But perhaps not as much as you would think. No use to begin from scratch — but some modifications do render.

It'll pay off and you'll be seen by people as a company that cares about what it shares.

And it shows you pay attention.

Make content optimal for each network. Tailor the channel to certain stuff. Use your captions with the correct vocabulary. It is easy to imagine terms which might not have a chance on LinkedIn to work on Snapchat. And for each site using the right (vs. same) hashtags.

If not, then you are going to look spammy.

Don't write over. Periodic Posting? Completely. Totally. Overposting on Twitter may be hard to do but for Facebook and LinkedIn it is easy to do. Various audiences have varying tastes. Know all of them, to cater to all.

Ignore certain canals. It. Just do it. Since sharing a cool new product on Pinterest could rock, but flop on LinkedIn.

11. Using data to decide when and how often to post

When is the time to post?

It depends on the social network. People can be on LinkedIn during normal working hours but Instagram is more of a forum for leisure time.

We have an entire article on social media dedicated to finding the best times to post. This is back by social data from the best brands.

Now, how much do you post?

Ultimately that's hard to tell. But, create social media reports to track outcomes for who is getting involved with your brand and posts. So, you should make data-based decisions, not hunches.

12. A / B testing the A / B messaging test (a.k.a. split testing)

This helps you to test minor variants in the messaging in order to figure out what works best for the audience.

How? How?

Separate the audience into two random groups Give each group a different message variation Compare the responses to the chosen metrics They key — change one thing at a time.

Otherwise, if you modify several aspects of the post, you 're back to speculation.

May you think what to test?

Posting email. Consider any of these for your A / B testing: A quotation vs a main statistic Using an emoji Organized vs. Unordered bullets Variations on punctuation Voice sound, say casual vs formal, passive vs active call-to-action. CTAs are critical, you are calling for action from the readers. Shift it to see what works best. 'Use App' versus 'Install Now' for example. Easy to do and results easy to see.

Picture use or video use. Work demonstrates the best output of photos, and videos. Ok, but which one of those works best? Try it and see, for your posts to go from theory to proof. For example, test: text-only versus posts with a regular image or video versus animated GIF Photos of people or products versus graphs or infographics Video length There is more to A / B test. Lots more. See our full Guide.

13. Using the right tools

There are tons of resources and applications for doing the right thing on social media.

There are of course the major networks such as Facebook, Twitter, YouTube, and Instagram. You need to get going there — at least with those that fit your brand and target audience.

You can then look at applications to get your posts and videos to the next level. Here's a few: Planoly is Instagram's visual planner for seeing your grid before you write.

Canva is an app for making (easily) beautiful images for your posts. No experience in graphic design required. Here's a guide to apps for social media images.

Story Slicer lets you cut, edit, and then post videos for stories from Instagram , Facebook, Whatsapp, or VK. It is easy to, for videographer inexperienced or pro.

Camping. The problem: Only one connection is available on your social profiles. The solution: a series of picture links to take users exactly where they want to go.

Check out the remaining tools to develop, post, track and customize your social media campaign.

14. Measure results and adjust your strategy as necessary

Did you identify your goals for your social media ...? Then have the correct metrics defined? The same is true for KPIs?

Yeah? Nice one.

Your next move then is to decide whether you receive more than you invest on social media. By compiling data from your accounts and campaigns to monitor performance — analytics and enhance it.

We wrote the full guide to the use of software for social media analytics.

I'll let you know the highlights below.

Facebook has a Dashboard for analytics. Use this to view your pages and posts with likes, fans, scope and interaction. Before and after a campaign note shifts.

Want to raise some advertisements but which ones aren't sure? To find that out, using the segment Promotions. There is more to it, so you get the picture.

Twitter also has a month-to-month dashboard to look at the details. Top tweets, followers, and mentions, like. For a given time span, see also commitments, reviews and promotions for your tweets.

Twitter reveals the viewer demographics too. Compare the audience with this, and how they vary.

Instagram offers enterprise profile analytics. Gain insights more than just content about who your followers are, when they're online, and more.

Reach: number of unique post views Website clicks: number of clicks on the link used in your Profile Visits page: number of times your username is clicked on You can find similar dashboards for LinkedIn, Pinterest, and Snapchat.

Using these tools to see what works, and what doesn't, and you can see and change to get more from the former.

You go there. Some methods, guidelines, and tips to make traditional best practices.

Engagement Opportunities For Each Platform

How to improve engagement

It is not necessarily rocket science to improve engagement, but it takes effort. Seek not to talk of social entrepreneurship or branding as something different. For decades, the form of marketing has been around.

Today, there is a huge audience out there ready to be targeted, dissected and reached by interaction with social media. The main thing is to know how to handle your audience, which is why we're offering five tips to boost your interaction with social media.

1. Start the conversation

Try to think of social media engagement as a long-term relationship as we have mentioned before. Any great relationship needs somebody to initiate the conversation to make things happen. And in some instances, the name has to be yours.

Blog posts that your audience really wants are a perfect way to open the dialog between both parties. Choose Chicago for example is a great brand to watch. They keep posting amazing Tweets with links to content on why you should visit Chicago. It helps to get people in their industry talking.

It is not always that easy to get a group to converse together, though. If you have issues with getting content engaged, consider hosting Q&As or Twitter Chats. But first try to join a couple of. Using social accounts from your brand to enter conversations within your field. Be helpful with questions and offer users information in the industry.

You will be shocked at the speed with which users will follow you. When people realize that behind the mark there is a individual, their level of confidence increases. It's all about confidence and dedication to creating brand awareness.

Pro Tip: Be careful of your early conversations. Don't advocate directly from the bat or you will notice few connections and involvement. Provide something of interest like an insight into the business or past experience.

2. Promote Your Brand Enthusiasts

Another way to show your ability to get the discussion started is by promoting the material of your brand enthusiasts. For instance, if you're on Instagram, you may want to ask customers to @mention you, or use a branded hashtag to display a new product or service.

Vans frequently uses the licensed hashtag # myvans to include consumers and get their own content shared with the hashtag. When posting content generated by users, you are essentially showcasing your customers and pursuing your social commitment. This also helps to push others on the fence into interacting with your brand by providing an avenue for communication.

Why do you want those hashtags for people to use? It all comes down to monitoring.

It's easy to monitor the success of a recent social giveaway through Sprout Social, or see how well your advertised keywords worked.

In our Instagram analytics report you can also see the top influencers involved with your brand. This helps you to be more careful about your social networking efforts – especially when working about marketing assets like hashtags, keywords or brand phrases.

You can see with the data which users are most engaged with your brand. And if these folks have massive audiences, helping both sides can lead to partnerships or co-marketing efforts. Having your hashtags, keywords, and @mentions present in a single stream platform makes the effort to manage engagement easy.

Pro Tip: Make sure your motives are fully clear, and how you intend to use the material of customers if you do so. Try using competitions on social media to give away t-shirts, swag gift packs, or the actual product. Encourage your audience to use similar hashtags to share your content.

A Better Way to Manage Social

Request a Demo

1. Jump on Current Events & Topical Subjects

You can use these topical events to bring new traffic into your social networks when something is trending, going viral or simply in the news. You can tailor it to your region for items like hashtag holidays, festivals, or live shows.

2. Be Receptive

With Your Audience

A problem many companies have with social media engagement is responding to questions in time. It's always sad when you see a social network of a brand going on years without any new content or interactions with customers. Not only can you inform your audience that you are not present, but you don't want to provide additional contact avenues.

It can be detrimental for your brand to just go one day without a response. You need to be careful and attentive to your current and future clients. So if you invest the time in engaging in social media, you have to be active. Otherwise people would think they don't care for you.

Your aim is to get as many eyes as possible on your brand. In addition, positive experiences inspire people to suggest your brand to friends and family, or post about the great social experience.

Home Depot does a great job in answering the full questions within minutes on Facebook posts. Providing fast and accurate responses to your customers shows you're completely invested. But answering them with a simple "yes" or "no" isn't enough to really engage anyone.

5. As you know, the brand will receive a multitude of different social issues, feedback and concerns. Make sure the social media team is well-equipped and able to manage incoming messages and ensure you're completely engaging users.

Break your team into specific categories to make the most of social engagement: Content Creators: These people develop, design and schedule your social content. Using a calendar on social media helps to plan across all teams and keeps you active in the social sphere.

Group Managers: Who is there for the company to manage a hostile consumer or big news? Hopefully, you've got group managers to monitor circumstances and keep positive interactions.

Public Relations: You need public relations managers to get the company the right publicity across bigger networks. That person would treat customers, customers and businesses alike.

Sales and enabling: If someone is interested in your brand but would like to know more, where are you going to send them? Sales and enabling will make relevant content accessible to drive interaction among stakeholders.

Support: Things break, so it's important to have somebody monitor so update the situation. The members of your team are always available in a crisis and ready to put fires out.

If you do not have enough members or you do not spend on this team, then that's all right. Knowing those managing social media interaction need to wear a lot of hats though.

How to Quantify Engagement

A big issue still unanswered is how to actually measure future commitments and benchmark stats. Don't worry – we already have you covered.

It depends on the network to calculate commitment, and as you know, each has unique aspects.

We are always going to tell you that it's not a good idea to take them all on at once. Start discovering the quintessence networks first, instead. To wet your feet with each social platform, bookmark our social media marketing guide, if you're still not sure.

Find Your Core Engagement Metrics

Marketers are always looking for the social media value and usually, the No. 1 spot is with the data. There are several main indicators to track and evaluate on a regular basis for ensuring the audience is fully engaged.

We provide critical analytical reports inside Sprout Social to better assess the overall engagement across networks. Some of the sensitive communication indicators include: Inbound vs. Replies: the total amount of responses sent within the defined date range vs the total expected inbound messages within.

Average daily response rates and times: Within your selected date range, this is shown per day and your total.

Time Distribution: This shows the percentages of messages that were responded to within specific timeframes.

Answer Time and Rate: Figures are also split out by weekday and hour.

Go In-Depth

Within Every Network To go even further, it is important to analyze every channel in social media where you are present. Know that each network differ, and could've a unique impact on your business.

Common engagement metrics include: Facebook: Organic Likes, Paid Likes, Unlikes, Mentions, Impressions, Post Engagements, Clicked Links, Reactions, Comments, and Shares.

Twitter: Organic Impressions, Clicked Links, Mentions, Direct Communications, Retweets, Replies, and Likes.

Instagram: Likes Received, Feedback, Press Engagement and Most Engaged Hashtags (including Live and Stories).

LinkedIn: Clicks, Views, Likes, Feedback, and Shares.

Okay, so how do I manage it all?

We feel you – Facebook, Twitter , Instagram and LinkedIn accounts are not easy to handle for a single company. No matter how large or small your company is, you need a way to handle the inquiries of your clients without looking at your social networks and hitting the refresh all day.

That is where we are coming in. Sprout Social has a Smart Inbox that is easy to use to better navigate inbound messages, @mentions, new followers and brand keywords. Ensure that monitoring your social networks is a high priority to make your communication techniques shape a long-lasting partnership with your clients.

One interaction isn't always going to change the view of those who see your company. Instead, when customers enter your company on social media, you have to take action and be ready to offer informative information.

Facebook Ads Vs. Adwords

U ntil recently, many advertisers took an adversarial view of Google AdWords and Facebook Ads. The long-standing rivalry between the two firms, frequently dramatized by technology media outlets, has been taken as irrefutable proof that the two platforms were in direct competition with each other, and that it was important for businesses of all sizes to make a tough decision as to which platform was correct for their needs; a false dichotomy that remains confounding and deceptive to those new to the Internet

Though the two platforms are often positioned as competitors, in a practical sense nothing could be further from the truth. In tandem, several businesses exploit the strengths of advertising on Google and Facebook Ads to achieve full exposure, increase leads and revenues, and attract new consumers, follow various approaches that fit with each platform's functionality and see impressive return on their advertisement spending.

In this guide, we will discuss what separates Google AdWords and Facebook Advertising, how the two ad platforms function and why you should consider using them as part of your broader digital marketing strategy.

What are the gaps between the Facebook and Google AdWords ads?

Until we look at the diverse strengths and features of Google AdWords and Facebook Ads, recognizing the primary disparity between the two ad networks is important.

Google AdWords: Google AdWords paid search is the world's largest and most common advertisement site for PPC. AdWords is so commonly used, it has become synonymous with the term "paying search." The two terms are used interchangeably, though other sites like Bing Advertising function in a similar manner.

Pay search relies on keyword targeting and the use of text-based advertising. Advertisers who use AdWords bid on keywords – specific words and phrases included in search queries entered by Google users – in the hope of displaying their ads alongside search results for those queries. Each time a user clicks on an advert, the advertiser is paid a certain amount of money, hence the name "pay-per-click advertisement." PPC bidding and bid optimization is a complicated subject and beyond the reach of this guide, but in essence users are paying for the opportunity to find new customers based on the keywords and search terms they enter in Google.

Facebook Ads: Paid Media Facebook Ads is a prime example of what's known as "paying media," or social networking advertising activity. With the highest number of active monthly users (or MAUs) of any social network in the world,

Facebook has become a highly competitive and potentially lucrative element in the digital advertising strategies of many companies.

While ads on Facebook can be considered similar to AdWords, in that marketers using both sites basically promote their company over the Internet, the similarities end here. Paid social assists users find businesses based on the items they 're interested in and how they're behaving online Unlike paid search, which helps businesses find new customers by keywords,

As far as the primary distinction between Google AdWords and Facebook Advertising is concerned, you can think of it this way: AdWords helps you find new customers, while Facebook helps you find new customers.

Now that we've covered the basic difference between Google AdWords and Facebook Ads (or paid search and paid social), let's look at the strengths of each platform and how those online marketing tools can be effectively leveraged.

Google AdWords Strengths and Advantages

As the most popular and widely used search engine in the world, Google is considered the de facto leader in online advertising. Google offers marketers with access to an unparalleled and unrivaled potential market of consumers who are actively searching for products and services, with more than 3.5 billion search requests every day.

Google's advertisement deals are split into two main networks-the Search Network and the Show Network. As a search engine, the search network includes the whole Google, and marketers will bid on millions of keywords and phrases to attract prospective clients.

The Google Display Network, that offers advertisers more visual ads such as banners, spans around 98 percent of the World Wide Web, Making it a better alternative for advertisers who want to accomplish campaign targets that are not inherently as conversion-driven as those of PPC ads, such as raising big-scale brand recognition through banner advertisements.

An Immense Audience

Its immense reach is one of the main advantages of using Google as a publicity platform. Google handles greater than 40,000 search queries a second, a total of over 1.2 trillion web searches each year. As Google becomes increasingly sophisticated – partly due to its growing reliance on its patented artificial intelligence and RankBrain machine learning technologies – this enormous search volume is likely to increase, along with the ability for advertisers to attract new customers.

Simply put, no other search engine can offer Google's future target market. This wide potential source of prospective customers alone makes Google an excellent addition to your digital marketing strategy, but it's easy to see why AdWords is the most popular and widely used

PPC platform in the world when combined with Google's increasingly accurate search results.

A Level Playing Field

One of the main myths for those new to PPC is that someone with the highest advertisement budget would necessarily "win" on Google ads in some way. Luckily, nothing could be further from the truth as AdWords mainly focuses on the quality and relevance of adverts, not how much the advertisers spend.

The more useful an ad is to the user, the better the user's experience – and therefore, the more likely they will continue to use Google as their go-to search engine. Google AdWords therefore mainly rewards importance and consistency above all other considerations. That is why smart advertisers with relevant, optimized, high-quality ads rarely have to bid just as highly as advertisers with poorer ads.

Some keywords that cost more than others — such as those in the financial industry, which is typical among the most costly of any professional sector — but how much advertisers have to bid would ultimately depend on the standard and relevance of their ads. Some indicators are more relevant to Google in its quality and relevance evaluation than others, such as the click-through rate, which is considered a reliable indicator of the overall quality and appeal of an ad To learn more about relevance and quality score, Google's ad quality evaluation framework, and an overview of how Google AdWords works, check out our free learning tools at PPC Unive

When AdWords first launched in 2000 (with just 350 advertisers in total), the text-based advertising that Google displayed alongside its search results were, to say the least, simplistic — but they included many of the same elements that can be seen in today's advertisements.

Although PPC ads remain text-based in AdWords, marketers can use an enormous amount of features to make their advertisements more persuasive and appealing to potential customers. Ad extensions, site links, social proofing like user feedback, location targeting, shopping advertising and a variety of other features are available to marketers, offering an unprecedented level of flexibility and control for marketers. Google has also introduced ad formats tailored to the unique needs of specific business types, such as vehicle manufacturers and hotels, that go way beyond the traditional text-based ad experience and integrate rich visual elements such as high-resolution images and interactive map data.

Whatever you sell or to whom, there is a good chance that there will be an ad format or feature that will make your goods or services more attractive to your target market. Google continues to implement new ad formats and features, empowering advertisers to reach new audiences and driving new businesses.

Facebook Ads' strengths and advantages compared to Google AdWords, Facebook Ads (as we know it today) is the scrappy pioneer, but in fact, Facebook has been improving and strengthening its advertising solution for many years now. Facebook Advertising is a leader in the paying social realm today, and has become a core part of the digital marketing strategies of many companies.

Unparalleled Granularity Audience

Close to Google AdWords, Facebook boasts a genuinely large global population. With more than 1.55 monthly BILLION active users – more than one-fifth of the world's population, and that's not counting inactive or uncommonly used accounts – Facebook has no competitor when it comes to its audience's enormity. However, instead of exposing advertisers and their messaging to this vast audience, the true strength of Facebook's immense audience lies in the potential granularity with which advertisers can target users of Facebook. From meeting and marrying partners to children's birth or making new career steps, Facebook users share every day with their friends and networks the joys and achievements of life's milestones. They also look for and consume content that aligns with a vast array of personal interests , beliefs, ideologies, and values, presenting advertisers with a unique opportunity to tailor advertising messages to target audiences in ways previously deemed impossible, or even unimaginable.

One of the most important uses of this feature is the ability of marketers to build what are known as "lookalike audiences." Marketers may upload consumer information from their own databases to Facebook, and then applies filtering to match users whose information is submitted by the advertiser based on their own data and information provided by third-party data brokers. This creates the users' "lookalike" audience, allowing advertisers to effectively double the potential reach of their advertisements by targeting new customers who exhibit the same interests and consumer behavior as their existing clients.

Many socially paid newcomers make the same enquiry, such as "Does Facebook marketing function?" By now, the reply should be clear – yes it does, very good. Instead of seeing Facebook as the largest biggest billboard in the world, however, advertisers should find Facebook as a way of getting closer to their ideal clients than they ever thought possible.

Inherently Visual Network

Facebook ads are profoundly visual in comparison to their PPC equivalents, which are comparatively flat, text-based. The very best Facebook ads integrate seamlessly with the videos, photos, and other visual material in user's News Feeds, enabling advertisers not only to exploit the highly persuasive qualities of visual advertising, but to do so in a way that conveys the aspirational message that makes advertising of high quality so compelling.

Just as Google is constantly experimenting with formatting its text-based PPC advertisements, Facebook is constantly examining how it can offer a superior marketing channel for marketers and a fulfilling, enjoyable online experience for users. During the past, Facebook required that ads on its website featured text that consumed no more than 20 percent of the total advertising area, a restriction that it has since relaxed. Despite this major shift in its advertisement governance, however, Facebook remains an inherently visual medium – a significant selling point for many advertisers.

Incredible ROI Companies and advertisers experimenting with Facebook Advertising are also fascinated by the granularity of their targeting choices as well as the resources at their disposal to produce stunning, engaging advertisements. One aspect of Facebook Ads, however, that consistently catches newcomers by surprise is the potential return on investment that advertising provides on Facebook, and how far savvy advertisers can extend a small ad budget on the site.

Although a Facebook advertising campaign's budget can vary widely depending on a variety of factors, such as reach, messaging, and overall campaign goals, Facebook ads are surprisingly inexpensive, especially when considering their potential effect and the granularity with which advertisers can target their ideal audiences. This extremely competitive pricing makes Facebook Advertising a very enticing idea for resource-limited small businesses and corporations – not just large brands with massive marketing budgets. Combined with the platform's impressive potential returns, Facebook Ads is one of the best-value online advertisement solutions available today.

Google AdWords and Facebook Ads: Which To Use?

Both Google AdWords and Facebook Ads are extremely effective advertising platforms that support virtually every business category. When assessing the strengths and possible implementations of each approach, it is also apparent that the two systems should be treated in a way that is complementary rather than adversarial. Some people insist on comparing Facebook Advertising to the Google Display Network and although the two networks have certain similarities (as outlined in this extensive Facebook vs. Google Display Network infographic), the ways in which the two platforms developed independently of each other shows that AdWords and Facebook should be used in partnership, not in opposition.

A remarkably effective publicity strategy is to harness the power of both paid search and paid social. It therefore needs a dual advertising strategy that aligns with each respective platform's strengths. While marketing messaging can – and should – remain consistent across both Google AdWords and Facebook Ads, understanding how best to use each platform to maximize ROI and increase business growth is vital.

Divided into 3 distinct tracks beginner, intermediate, and advanced users, PPC U has everything you need to master paid search and socially charged, and to make it easier and smarter for only the most modest advertisement budget.

Instagram Ads And Story Ads

When Instagram revealed this March that it would introduce full-screen, vertical story ads, advertisers had reason to be excited. Story ads offered an alternative to News Feed ads — which had lost a little bit of novelty while still successful. They would also have become more competitive: the 2 million monthly active advertisers of Instagram (up from 1 million in March '17, and just 0.2 million in Feb '16) were all limited to News Feed in September of last year. Story advertisements were not only a new positioning but an attractive one. Advertisers abruptly had access to a super immersive format — when that platform is ultimately monetized, future Instagram TV advertisers can expect the same format: Fullscreen. Vertical: Vertical. Immergeant. 400 million Instagram accounts—businesses and customers alike—leverage Stories to keep their fans updated on what they are doing. Story ads provide exclusive exposure for advertisers to the pool of viewers. The results that we are going to be getting into were encouraging. They also bode well for advertising on Facebook Post, which are expected to drop shortly.

We're going to give you the full skinny — how Instagram Stories function, how they can be set up, and how they can be leveraged in combination with your current News Feed ads to maximize return on ad spending.

What are Ads on Instagram Story?

Within Instagram Posts, there are Instagram Story Ads that live above your News Feed. Naturally, Instagram stories are both full-screen and vertical — so when you watch them, the story itself is what you see on your mobile device. When one story ends — simply ending or you swipe through it manually — the next one starts. That way, once you're in the format, a continuous stream of full-screen content is super easy to navigate.

Story ads act as dividers between Articles themselves — but, like News Feed advertising, it's hard to tell them apart from the rest of the organic content in the format: they look just like organic posts apart from the "Paid" denotation and, possibly, a increase in output value. As you can also see in the above picture, Story ads give you the opportunity to connect within your post — which is a feature reserved for accounts that are either confirmed or have more than 10,000 followers in the world of organic posts.

Users simply need to swipe up on their CTA arrow to access your post connection, at which point they'll be taken to your landing page. If this is a functionality that you are interested in — if you want to send prospects to your product page, blog, or a lead form — you were once limited to the four of the six marketing goals that Story ads were available for. Instagram Story advertisements are now available for seven reasons (Brand Recognition has been added recently), and you can add CTA links to all of them: Brand Awareness: Raise visibility for your brand by finding people more likely to be interested in it.

Reach: Reveal the maximum number of people on your ad.

Video views: Allow more viewers to see the content of your video.

Conversions: Push useful behavior to your website or app.

Installs the Software: Get more people to install the device.

Lead Generation: Sales push leads such as email addresses and phone numbers.

Traffic: Send more to your account.

Instagram Story ads can be generated in Creative Center or Advertising Manager. Let's run through the ads manager development process.

How to Make an Instagram Story Ad

Pick your marketing target in a new or ongoing campaign. Name your ad collection, then optimizing your market, targeting, and budgeting – just as though you were making a Facebook ad. You'll then want to turn off Automatic Placements, press Edit Placements, and pick Instagram Stories: Note: You may run Instagram Story advertising in tandem with other placements — but you'll have to make some granular changes when you actually create your ad because of the special nature of Story ad creative. For eg, if you run a single image ad, you would need to upload different images for both Facebook News Feed and Instagram Stories. The good news: if that's the case, Facebook will tell you: That said, your target shouldn't be to find a few really similar iterations of the same ad to run on multiple placements. Given the unique potential of Story ads — a modern medium with new innovative criteria — you really should take the time to carve it into your own ad collection.

We're going to speak a little bit about the kind of imaginative that a jif in this format succeeds. For now, here are some simple sizing and spec criteria to ensure you stick to: Instagram Story Ads Sizes and Specs You have three scale formats to choose from when you create your story ad: Square (1 ratio 1), Landscape (1.91 ratio 1), and Vertical (4 ratio 5).

Recommended resolution is 1080 by 1920 pixels, but if you need to, you can go as low as 600 by 1067. Other specifications to be aware of: Image Creative File Type:.jpg or.png File size: 30 MB max Length: Images display 5 seconds by default Video Creative File Type:.mp4 or.mov File size: 4 GB max Length: up to 15 seconds Compatible codecs: H.264, VP8 Meets these basic requirements, and you have a working Story ad for yourself. Now, you may be getting a little creative.

How to Avoid Swipe- Through Advertisers New to Story Advertising will experience a common question: How can I create an ad that is not disruptive but that still prevents the proverbial thumb? There is not much difference, as described earlier, between an organic post and a paid post — if you're scrolling through stories or feeding news. In the two formats, advertisers face the challenge of standing out from the crowd by not representing a complete break from the content users go to the web to access — knowledge that often comes from friends , relatives, and products that they already know and trust.

That said, here are some suggestions that will really be watching to build a better prospect for Instagram Story ads.

Using a Custom or Lookalike Audience

The best way to stop new prospects from swipe-through for your brand? Do it not! Use Facebook Custom Audiences to identify prospects your brand is familiar with. You can target Instagram users using Custom Audiences, based on the following five segments: Customer File: email addresses, telephone numbers, or any other information that you have in the lead generation process.

Traffic on the website: people who visited your website , blog, or a similar landing page.

App Activity: People who communicate with your program.

Offline Activity: Individuals who communicate with your company, either in-store or by phone.

Engagement: People who use Facebook or Instagram to engage with your content.

An example: To produce this ad, Michael Kors used the Carousel ad style (more about these in a second).

You can see the innovative visually elegant but the targeting is what's important here. Michael Kors sold his new Carousel to a lookalike audience focused on the features of his current customers in a campaign that generated 20 per cent higher return on ad spending. The campaign also yielded a click-through rate of 3 per cent. By putting your Story ads in front of more skilled eyes you will produce similar outcomes by targeting custom and lookalike viewers.

Try a Carousel

Carousel ads are perfect for Facebook, and they are equally well suited for ad campaigns on Instagram Story. One thing to bear in mind — Instagram Stories carousel ads can not run with any other placement, so they need to be rolled out in their own campaigns. Not that would stop you; Carousels provide a distinct competitive advantage in a environment in which air time is sought. There are up to three panels in each

Carousel, and each panel can contain up to 15 seconds of video.

Instagram stories are quick-hitters, obviously. Carousels will give you the ability to give your brand a deeper and more convincing view of prospects — or to deliver 3 special, insightful insights. That is precious air time.

Like Facebook Carousels, Instagram Story Carousels offers you a chance to connect from each card to another landing page. They also endorse by-card metric reporting — so if you're curious about which cards your prospects are viewing for, how long they're viewing them for, and where they're sliding up, that information can be easily obtained inside the Advertising Manager.

Own the First Few Seconds

Given the predilection of users for quick-fire swiping (thanks, Tinder), it 's important to own your video for the first few seconds. That means hitting a few checkmarks: build with volume something. With the sound on, 60 percent of stories are presented. Hit your prospects with an early hook reflecting a welcome step away from soundless boomerangs and brunch pics.

Put it on your stamp. Your logo appears at the top left of the ad in the form of your account name / icon; but if the consumer swipes through immediately, they will not be bothered to look. Within the first few seconds of your Story, display your brand name / logo prominently in your creative.

Tell prospects what your sales are like. Even if it takes 45 seconds of a Carousel ad to say your brand story — do not bother saving your company until the very end. Beats By Dre found that their product-centered story advertising, which expressed stronger call-to-action and more imaginative product, performed better than their lifestyle-centered stories.

The Future of Brand Storytelling

A fascinating, ahem ... story tells the start of Instagram TV, the imminent decline in Facebook Story ads, and the rise of Instagram Story Ads. People are engaging with brands on their mobile devices more and more meaningfully — and they increasingly want to do so in a format that's simple, comfortable, meaningless, and captivating. Vertical, full-screen video is ideal for content consumption of that kind. We are already seeing that the change from News Feed advertising to Story advertising is going to be more drastic than the move from web to mobile.

Long story short: get into the movement's vanguard, otherwise advertising will soon saturate News.

Youtube Marketing

If I had you compiled a list of the most important to least important social media channels right now, which would rank at the top? The answer would be Facebook, for almost everyone.

Now another question — which at the bottom of it will be? This will actually be YouTube for a significant number of companies (and I mean a lot of them).

Incorrect. Since YouTube can do a lot for the companies that make successful and regular use of it.

To do this, you have to understand how YouTube marketing is different from other social channels, and how you can use it to your benefit.

This guide is friendly to beginners -because it can help you build your YouTube channel from the ground up, but it also provides an advanced marketing strategy that can benefit everyone.

We're going to go over setting up your site, optimizing and editing your content, thinking outside the box with new approaches, monetizing, and ads on YouTube, all with lots of great examples and screenshot tutorials.

If you want to learn how to promote your company using YouTube, then this guide is for you!

Set for dive in?

Let's kick-off.

YouTube Marketing: The Fundamentals

Prior get to the how-to, let's cover the basics that everyone will learn before the actual platform begins. Trust me, even if you already have a channel up and running, you do not want to miss this segment.

Why You Should Be Marketing On YouTube

It only makes sense to cover why you would like to do so before we delve into how you can expand your channel. There are plenty of great advantages to YouTube marketing that many companies don't fully consider.

The former is almost self-explanatory. Currently video is huge. It dominates the marketing landscape, and if you don't use video, you'll almost certainly lose out on your rivals. That's not a hyperbole; consumers are more likely to identify and respond to businesses using video with higher video ranking on all social media and performing well in advertising.

You will have a whole list of videos while you are using YouTube. The video files can then be uploaded native to each website. With only a few taps, you can even embed the YouTube videos into your blog posts, making your blog posts more social and engaging.

YouTube also has an huge and very diverse audience, which happily uses both YouTube's and Google's own search engine to find content they're searching for. If you're able to search for the right keywords (and I'll show you how to do it later in this guide!), you'll be able to communicate with the audience immediately, instead of hoping a Facebook Ad shows up in their stream. This helps them to discover and has an huge and very diverse audience, who happily uses both YouTube's and Google's own search engines to find content they're searching for. If you're able to search for the right keywords (and I'll show you how to do it later in this guide!), you'll be able to communicate with the audience immediately, instead of hoping a Facebook Ad shows up in their stream. It helps them to find you, not the other way around.

Because YouTube videos will show up early on in Google's search results and YouTube is the second most commonly-used search engine after Google, you want to have this huge advantage on your side.

One last benefit?

YouTube is used by only 9 per cent of small businesses. Here, you will have less competition from industry than any other platform, giving you an edge.

YouTube Demographics I mean it when I say that YouTube has a wide, diverse audience. They've 1,300,000 active users, and every single day, the site receives over 30 million visitors. We know YouTube's audience watches more than 3.25 billion hours of content per month, and more than 1 billion video views every day. That is a lot of photographs.

Still, what about the audience itself? Here's what we know, thanks to the amazing statistics of

FortuneLord: 11 percent of YouTube's audience is 18-24 23 percent is 25-34 26 percent is 35-44 16 percent is 45-54 8 percent is 65-64 3 percent is 65 + 14 percent is undetermined, because we know that eight out of ten people between the ages of 18-49 are watching YouTube at least once a month, that gives you a huge audience waiting for you.

We are also aware that mobile video views are increasing across all platforms, but that this is particularly true for YouTube — and that users here are willing to stick around for a little longer; on YouTube, the average mobile viewing session lasts about 40 minutes, which is considerable. So, keep the mobile viewers in mind when creating your content.

YouTube: Unlike all other social media

You need to do it differently than other social networks in order to truly thrive on YouTube. Facebook, Instagram and Twitter all create and share great content with the goal of creating awareness, engagement and conversation. (That's a simple definition but it's going to work for now for this argument). It's about socializing in reality.

I don't think most people use YouTube this way. YouTube videos are more like blog posts, which fit well into the content marketing niche. Sure, people will comment — but they do so in a manner similar to how blog posts are commented upon. They come to watch and absorb videos, and don't actually express their day thought. Because of that, instead of social media marketing, you should approach YouTube as content marketing.

To highlight this, some main differences: people are more likely to find your videos on YouTube by searching for them or watching other similar content. In most social media platforms (the exception is Pinterest) they will see you from ads if they follow you, or from a friend's interaction on your content.

YouTube's focus is on watching videos, and not thinking about them. You don't even see people in the comments tagging each other as you do on other pages. It is about the experience of the audience and not a social one. If people want to do this, many people come to YouTube with the intention of sitting down and watching some serious video on their own social media. They don't automatically go idly on and swipe through a feed the same way on Facebook they do.

Through treating YouTube as a content site rather than a social one, you would be able to produce better videos that perform well.

YouTube Updates

That's the last thing we need to cover before jumping into the how-to, but it's an important part. YouTube has made some improvements on the web recently and it's necessary to fix them so that we're all on the same page.

Within this book, we'll cover many of these updates, but here are some of the most relevant ones to note: As of May this year, you can no longer make annotations. Instead, a new feature named "End Screens" will replace them. They are still available if you have annotations on your videos that you created before May.

Mobile users could speed up or slow down videos

YouTube is presently working on a way to adapt videos easily to any device , making the site more mobile-friendly There has been a recent redesign of ad content due to controversies when advertisements were shown on videos that included violence, hate speech, and other material companies did not want to be associated with it. Today, gun sellers, political analysts, and even video games networks have seen less advertisements for their content. It just really affects those who seek to monetize their YouTube by putting advertising on their channel, not so much for those who run the ads.

You need 10,000 views on your channel now, before applying for monetization. This will present a challenge for small businesses seeking to use YouTube as "passive income." However, most businesses benefit most from using YouTube for content marketing purposes, so this isn't going to affect many people reading this post.

Last year, youTube enhanced their comment filtering software in the event you skipped it, making it easier for channels to filter out or discourage comments that include those phrases or words from appearing on their posts. You can read more on moderation of the comments here.

And now, we 're done with the basics. Let's get right into marketing at YouTube, starting with how to optimize your channel.

How to Optimize Your YouTube Channel

The early obsession with search dates back to the earliest days of the Internet, when algorithms did not reign supreme. It was much easier to find oneself on the network back then. To be discovered relevantly in an online search, it did not require all the technological know-how, depth and knowledge of hundreds of ranking factors.

No, it was much easier back then.

Today, however, with the development of Google's core search algorithms, and in the midst of significant changes that have gone by names like Panda, Penguin, and Hummingbird, discovering themselves on the web has become comparable to gaining a Ph.D. in physics or mathematics.

As marketers, we all know that the easiest way to market any company online is to find it organically through a search at the top of the results pages of Google's search engine (SERPs). It's free and provides almost boundless traffic to anyone who can master this highly engaged area of online searching. But this too has been a monumental undertaking.

A lot of us are online-searching sleuths on the other end of the spectrum. We are experts, able to navigate the world's knowledge annals with ease and effortlessness. At a moment's notice, we can draw on the vast information available from strong, blazing-fast pocket computers, on cue and at any time. Yeah, we sure know how to conduct a quest.

Whether a company owner or specialist, however, you know full well that this is not the case to be found. Appearing relevantly for keywords that are highly competitive has become an increasingly difficult task. But how else can we market our companies online if we can not rely on Google's SERPs? So how do some people appear to control searches on Google while others tend to falter so fail?

It's clearly not easy. This may also be why the world's leading SEO specialists can order thousands of dollars an hour to study, modify and customize pages for unique keywords. This is definitely no small feat. What people don't know is that there are basic building blocks in place which make it difficult to tract considerably over a period of weeks or even months.

Übersetzung? Anyone who is interested in winning search needs to know that it takes years and years to build up the form of link profile, authority, and content to rank for specific keywords almost without effort. The veracity of the matter? If you are serious about gaining some traction with organic marketing online, you need to do the most research for the least initial return.

The Issue?

We're the result of a world of instant gratification. We want things and now we want them. This is partly born from our genetic makeup but further fostered by media and social standards that emphasize the hedonistic pleasures associated with fulfilling the most primitive desires of life to feed, gain and procreate.

And, to be good in business or life, you need to do the most work for the least initial return, not the other way around. If you want to feel the joy you must bear the pain. And when it comes to marketing your company, you'll most likely experience massive amounts of pain if you don't know what you're doing.

How do you market your business online?

What does your company need to be advertised online? How will an entrepreneur get the proverbial word out without waiting years and years to step up the ranks on Google's SERPs? There are certainly some ways to market your company, which will offer a better return on your time investment than others. Some take weeks to pan out, while others take months and years to pan out.

Whatever strategy you use to market your company on the web, as long as you make sure that you add value along the way, and adopt the right collection of marketing habits, you can ultimately reap the benefits of your work overtime. This is not going to happen overnight. But then again, never does anything worthwhile. Here are some of the best strategies for driving this all-important traffic to your web and online pages — in both the short and long term.

1. Creating a blog and regularly posting high quality content.

Clearly, the most important way you can promote your company online is by creating a blog where you can regularly post and share high-quality content that adds an incredibly high value. This is certainly a very long-term strategy, and will not pay off immediately, but every entrepreneur needs to realize the value of adopting this form of online marketing.

Creating a noteworthy blog in any industry or niche not only helps drive traffic by peaking Google's attention but also builds authority. When you can become an expert in your field, the attention of customers, media owners and business owners alike will be drawn. That, in effect, will snowball, create more authority, and ultimately, gigantic exposure and sales volumes.

2. Market your web- and quora material.

If you are looking for some early traffic, and you have a fairly young domain — less than 2 years old with little authority built up — you should be focusing on promoting your content on sites such as Medium and Quora. How's that working out? Write one piece of high quality material on your website. Make sure it's keyword-centered, concise, unique, and adds considerable value. Make sure that whatever you're thinking about in some way, shape or form helps people.

Write another article on a platform like Medium or Quora once you've done that, and always make sure it's keyword-centric, informative, creative and adds a lot of value. Using a primary or related keyword to build one link from that article back to the main article on your web or blog. That's called content marketing, and it's the most effective way to get traction on Google's SERPs, while still targeting large established audiences through these authority pages.

3. Connect on LinkedIn Groups with others.

LinkedIn groups are a great way to communicate easily with other people in your industry or niche to help spread your word. You can use LinkedIn groups to promote your content as long as you don't come across as spam. It is best to add value to a chat or conversation before attempting to drop your ties.

LinkedIn groups are also a perfect way to reach out to people with whom you do not have shared connections. Without being linked, you can message every other participant of the community which can become a huge advantage depending on the specific circumstances. Share updates in the community, sometimes, and be sure to stay in the spotlight without oversharing.

4. Using Facebook advertising and landing pages which are strategically focused.

Although not free, Facebook ads provide a great opportunity for your company to target the right audiences. As long as you are well acquainted with your customer, you can use metrics such as interests, geographic location, marital status, age and many others to locate potential consumers to send to strategically targeted landing pages, also known as squeeze.

Micro-spend experiment to see which ad copy and squeeze page gets the best answers to drop consumers into your sales funnel. When it comes to ads on a site like Facebook, it may take a significant amount of time to find the right combination or formula, but once your campaign is successful, all you need to do is keep on scale.

5. Leverage the impact of influencers on Instagram.

Today, with the ever-penetrating power of social media, at a moment's notice, you can instantly meet droves of people from around the world. But we also know that algorithms and popularity work against us, especially when we don't have the reach of hundreds of thousands of followers or millions.

We need amplifiers, power users and influencers to help spread our messages, to meet certain people. Although this won't be free, so long as you pick the right Instagram influencer to help spread your post, it will give you direct exposure to a large audience in your particular niche.

YouTube offers a great resource to market your company on the web. While at the beginning you might find some friction for building your audience, if you focus on creating useful video tutorials, you will eventually reach a vast number of people. Finally, you need to concentrate on adding value without much consideration for income generation.

YouTube is a fantastic tool for videos, and in an easy-to-understand format you can show people just about everything. If you're sharing a screen to teach a digital ability, or capturing something in the real world, just make sure the recording quality and the overall content is good. Also, be sure to drop a link back to related content on your site within the definition.

6. Using email marketing to build a partnership with your customers.

Email marketing is something that should involve any business owner, but it's not an easy feat. To be effective with email marketing, you must give away something for free in return for the email address of the user. It has got to be something worth it. If you're serious about gathering emails, take the time to create a free report or ebook to support people in your niche or industry. Instead, through drip-fed promotions, build a partnership with that user using a program such as Aweber, Get Answer, Constant Contact or Mailchimp. Try not to sell at every turn and corner though. First bind, then concentrate on sale.

Creation of videos that offer your product as a solution to the problem of a customer

There is plenty of room to be creative with strategies here. Nevertheless, the key is to focus on specific goals and create videos to achieve them; not the other way around. Hold in mind the digital selling funnel, just as you would on your blog, and nudge users to convert accordingly.

YouTube Monetization When a client asks me "Can I monetize my channel?," I always ask "do you mean monetize like show ads and try to get paid?" I don't suggest this course of action for most businesses. There are a few valid explanations why I have.

The first is that the lengths- and loyalty-of the viewer's attention are slut. I'm also lumping online here with my own impatience; as a customer, if I click to watch a video, an ad pops up and I see a similar video in the "You Might Also Like This" list, I'm going to give that one a shot. I don't giggle. This I did twice today. You don't want to do something that will cause viewers to lose interest in your video, or worse, then click on a video of a rival.

YouTube advertisements are in the majority of cases more valuable to the advertiser than the viewer of the videos the advertisements play on.

Plus, as a result of these monetization options, the money you'll make isn't exactly going to push you into early retirement. You could make anything like $1 for every 1,000 views, and you won't even get paid until you reach the $100 mark. That takes ages for most businesses. Many think the chance of losing viewers for pennies of future income isn't worth it.

The target for most YouTube businesses is to monetize, not actual pay-per-video view advertising, through soft-selling and lead generation. Focus on this strategy that we've discussed in other sections and you're going to make a lot more profit from YouTube than running ads on your videos.

The two exceptions here are

1) if you have built up a broad user base that you know would happily wait for your content through the ads and

2) if your company is semi-famous on YouTube. Even, wait for the latter to have at least 5-10,000 subscribers before you allow advertisements.

How to Monetize YouTube

Here's how to monetize YouTube videos if you believe that monetization is the best option for your company and/or if you vehemently disagree with me.

Go to the Studio of your Creator, and then click on the tab Channel. You will see the box for monetization, where it says "Enable." Click it.

You'll see what YouTube's requirements are. These are: You have accepted the terms of the YouTube partner You requested access to AdSense You set your preferences for monetization Your channel has 10,000 views While you need at least 10,000 views to be able to monetize the account, you can start the submission process before it. There's a good chance that you have already accepted the terms of your YouTube partner when you create your account, and that you have access to AdSense for your site (if not, you can do that here).

If you set your expectations for monetization, you'll see many choices. Select the ones you need to use and click "close." These include: show ads (only on the desktop) that you need to pick to monetize. These appear above the videos about "what you might want to do."

Overlay ads that are mobile-only, and show up in front of your videos as a tiny overlay.

Supported cards which can be viewed on all devices to users and will appear on the side of your images.

Skippable video advertisements that play before your video and will be available to desktop and smartphone users alike.

If your channel receives 10,000 views, if accepted, you'll start earning money on video views. Assure that the account is in good standing and that you follow the rules of the Trust.

How to market on YouTube

What if you'd like to be on the other side of the monetization- if you want to use advertisements to promote your business rather than taking advantage of the views of those ads? I will happily recommend this for companies. Here's how to advertise on YouTube: Click here to get started. This takes you to the ad site at YouTube. YouTube Advertisements are currently running via Google Adwords, so if you don't already, you're going to have an account made. Click "Start Now" once you do so. The YouTube / Adwords ad maker looks a little different from what ad managers look like in Facebook / Pinterest / Twitter / Quora. They view all four steps of development on one page, and you click on each to add and edit the content there. First, choose your own video.

You can search for the YouTube video title or URL which you wish to promote.

Next, add text to your ad, and select your thumbnail. Recall that this text is designed solely to act as a CTA; it need not be a video title or description.

Decide where you want users to submit their click on the ad. They can be sent to your screen, or to your blog. Sending visitors to the web site would be the most effective in most situations.

First, set your (optional) budget and CPC limit. YouTube Advertisements work like all other PPC systems on a bidding system, and you will only pay if viewers watch the commercial.

The last step here is especially important: the focused portion of designing the campaign. You may target on the basis of their venue, gender, age group, web activity and interests. Take all of these into consideration; targeted interest maybe even more relevant here than on Facebook Ads.

After you've done all of this, you'll check the ad with an entry in the billing records. Then submit!

We are all familiar with Facebook contests, Instagram contests and even Pinterest contestshttps:/blog.hootsuite.com/secrets-youtube-contest/. But what of contests on YouTube? They aren't as simple, but a great strategy. Since they aren't as popular, if you want to use them, this gives you an advantage. A YouTube contest, like all other social competitions, can do a lot to help raise viewers, participation and social shares. And, when properly executed, the content created by the generation and/or the user will lead.

Different can YouTube contest forms include: contest commenting, where viewers leave a message as their entry; this is intended to drive interaction.

Subscriber competitions where non-subscribers can join their video competitions by subscribing to your Answer page, where viewers are encouraged to make and post their own videos in answer to yours. They will be easier to find by requiring them to make "response videos" of them.

Vote contests, where users vote for their favourite alternative, here similar to the idea of Pinterest. That can take users off the website.

If you want a YouTube contest to allow lead generation, you're in luck. ShortStack recently released a new template contest software just for contests on YouTube. This prototype helps you to collect lead details just as you would on competitions using the app using Facebook or Instagram. Users can potentially receive entries by voting, or by sharing with mates. You also have the choices, including setting age limits, that comes with the rest of ShortStack apps. If you are going the route of the contest to improve your plan and dedication, I suggest that you try the ShortStack templates.

YouTube marketing is often totally ignored by most businesses, but it may be just the weapon you need to set apart from your competition.

By approaching YouTube as a further leg to your marketing plan for content, you will be able to create fantastic video content that will boost content and social media marketing.

Video is the hottest thing about marketing right now, and I don't think it's going away; accept it by signing up for your YouTube company and jumping into today.

Linkedin Marketing

Linkedin is not just for job seekers and professionals. Certainly, millions of professionals use LinkedIn to develop their networks and careers every day, but did you know you can use LinkedIn to develop your company, too? LinkedIn makes an invaluable addition to the digital marketing strategy, from making connections to generating leads, forming partnerships, and building a stronger brand image.

LinkedIn is at its heart a technical, social network. It's all about career growth, professional relations, conversations with industry, and other business-related activities. It's not like other social media marketing sites like Facebook, Twitter, or Instagram; there, companies have direct access to users who they can quickly appeal to with status updates, pictures, and other casual content.

In fact, unlike LinkedIn, brand followers on these other social networks are either expecting or at least becoming informed that companies are marketing their goods and services using the platforms. This is certainly not the case on LinkedIn, where it is highly frowned upon to openly push your company, spamming, and obvious hard selling. Since the network consists of a completely different audience, marketing with LinkedIn needs a particular form of strategy to achieve the results you want. [https:/www.businessnewsdaily.com] You can use 15 LinkedIn marketing hacks to find new customers, create new contacts, and ultimately grow your business to help you navigate LinkedIn as a marketing platform.

1. Find highly targeted customers and connections

In the realm of digital advertising, the targeting on LinkedIn is unparalleled. Small companies will purchase their product or service at zero in on the exact market, company size, and job position [of the people] they normally know should. For example, if you offer customer support software to small businesses in the U.S., you can set your promotional strategies only to display businesses [that are] under 100 employees, located in the U.S. — and within that category, only to executives in those businesses with a customer service name. — Tim Peters, Sales Manager, IntelliResponse

2. Keep on the radars of customers.

My firm is helping small businesses produce leads on LinkedIn. Clients inform us of what kind of people make customers of high quality to them. We scan for people who match their requirements on LinkedIn and then add them. (We do it, so this looks like the customer is introducing himself, but we're doing the totality of the work for them.) Then we keep in touch with the people who have expressed interest, using LinkedIn once again. We do regular status updates, and weekly blog posts from LinkedIn to keep the name of the company in front of their network. We also send monthly emails that provide information about the kinds of issues our customers should solve for their customers and provide the outcomes with other customers that they have achieved. We also make deals such as inviting people to a webinar or a white paper package. The result is an easy, inexpensive, systematic process with all the work done through LinkedIn, to do lead generation

3. Grow your email marketing list

I highly recommend that everyone write a customized letter on Linked, saying thank you for connecting to LinkedIn and inviting them to be part of your email marketing list. Excuse yourself for not being customized in the email. This way, LinkedIn lets you send messages to 50 people at a time. With this approach, I've added about 300 people to my email list. Have a direct connection for email signup through your account. It is imperative that the message includes reciprocity:

1. Tell them what they are going to get by signing up for the email list, and
2. Offer to look at theirs, which is a relatively non-committal way of acquiring goodwill.
   — The creator Bradford Hines, YumDomains.com, and HungryKids.org
3. Using Sponsored Updates

With Sponsored Updates, the companies pay to force their post on the LinkedIn feed of a person. This "pay-per-click" or "pay-per-1,000" impression feature provides similar demographics to other social networks (location, gender, and age), but one main difference is the ability to customize based on the company name, job title, work role, abilities, schools, and groups. Without competing with the noise of other irrelevant companies and messages, users can target interested industries. A funded update can be an excellent way to encourage thought-leadership material with a clear call to action that is mainly useful to the target audience. People no longer want to see pure advertising and want something useful free of charge. By promoting a company's content (white paper, guide, etc.) with a LinkedIn Supported Update, a company may target a targeted audience, increase traffic to the website and generate sales leads if the content is sufficiently convincing. — Company principal Jeremy Durant, Bop Concept

4. High-quality content publishing Good content can be strongly targeted and can accomplish two goals. Firstly, it will teach us how to properly solve a problem or how to do their work. And then, it establishes

you in that room as a leader of thinking. Naturally, everything leads to more company, if you give real value to them. It's fundamental psychology, and it has real results. — Co-founder Michael Riley, boxter

5. ... and go viral

The most effective resource available on LinkedIn today is Posting directly on LinkedIn. If a post starts to gain some momentum, LinkedIn will put a spotlight behind it in one of its categories, and tens of thousands of readers (or more) can get it. This is a good way to improve your visibility while reaching readers in a way that was not possible on your own website/blog, or even posting a link to an article on LinkedIn. — Lavie Margolin, author, "The Butterfly Effect of LinkedIn" (H. Delilah Company & Career Press, 2013)

6. Give your employees a face On LinkedIn, get as many of your employees as possible to create and complete their profiles. These should consist of appropriate photos, relevant job history, including a summary of how they are helping your company and professional contacts. My current organization is setting up a LinkedIn Day, where we will have a photographer available to take photos of the profile, and we will help workers set up their accounts. — Tam Frager, Director of Marketing and Communications, Front Range Internet, Inc.

7. Join groups — and remain involved. One tip I often share with small business owners is to enter LinkedIn groups, which are important to their demographic target. Facebook is not just a perfect way to "listen in" to what your audience is thinking too, there might be opportunities for small business owners to connect or

give advice. Most importantly, even if you are not related, you can message the leaders of groups you are in. LinkedIn InMail easily adds up, and this is a perfect way to save money while developing relationships with potential customers. — The Content Marketing Strategist Lauren Covello, Ripen eCommerce

8. ... and build your own LinkedIn party, too Here's a secret sauce to find your perfect, ready-to-buy prospects on LinkedIn right away: start with your own LinkedIn group. After you have set up your LinkedIn party, go out and join as many groups (LinkedIn allows you to be in a total of 50 groups) where your prospects hang out.

9. The next thing is to pick one of the new groups that you have joined and start working on the Members' page to find prospects. Click on Members once you are in the group and accepted as a member, then filter the members' list by looking for

certain work titles or something else to win the list to your ideal prospects and then invite them to join your group (tip: submit custom invitations). You have all your proverbial fish in one tank until these invitees join your LinkedIn party — all your best prospects in one location! This LinkedIn community can be managed so that no rivals get in, and you can share great/valuable content within the community that your prospects would love. You can also show them your value/expertise while avoiding blatant sales pitches or spam. Plus, you do have a built-in email list, the core prospects/clients focus group, and so on. This is a perfect brand-building strategy and generating leads to improving your small company. — Ali Liaquat, marketing director, IT-Serve.com

10. Make your Company page matter

It's additionally imperative to have a refreshed and predictable nearness for your image with its own Company profile page. Symbolism, hues, and pictures on this page will be perfect with the site, and some other web-based life accounts the organization has. The page should be updated frequently, so the brand is successful and appears to be a current company. We have all experienced coming by a client social media profile that's updated once a month, or worse, hasn't been updated in months. Creating a LinkedIn presence then not sustaining it would be worse than not getting one at all. — Carrie Booher, chief marketing officer, Web Optimism

11. ... and don't forget to assert your custom URL Everyone will assert their custom URL and ensure it contains their name (e.g., http:/linkedin.com/in/davideerickson). This is particularly relevant for people who have a lot of contact with potential

clients — particularly for those who [are in] professional services and the B2B field — because when meeting with someone they have not yet met, Lots of people will search Google for the name of the person they encounter to know more about. Claiming your custom URL makes your LinkedIn profile more likely to rank high in those search results. — David Erickson, web marketing vice-president, Karwoski & Courage

12. Fill in the Summary section on your own profile

The most overlooked section is the overview section. You have 2,000 characters to converse simply and persuasively with the target audience. Using full sentences, speak in the first person, and answer their pain points simply and succinctly. Many people tend to go to LinkedIn than a website. People tend to interact with the person before the product or service most of the time, and this is your chance to introduce yourself to prospective customers. Also, at the end of the summary section, include your contact information. Even if it is on your profile somewhere, make it easy for people to get to you. — Susan Tabor-Kleiman, Queen, creator, Your Expert Writer

Think of it as a game of numbers.

I've discovered that marketing LinkedIn is more science, less art. In other words, it's a game of numbers. I know I'm going to hit at least 2,000 C-Level executives every Wednesday. Such contacts will result in approximately six replies, and two of the six will become clients. Instead of attending trade shows, presenting, and speaking at the expense of about $10,000 a year, I've set up my own marketing company for less than $1,000 a year, of which $250 goes to LinkedIn for a Premium account. I can spare a few hours of my time per week more than I would like to take the $40,000-per-year pill I know most of my colleagues pay, attending an average of four conferences per year. — Greg Taylor, director, solicitor for telecoms law

13. Evite hard-selling Treat LinkedIn like every other type of marketing you do and be clued to the latest trends. People don't want to get bothered, so do your hardest on LinkedIn to be "discovered." Learn up and apply these approaches to this network on content marketing and inbound marketing. There's plenty of people on LinkedIn behaving like hard-selling 1980s sales reps, so be wise and don't become one of them. — Nikki Hammett, Director of digital marketing, Blur Party

14. Start with contacts, then create relationships. Understand that LinkedIn is a professional social network for communicating with other professionals. A business owner will and should be

communicating with clients, strategic partners, referral partners, and other business owners. And once such connections are made, the business owner will determine how different relationships can be nurtured to improve the relationship. — Charlene Burke, CEO, Search by Burke, LLC

Marketing Statistics That Give You An Insight To Each Platform's Strength

Marketers are always looking for the latest social media statistics that might help shape their existing strategies on an ever-growing platform like social media.

Within only a matter of months or years, the social world will experience dramatic shifts, which means it is important to remain constantly on top of where the customers are and how to respond to them.

For marketers looking to gain more on social in 2020, here's a compilation of 100 social media statistics that can help determine the best platform and provide better transparency in channeling capital like time, energy, and money.

Global Social Media Marketing Statistics

The social media landscape is fast-paced, and understanding what noise is and what really produces results can be hard to say. To stay aware of the continually changing media condition, here are some broad insights via web-based networking media to update you.

With greater than 3.5 billion users worldwide in 2019, social media accounts for virtually 46 percent of the world's total population. An average person has an account on more than nine different social media networks and spends an average of 2 hours and 16 minutes on social media 91 percent of social media users access social channels via mobile devices, making smartphone publication important. In only two years, Instagram stories have long dominated social media as the most popular channels, rising from 150 million to 500 million daily active viewers Facebook and Instagram. However, several other niche media networks have not only arisen over the past few years but have also quickly shot up to prominence.

TikTok is one such site that began only three years ago and has more than 500 million active monthly users Most Popular Social Networks With 2.41 billion active monthly users as of Q2 2019; Facebook is the world's largest social media network.

As indicated by the most recent insights, there is currently a sum of 17 internet based life locales with 250 million or more dynamic month to month clients (MAU): Facebook — 2.41 + billion YouTube — 2.00 billion WhatsApp — 1.60 billion Facebook Messenger — 1.30 billion WeChat (Weixin) — 1.11 billion Instagram — 1 billion QQ — 823 million QZone — 572 million TikTok (Douyin) — 500 million Sina Weibo — 465 million Reddit — 330 million.

Facebook is the third most visited site, outranked distinctly by Google and YouTube 74 percent of Facebook clients sign in day by day and spend a normal of 38 minutes per day on the stage In a month, a normal Facebook client sees ten updates, offers four remarks, and taps on eight advertisements 300 million individuals use Facebook stories day by day, which is just behind Instagram stories. Instagram posts can likewise get you more natural commitment with merry go rounds than customary posts.

Watch out for these subtleties as you set up your Instagram Marketing Plan for 2020 to guarantee you are centered around the most recent patterns.

Instagram clients will spend a normal of 28 minutes out of each day on the site in 2020 More than 200 million Instagrammers visits, in any event, one organization profile ordinary Engagement with Instagram brands is multiple times higher than Facebook, multiple times higher than Pinterest and multiple times higher than Twitter Carousels get more natural collaborations than all recordings and photographs on Instagram More than 150 million

Given its short life cycle (3.39 minutes per session) and daunting character limit, Twitter marketing statistics marketing for businesses on Twitter can be especially complicated.

Brands looking to boost their content on Twitter need to provide timely engagement and customer support to their users. Partnership with an influencer will offer tremendous benefits, too.

Bear these Twitter figures in mind when implementing a social media marketing strategy for your brand in 2020.

Since network inception in 2006, more than 1.3 billion Twitter accounts have been established. Twitter is the third most populous social media network with marketers in 2019, with 330 million people using Twitter every month sending 500 million tweets, with 59 percent of marketers actively using the Tweets platform that includes photos or videos being 394 percent more likely to be retweeted An average Twitter user follows at least five businesses. 60 percent of Twitter users expect a brand or a business to respond to their question within an hour Tweets that contain hashtags will result in as much as 1.065 percent higher interaction compared to a comparable hashtag-free tweet 40 percent of Twitter users claim to have made a purchase directly from Twitter's influencer tweet users spend 26 percent more time on advertising than others

As a marketer or company owner, creating a YouTube presence will do wonders for the brand; 80 percent of users listed a brand in a tweet 77 percent of Twitter users feel more optimistic about a brand when their tweet is replied to YouTube Marketing Statistics. Check out these new YouTube statistics to gain an advantage on the competition and set yourself up for 2020 success.

YouTube is the 2nd largest search engine in the world only behind Google 82 percent of Americans report using YouTube, making it the most popular social media site in the U.S. With 2 billion monthly active users, over 1 billion hours of YouTube videos are watched daily The average length of a first-page YouTube video is 14 minutes and 50 seconds. The platform will produce 3-fold more conversions than other social media sites already.

Learn how to maximize your marketing campaign with LinkedIn by taking a peek at these new statistics.

More than 100 million work applications are posted on LinkedIn every month Posts on LinkedIn containing photos have a 98% higher comment rate, and posts with links have a 200% higher engagement rate With 630 million professionals on LinkedIn, 90 million users are senior influencers and 63 million in decision-making roles 49% of LinkedIn users earn at least.

Marketers looking to generate more Pinterest sales may create themed content around their product or service.

According to Pinterest, the site currently has more than 300 million active monthly users Pinterest ad revenue is expected to reach $1 billion by 2020 The average time spent on Pinterest is 14.2 minutes 7 out of 10 Pinterest users are women With more than 14 million products pinned per day, more than 200 billion pins saved on Pinterest 50% of millennials using Pinterest every month. Marketers seeking to attain millennials will benefit in particular from targeted advertising.

Global advertisement spending on social media is projected to reach $98B by the end of 2019 The total percentage of marketing budgets devoted to social media ads is projected to nearly double by 2023 Different social networks are critical for small businesses, with 40% of small businesses depending on revenue-generating social media advertising 26% of those clicking on Facebook Keeping an eye on the latest data on social media about interaction trends is an excellent way for brands to reconfigure their social efforts.

Instagram beats out all other user engagement platforms Visual content is 40x more likely to be posted on sites such as Facebook, Twitter, and Instagram Post on Facebook with less than 250 characters having 60 percent more exposure Social Media Figures For Company Social media has fully changed the nature of doing company and helped people make a fortune. With more and more people turning in the buying journey to their smartphones and social media, there are many explanations why the company should be involved in social media.

Eighty-five percent of businesses use software and resources from third parties to better monitor their social media activity. Statusbrew provides a variety of social media strategies for companies to control their social media effectively 50 percent of consumers claim they follow brands on social media to learn about new goods or services 61 percent of consumers claim brands may promote shopping by creating posts that provide deals or social media trials 21 percent of consumers prefer a brand on social media rats As a brand, creating a social media strategy that stands in contrast to the latest trends is beneficial to your company.

Using those figures to make the most of your social media budget in 2020. Optimize your marketing plan and use a social media management tool such as Statusbrew to efficiently control your network.

Creating A Social Media Marketing Strategy

G etting a plan is the main ingredient in doing social media marketing well.

You may be posting on social media sites for the purpose of posting without a plan. It would be difficult to achieve success on social media without knowing what your goals are, who your target audience is, and what they want.

If you want to grow your brand through social media or level up as a social media marketer, it is essential that you develop a social media marketing strategy.

Here's one way of doing it.

How to develop a marketing plan for social media

It is important to notice that there are a number of crossovers between a social media marketing strategy and a social media marketing plan.

You can think of it this way: Where you are going is a policy. One plan is how you are going to get there.

One of the easiest ways to build your marketing strategy for social media is to ask yourself about the 5Ws:

Why do you want to be on social media?

Who are the target audience?

What do you partake of?

What do you partake of?

When do you partake?

I've created a simple social media marketing strategy template to help you build your strategy. Feel free to use, add or change it (after making a copy of it) as you see fit.

Here's another interesting thing about strategy (or strategies): You can also have a plan for each of your social media platforms, like a Facebook marketing strategy, an Instagram marketing strategy, and so on, all of which contribute to your overall social media marketing strategy.

But let's get started with the overall plan.

1. Why would your company want to be on social media?

The very first question to answer the question is Why.

This applies to your ambitions on social media. Do you want to sell your goods on social media? Moving traffic to your site? And for helping your clients?

Generally speaking, there are the nine social media goals you should have: Increase brand recognition Drive traffic to your website Generate new leads Increase revenue (by raising signups or sales) Increase brand engagement

Create a community around your company Offering social customer support Increase mentions in the press Listen to discussions about your brand.

In general, concentrating on only a couple of goals is nice when you have a team where different individuals or groups inside the team will take on different goals.

At Buffer, for example, the marketing team uses social media to increases our brand recognition and drive our web traffic while our advocacy team uses social media to provide timely customer service.

2. Who are the target audience?

When you've worked out your How, your target market is the next thing to remember.

Understanding your target audience will allow you to answer the following questions more effectively about what, where, and when you will be sharing.

For example, if a travel and lifestyle brand (like Away) knows that their target audience likes to read about new places and travel tips, they might share these content on their profiles on social media.

It's a perfect exercise to try to develop marketing people here.

There are various ways to build people's marketing. My own favorite solution is to use the 5Ws and 1H again.

Who are they, then? (E.g. work title, age, gender, salary, place, etc.) What's their value in you able to provide? (Examples include entertainment, educational content, case studies, new product details, etc.) Where do they normally hang out online? (Facebook, Instagram, etc., or niche sites, for example) When are they searching for the type of content that you can provide? (E.g.

weekends, daily commutes, etc.) Why do they eat the content? (E.g. getting better at work, becoming healthy, staying up-to-date with something, etc.) How do they consume the content? (E.g. read posts on social media, watch videos, etc.) You probably don't have to start from scratch. If you have been running your business for a while, you most likely already have a good sense of your target audience. Writing it down so you can share it with the team or using it for your future reference could be helpful.

Kevan Lee, our Marketing Director, has written a complete guide to market people to help you build your marketing persona.

3. What do you partake of?

You may be thinking about what types of content to share when you see this question. Want to share videos or photographs, for example?

But hold on for a second!

We are talking about the marketing campaign for social media here, so let's take a step back and think at a higher level. "Style" may be a better term rather than the types of material to share.

Here are a few brands and their theme(s): MeUndies, an underwear brand, shares pictures of their customers on their Instagram profile and images of their products.

Huckberry, an outdoor and adventure brand, shares its editorial content on their Facebook profile and high-quality outdoor images.

Burrow, a luxury couch company, shares mainly memes in their Instagram profile.

If you browse through the aforementioned social media pages, you may have found more than one key theme for the brands. Having a handful of themes is perfectly fine as it allows you the opportunity to share a variety of content to keep your audience interested without seemingly being distracted.

That is where it would help to have a clear understanding of the target market. Look at the marketing staff, and ask the following questions: What are their priorities and challenges?

How do you help solve those problems?

For a brand of fitness apparel and accessories (like Gymshark), its target market could be trying to keep up-to-date with the new fitness gears. In that case, on their social media pages, it can share the new items.

(Would that be too promotional? Maybe not. Piper Jaffray Investment Bank surveyed more than 8,600 American teenagers and found that 70 percent favored brands to message them about new goods via Instagram. The trick goes back to knowing the target audience.)

4. What do you partake of?

The next step is to decide where you'll post your content. In other words, what channels does your brand want to be on social media?

Note that your brand doesn't have to be on every social media network before we go any further. We've made the error before. Being on fewer channels gives you greater concentration and more time for content development.

Fast tip: That said, it'll be smart to have at least a full profile on the Big Four — Facebook, Instagram, Twitter, and LinkedIn — because they will always appear on Google's first search results page as people search for your brand.

Your knowledge of your target market will once again come in handy here. What channels are your most active target market on? Why is it that makes them use this platform? For instance, teens and young adults may like to scroll through Instagram when they are bored to see what their friends are doing, or if their favorite brands have new items.

Another thing to consider, albeit smaller, is, what is the "X factor" of your brand? Are you great at blogging, videos, or photography? Some channels lend themselves well to other types of content. Photos on Instagram, long-form videos on YouTube, articles on the Web, for example, are fantastic. But this is a minor point since social media sites are developing nowadays to offer almost any type of content.

Lastly, find even smaller, niche sites. Zwift, for example, an online cycling training software company with multi-players, has launched a club on Strava, a social network for athletes. Their club has more than 57,000 riders, and thousands of riders are participating in their Strava messages.

5. When do you partake?

The last important part of your plan is to find out when you want your content posted. You can be tempted to jump to the best time(s) to post on a study.

Split. And just breathe.

Let's take a step backward and look at this again from a higher level. Consider the habits of your target audience before determining precisely which time of the day and days of the week you plan to write.

How do they usually use social media to find the sort of content you are going to share?

Below are a few reasons to consider: Sports enthusiasts are likely to find and engage with information about the event on social media just before, during, and just after sporting events.

Athletes can be on Instagram when making their morning or evening workouts cool down.

People who love to travel can be more involved in social media during the weekends when they prepare for their next trip (or when they dream about their next trip during their work breaks).

Baby mothers might scroll through social media while they're breastfeeding in the middle of the night.

From these few examples, you could have inferred that there may not be a universal best time to post. It depends on your audience, really. So for this move, concentrate on your target audience's general behavior patterns.

When you have developed your marketing plan for social media, you can then find the best time for your brand to post by experimentation.

Finally, how is the plan going to be implemented?

And you've got it there-your marketing strategy for social media!

This is not the finish, however. As already stated, a strategy is where you're headed; a plan is how you're going to get there. You decided where to go; now you need a plan.

How are you expected to complete your social media profiles? What kind of tone and voice should be like? What type of posts would you use (i.e., picture, connection, video, etc.)?

We've got a step-by-step guide to creating a social media marketing plan to help you with the next step and your social media success. Here is a sneak peek of the infographic that you will find in the guide:

Focus on the big picture

Developing a strategy for social media marketing is probably one of the most difficult things to do because it requires you to step back and look at the big picture. You have to change your attention away from your regular activities, such as arranging and answering higher-level thought comments.

But having a social media marketing plan, so you're not just posting content just for the sake of posting content, is really satisfying and beneficial. This will help you achieve your corporate and social media targets.

How To Make Your Platform The Most Popular Platforms On Facebook, Instagram, Linkedin To Youtube

The early obsession with search dates back to the earliest days of the internet when algorithms did not reign supreme. It was much easier to find oneself on the network back then. To be found relevantly in an online search, it did not require all the technological know-how, depth, and knowledge of hundreds of ranking factors.

No, it was much easier back then.

Today, however, with the development of Google's core search algorithms, and in the midst of significant changes that have gone by names like Panda, Penguin, and Hummingbird, discovering themselves on the web has become comparable to gaining a Ph.D. in physics or mathematics.

As marketers, we all know that the easiest way to market any company online is to find it organically through a search at the top of the results pages of Google's search engine (SERPs). It's free and provides almost boundless traffic to anyone who can master this highly engaged area of online searching. But this, too, has been a monumental undertaking.

A lot of us are online-searching sleuths on the other end of the spectrum. We are experts, able to navigate the world's knowledge annals with ease and effortlessness. At a moment's notice, we can draw on the vast information available from strong, blazing-fast pocket computers, on cue, and at any time. Yeah, we sure know how to conduct a quest.

Whether a company owner or specialist, however, you know full well that this is not the case to be found. Appearing relevantly for keywords that are highly competitive has become an increasingly difficult task. But how else can we market our companies online if we can not rely on Google's SERPs? So how do some people appear to control searches on Google while others tend to falter so fail?

It's clearly not easy. This may also be why the world's leading SEO specialists can order thousands of dollars an hour to study, modify, and customize pages for unique keywords. This is definitely no small feat. What people don't is that there are basic building blocks in place, which make it difficult to tract considerably over a period of weeks or even months.

Übersetzung? Anyone who is interested in winning a search needs to know that it takes years and years to build up the form of the link profile, authority, and content to rank for specific keywords almost without effort. The veracity of the matter? If you are serious about gaining some traction with organic marketing online, you need to do the most research for the least initial return.

The Issue?

We 're the result of a world of instant gratification. We want things, and now we want them. This is partly born from our genetic makeup but further fostered by media and social standards that emphasize the hedonistic pleasures associated with fulfilling the most primitive desires of life to feed, gain, and procreate.

And, to be good in business or life, you need to do the most work for the least initial return, not the other way around. If you want to feel the joy, you must bear the pain. And when it comes to marketing your company, you'll most likely experience massive amounts of pain if you don't know what you're doing.

How do you market your business online?

What does your company need to be advertised online? How will an entrepreneur get the proverbial word out without waiting years and years to step up the ranks on Google's SERPs? There are certainly some ways to market your company, which will offer a better return on your time investment than others. Some take weeks to pan out, while others take months and years to pan out.

Whatever strategy you use to market your company on the web, as long as you make sure that you add value along the way, and adopt the right collection of marketing habits, you can ultimately reap the benefits of your work overtime. This is not going to happen overnight. But then again, never does anything worthwhile. You'll find below some of the best strategies for driving this all-important traffic to your web and online pages — in both the short and long term.

1. Creating a blog and regularly posting high-quality content.

Clearly, the most important way you can promote your company online is by creating a blog where you can regularly post and share high-quality content that adds incredibly high value. This is certainly a very long-term strategy, and will not pay off immediately, but every entrepreneur needs to realize the value of adopting this form of online marketing.

Creating a noteworthy blog in any industry or niche not only helps drive traffic by peaking Google's attention but also builds authority. When you can become an expert in your field, the attention of customers, media owners, and business owners alike will be drawn. That, in effect, will snowball, create more authority, and ultimately, gigantic exposure and sales volumes.

2. Market your web- and quora material.

If you are looking for some early traffic, and you have a fairly young domain — less than two years old with little authority built up — you should be focusing on promoting your content on sites such as Medium and Quora. How's that working out? Write one piece of high-quality material on your website. Make sure it's keyword-centered, concise, unique, and adds considerable value. Make sure that whatever you're thinking about in some way, shape or form helps people.

Write another article on a platform like Medium or Quora once you've done that, and always make sure it's keyword-centric, informative, creative, and adds a lot of value. Using a primary or related keyword to build one link from that article back to the main article on your web or blog. That's called content marketing, and it's the most effective way to get traction on Google's SERPs, while still targeting large established audiences through these authority pages.

3. Connect on LinkedIn Groups with others.

LinkedIn groups are a great way to communicate easily with other people in your industry or niche to help spread your word. You can use LinkedIn groups to promote your content as long as you don't come across as spam. It is best to add value to a chat or conversation before attempting to drop your ties.

LinkedIn groups are also a perfect way to reach out to people with whom you do not have shared connections. Without being linked, you can message every other participant of the community, which can become a huge advantage depending on the specific circumstances. Share updates in the community, sometimes, and be sure to stay in the spotlight without oversharing.

4. Using Facebook advertising and landing pages, which are strategically focused.

Although not free, Facebook ads provide a great opportunity for your company to target the right audiences. As long as you are well acquainted with your customer, you can use metrics such as interests, geographic location, marital status, age, and many others to locate potential consumers to send to strategically targeted landing pages, also known as squeeze.

Micro-spend experiment to see which ad copy and squeeze page gets the best answers to drop consumers into your sales funnel. When it comes to ads on a site like Facebook, it may take a significant amount of time to find the right combination or formula, but once your campaign is successful, all you need to do is keep on the scale.

5. Leverage the impact of influencers on Instagram.

Today, with the ever-penetrating power of social media, at a moment's notice, you can instantly meet droves of people from around the world. But we also know that algorithms and popularity work against us, especially when we don't have the reach of hundreds of thousands of followers or millions.

We need amplifiers, users of power, and influencers to help spread our messages and get to know some people. Although this won't be free, so long as you pick the right Instagram influencer to help spread your post, it will give you direct exposure to a large audience in your particular niche.

6. Build valuable youTube video tutorials.

YouTube offers a great resource to market your company on the web. While in the beginning, you might find some friction for building your audience, if you focus on creating useful video tutorials, you will eventually reach a vast number of people. Finally, you need to concentrate on adding value without much consideration for income generation.

YouTube is a fantastic tool for videos, and in an easy-to-understand format, you can show people just about everything. If you're sharing a screen to teach a digital ability or capturing something in the real world, just make sure the recording quality and the overall content is good. Also, be sure to drop a link back to related content on your site within the definition.

7. Using email marketing to build a partnership with your customers.

Email marketing is something that should involve any business owner, but it's not an easy feat. To be effective with email marketing, you must give away something for free in return for the email address of the user. It has got to be something worth it. If you're serious about gathering emails, take the time to create a free report or ebook to support people in your niche or industry. Instead, through drip-fed promotions, build a partnership with that user using a program such as Aweber, Get Answer, Constant Contact or Mailchimp. Try not to sell at every turn and corner, though. The first bind, then concentrate on sale.

8. Using the TripAdvisor or Angie's List.

Sites like Angie 's List and TripAdvisor are providing an avenue to reach a vast audience of potential customers for just about every company. Such platforms are a great way to find your local company, enabling you to have customers leave feedback based on their interactions with your company.

Use Angie 's List if you sell the facilities. If you are in a sector relating to travel, why not list on TripAdvisor? Not only are these ties perfect for

SEO, but you'll also gain access to a wide range of customers in your industry or niche looking for goods or services. Take the time to build a good list and invite customers to post honest feedback based on their interactions with you.

9. Build consumer confidence on platforms such as Yelp, and Trust Pilot.

One of the barriers which hold back business owners and professionals alike is that of confidence. Consumers are hesitant to trust organizations. They have no prior knowledge of or know someone who has worked with them. Sites like Yelp will obviously help with this, but so can a platform like Trust Pilot.

Trust Pilot and Yelp are primarily committed to helping customers choose the best business to partner with, and by having previous customer feedback with the business, it improves accountability. Such sites are the largest online review sites in the world and can be leveraged to help create trust with potential customers.

10. Using rich snippets like AMP and FBIA.

You can use rich samples, Accelerated Web Pages (AMP), or Facebook Instant Posts (FBIA) to help with some early exposure if you're trying to gain some traction with your material. Rich snippets apply to a no. of content forms, including AMP specification articles, local businesses, music, recipes, reviews, television, movies, and videos.

In addition to plugins for both AMP and FBIA, there are Wordpress plugins that you can use for rich snippets from Schema.org specifications. With, for example, Google and Facebook's recent emphasis on phones, getting AMP and FBIA posts will give you a small advantage over those who don't, increasing your exposure on SERPs and news feeds.

11. Collaborate with the famous niche bloggers.

To reach out to popular bloggers in your niche could be an effective way to market your business online, especially if you have something worth adding to one of their posts. If you discover a popular blogger who often writes about a specific topic that is directly correlated with your line of work, why not reach out and look for ways to work together?

Offering your services as a guest blogger is one great way to make this happen. Clearly, you'll have to have a decent background in writing yourself, so it might be hard to find a common blog willing to let you do that, but if you finally secure a guest post, it will be worth a shot.

12. Contribute periodically to sector-specific fora.

Many people have everything wrong, posting the whole forum-strategy for SEO. We are going out there and dropping spammy links and asking why they're kicked off the forums. You couldn't do it. If you're serious about selling your company online, join the discussions, and add value while you're seeking an industry-specific platform before attempting to link-drop.

Nobody likes someone who comes into a forum as a new guest and starts spamming links. Again, for the minimum initial return, you have to think about doing the most research. Price Added. Chat and speak with others. Provide ideas. Reply to questions. I don't associate with spam. Add your connection to your signature after a few posts, or the forum rules require you to do so but do not attempt to guide people to your site at every turn and bend. If you do that, it won't fit well for you.

13. Offer the customers a free product or service.

Studies also have shown that people are more likely to accept something free of charge than charging a nominal price for it. So, why not give your customers a free service or product? You could be giving a free 15-minute consultation or an entry-level product you wish to give away.

Whatever you do, make sure that the contact details of the customer are saved so that you can contact them later. When you give away a service for free, you have a chance to upsell those customers to your paying services right then. People are more likely to feel as if they owe you when they also take anything for free.

14. Use sites like Yahoo Local and Google Local for business listings.

You can list your company on local business listing sites such as Yahoo Local and Google Local if you are running a small business and are trying to draw nearby clients to a brick-and-mortar location or provide a geographically relevant professional service.

Google Local is a particularly powerful way to list and check your business information, including public details such as the address of your company for appearances on Google Maps, storing times, and other business-related information. Make sure you keep the information correct and up to date.

15. Optimize your SEO Website.

Clearly, an important part of promoting your company online is optimizing your site for specific keywords. The one thing to keep in mind, though, is that if your company is young — less than two years old — and you've developed very little authority or content, you're going to have a hard time ranking for any keyword that's mildly competitive at the top of Google's SERPs!

The aim is to create excellent content, but also to optimize the On-Page and Off-Page SEO of your site. As this can become a very lengthy topic, pay attention to issues like the speed of your site, mobile accessibility, meta descriptions, the profile of links, level of reading, quotation of sources, quality of content, perspective, and so on. This is more like a marathon than a sprint, so don't be disheartened in the short term if you don't see huge results.

16. Co-sponsor a contest award or giveaway.

Find something you can give away and co-sponsor an award or contest in your field with another client, community, or professional. Use tools such as LinkedIn and Facebook to network with others, and locate with you another like-minded company or professional willingness to hold an award or giveaway. The whole point here is to add value to the public eye once more.

17. Give a talk at a conference or on a webinar.

Why not offer a talk at a professional conference or webinar, if you're an authority in your area? Of course, the first recommendation for professional conferences would be TED Talks, but you might speak at a variety of other forms of conferences or even webinars held online.

As far as online marketing is concerned, webinars are one of the most effective resources for selling almost everything to a highly engaged audience. And the greater the market, the more likely you will offer your goods or services. Long-term, this will definitely give you exposure and allow you to develop more authority over time, and it is an excellent piece of portfolio or resume item that can also be used, particularly in the case of professional speaking commitments.

18. Use press releases to communicate important news or events inside the organization.

Press releases won't get you media coverage straight away. While some media professionals are going to use resources to Help a Reporter, or even scour press release pages to PR Web, you probably won't get some sort of instant news attention by sending out a press release.

Nonetheless, a well-written press release with a healthy connection profile can help you moderately with SEO, but it can also allow you to communicate important company news or events that you can then use to aggressively target media outlets through the correct PR channels.

19. Create an email signature with a brand name.

One of the greatest ways you can advertise your company online is via a branded signature email. Place your ties and any potential accolades that your organization may have received directly into your signature account. This helps the people you are in daily contact with to passively promote your business.

In your electronic mail signature, you can also include social media links, along with any related links to important pieces of company marketing

— digital brochures or news articles about your product. Often drop a brief catchphrase or one-sentence tagline about your company and its purpose.

20. Implement the 80-20 rule to recognize high-value clients and market them to them.

The 80/20 rule, or the Pareto Principle, states that 80% of outcomes come from 20% of the effort. Basically, it's only a tiny portion of what we're doing that really produces results. That also refers, however, to sales, which states that 80% of your revenue comes from 20% of your customers.

By giving them additional deals and discounts for other services and goods, if you can identify which customers produce the most profits for your company, you can increase your sales. You can also directly link your online marketing to these customers if they are logging in using a login system or if they are monitored by cookies.

21. Post photos and videos on Pinterest, Flickr, Tumblr, and Instagram, with relevant hashtags.

There is a range of high-domain authority sites on which you can post pictures and videos to create a following. First, remember Pinterest, Flickr, Tumblr, and Instagram. Use specific hashtags and explanations to better categorize what you are posting about, and follow with those hashtags other people in your industry or niche blogging.

This is not a strategy in online marketing that will offer you instant sales or even instant traffic. It'll take quite some time. But as long as you add value and are enthusiastic about what you're doing, you're going to build up the follow-up in the months and years to come. Be sure to comment, like, and connect as much as possible with posts from other people to get yourself out there at the outset.

Ways To Grow Your Company On Instagram, Youtube, Twitter, And Facebook

As someone who's grown up with social media for virtually all of my life, I've found myself taking it for granted time and time again.

I think back to having my Facebook page, and how happy I was about my real-life friends being digital friends.

It now looks ridiculous, but it felt like a major moment.

Over time, among other items, I went over to Twitter, Instagram, and LinkedIn because I wanted to have an account on all these platforms.

As I grew older and started my digital marketing career, I now realize how impactful social media has become a culture in everything we do, and how different life is because of it.

Never before has a person been able to remain in real-time linked with hundreds of thousands of millions of people all over the world.

For me, I can imagine going back to a time when I was maybe 13 or 14. I had a group of friends that I met on a Gaming Facebook page. When I lived in Connecticut, one lived in California, two lived in Ohio, and two were in Poland.

It can be hard to understand that social media has brought us all together and helped us to become long-term friends who have been linked for over eight years.

But those kinds of interactions don't just end with individuals. Via social media, brands create the same personal relationships with their customers.

As a brand, you have incredible opportunities to share exciting news and perspectives about your company, build an online community of people who are passionate about your brand, and connect with customers on a more personal and human level than ever.

If you don't know how to start, building the follow-up and interaction with your audience can be difficult for brands, though.

This book will educate you on the fundamentals of building a following social media and will provide you with the tools and tactics that brands use today to win on social media.

First things first, realize that just because there's a social network, it doesn't mean you need to be on it.

You need to understand what the platform actually does, who uses it, how it is used by people, and whether it makes sense to have a presence for your company.

Can you say with certainty that your target customer uses any available social media platform? The response is possibly no. Having said that, your brand will be on the platform(s) on which your customers are. Getting fantastic Facebook material and a highly active profile doesn't mean anything if the buyer persona isn't there too.

Let's take a closer look at five of the biggest social networks as of September 2019 to help you decide.

Facebook The fact that Facebook remains the pioneer in social media space can not be overlooked. With the 2.5 trillion active users mark fast approaching, it should be no surprise that keeping users on the site longer is the highest priority.

Over the past years, Facebook has launched a range of new features that allow users to do more without leaving for another site, including reinvigorating Facebook Groups, live video streaming features, creating a comprehensive ad network (more on that later), and adding news publishers.

I know what you're thinking. "But my company's different and these latest apps don't support me. We would not be able to use Facebook to advertise ourselves because our customers won't find our content online." Even though your customer might not be able to use Facebook in the workplace, they will still use the site personally — maybe as a mental break throughout their working day.

Through that way, you can always be identified and make an impact.

SurveyMonkey, for example, created a brilliant Facebook post about using surveys to create winning advertisements, logos, and packaging using puppets (still a win in my eyes). It is up-to-the-point, eye-catching, and provides an enticing brand for customers.

YouTube Some may hesitate to think youTube is considered a forum for social media. And I'd say on the surface there's truth to that.

Consider the fact: YouTube is Google's second-largest search engine. With video proceeding to surge as a preferred medium of content, it's no wonder that YouTube is now the second most visited website on the internet, again, only behind Google itself.

However, if you dig deeper into the platform's heart, YouTube has hundreds of millions of personalities putting content out every single day for their viewers' enjoyment and interest. As with every other social network, this is.

YouTube content creators publish 400 hrs of video per minute, and everyday users view more than 1 billion hours of YouTube videos.

Personally, I know that YouTube is a good place to come back to, and there are a variety of content creators that I watch on a weekly basis, sometimes even hourly.

Now, as a company, I'm sure you think it's hard to justify using YouTube because you may be in an industry, or offer a niche or less flashy product or service than others.

I'm going to play Devil's advocate and say the four most popular content categories on YouTube are entertainment, music, pop culture, and "how-to" videos.

Reflect on your brand and ask yourself, "Have I got" how-to "knowledge or tutorials my clients might consider valuable?" If so, make a video and post it on YouTube!

It will only benefit your brand and give you a greater chance that customers will find it.

YouTube videos also have a good chance to appear as the top search result in Google when a user searches for a query like "How to ..." I searched "How to use HubSpot 2019" in the example below, and the first results were all YouTube videos displayed above the first text-based search result, which was from HubSpot itself!

Instagram

What used to be a casual social media site to share filtered images has skyrocketed into the world's third-most trafficked website.

After its acquisition by Facebook in 2012, Instagram has now achieved more than 1 trillion active monthly users. More interestingly, when compared to Facebook, Instagram posts have seen results as high as 10x engagement.

Instagram had launched Instagram Stories in August 2016. More than 500 million Instagram users use Stories every day in 2019, equaling more than half of the total users of Instagram. And, more than 1/3 of Instagram's most-viewed stories actually come from businesses!

Instagram also launched shoppable tags in Stories as well as daily posts. Brands can now add their goods with links to their e-commerce sites through an Instagram business account, which enables users to make transactions directly on the site. This is a powerful feature for e-commerce businesses.

Twitter

It gained enormous popularity when Twitter launched in 2006 by adding a 140 character cap to tweets (now revised to 280 characters). It revolutionized how social media was invented by becoming the first medium to fully accept being in real-time.

When Twitter has expanded to 330 million active monthly users, having the most up-to-date news and updates in real-time has become increasingly popular. In reality, twelve percent of Americans are using Twitter as their primary source for news.

However, when it comes to its international scope, where Twitter really takes flight (get it, because birds fly) is. Eighty percent of Twitter users are outside the U.S., and Twitter supports 34 different languages.

Global brands should take advantage of the international scope of Twitter, in particular, when it comes to major announcements or product releases.

LEGO took advantage of the international scope when announcing their latest game LEGO Star Wars: The Skywalker Saga, having over 500 retweets and more than 2,300 comments.

Advertising and the capability to upload videos and live streaming were also added to the website.

LinkedIn

"The Technical Social Network." That is how many people describe LinkedIn, and it makes sense to see that 80 percent of advertisers use LinkedIn for professional purposes.

Think about the vision of a B2B Marketer.

You can link and sell directly to people in your target industries (even as broad as the target companies that you want to work with). Or, if you're looking to develop your business, you can use LinkedIn to hire your company's quality talent.

Not only that, but LinkedIn has now become more and more focused on content.

LinkedIn opened the platform to native video, enabling users to either record live video or upload a video and post it on their newsfeed. You can simply click on the video icon at the top of the page and directly add a video to your message.

LinkedIn makes it easy for all my fellow bloggers to post their long-form content on your profile. Instead of copying and pasting a long article into the regular "Begin a post" section, click on "Write an article on LinkedIn" instead, where the site has built-in blog publishing features.

LinkedIn updated LinkedIn Groups as well.

LinkedIn Groups are close to Facebook Groups, where like-minded professionals meet. This could be a great way to find and interact with people working in the same business, sector, or having the same interests as you.

Although these are the five most prominent social media sites, you can also consider for marketing your company, including Pinterest, Snapchat, TikTok, and more.

Be sure that you do your homework and have a good understanding that the site you select is a frequenting location of your ideal prospects. The selection of the right social media represents the first step towards creating a strong profile and following.

Analyze your competitors

There's something you should be doing regularly in marketing that analyzes your competitors — and that's relevant for social media too.

What platforms do they work on? What kind of content do they share? How much do they partake?

Understanding the social media tactics and involvement of your rival will help you draw up a roadmap on what you can also do.

Most importantly, you will find opportunities by studying your rivals to distinguish yourself as a brand in the eyes of the target customers you compete for.

Finish up your profiles (yes, your personal ones too)

Now that you've found out where to create your profiles, it's time for the dirty work.

Be accurate and up-to-date Nearly every social media site has a summary region, profile image, and cover photo where you can enter and view information about your company — make sure this is accurate and up-to-date across all platforms.

Nothing is as frustrating as seeing your website with one address and your Facebook profile with another.

Establishing this general knowledge helps add transparency and allows people to take decisive action if they so wish.

Creating profiles should not only be siloed on company pages. Depending on the site, each of the employees should have completed profiles so that they can exchange business news, industry perspectives, etc. Think of how much more impact you would have by setting up a job advocacy program!

When every employee becomes the company's brand advocate — sharing content through their personal platforms — you have the ability to reach out to all of their fans and connections.

It's important to note when you create these profiles, that your company and personal profiles are never really complete.

Tweaks and changes should always be made that will enhance the customer experience and show the business in a positive light.

Be consistent with your brand.

I mean, the overall tone your social media presence needs to suit your defined personality, values, and voice when I say consistent.

Your written bio should match the picture of your profile, which should match the photo of your cover, which should match your content.

Therefore, if you are using several social media sites, make sure that each account tells the same story about your organization and projects the same sound.

Consumers want to communicate with your brand in a meaningful way, and posting mixed and conflicting messages would just confuse your followers and potentially discourage them from sticking around.

If you're a law firm, for example, don't act fun and exciting in your bio if the content of your posting doesn't represent a similar attitude or personality.

To summarize their brand, they need each work applicant to have "a picture of an octopus battling a pirate (not joking)." Yes, it's a really specific brand, and yes, this example probably isn't directly applicable to other companies.

You could learn a lot from them, though. Goodr is doing a great job of being consistent across their profiles and the content they share with their fun, colorful brand through their social media pages.

For example, Goodr's Twitter profile uses a cover image featuring their famous flamingo, Carl, wearing his favorite pair of Goodr sunglasses, and chilling alongside a pineapple.

"We are recklessly committed to fun ... blah, blah, blah, sunglasses. Route. Street. Drink. Mile." Whatever the tone of the business is, be consistent.

Creating a social network afterward relies heavily on transparency and trust, and that comes with both your profile and the content being shared.

5. Share awesome content. Can I get a "hey, duh?" While this may be one of the most "no-brainer" ways to create a following, it 's important to have content that your followers want to see and connect with and can't be ignored.

Sharing quality content for members of your audience will help build your business — and personal brand — as a leading think tank within your industry.

Sharing awesome content is the difficulty of understanding what great content really is!

What is it you would share?

It is your own material; that is the obvious thing to post. However, a lot of businesses are used to posting their content only, which can potentially damage you in the long run.

Don't be a snob on the stuff.

If you just share your own stuff, then you don't do it right.

Best-practice practice? Employ regulation 70-20-10.

The content you share should add value and build up your brand 70 percent of the time, should be posts and suggestions from other people 20 percent of the time, and should only support yourself or your company 10 percent of the time.

Let it sink in.

Just 10 percent of social media posts should be self-promotional.

Why? For what? As this helps you to create trust and provide genuinely useful content and knowledge to your followers. Will you be following an organization that constantly bombs you with promo offers? Probably not.

Aside from that, here are a few tips on what to write.

Get visual with the contents.

Add visual content to your posts, such as photos, gifs, and videos to make them more enticing. Think of the term "showing versus saying." People want to see much more than text, and to catch their eyes need something visually appealing. Users on FB, IG, and Twitter all showed huge interaction with visual content for both image and video: using live video to try and relate and your audience in real-time. Reports have shown people are spending three times more time viewing live videos than pre-recordings. Take advantage of the emerging trend and talk to your followers directly!

But above all, pay attention to the forum, and how it is used by your audience.

Consider the strengths of each site and their common behaviors. If you have content that moves in real-time, a site such as Twitter will work better for you than Instagram.

Or, if different sites are sharing the same content, be ready to adapt accordingly. If a long-form LinkedIn status gets a lot of attention, but the same post on Facebook doesn't get a lot of interaction from your fans, they tell you they 're not interested in that type of content on Facebook, and you need to make a change.

When do I want to share content?

Knowing when to post to your social networking sites depends on your audience, but there are some general guidelines that you can use when you first start.

For example, HubSpot found that for Instagram, "B2B organizations have the most times of high-clickthrough rates to choose from 12 p.m. to 1 p.m., 5 p.m. to 6 p.m., and even as late as 8 p.m. to 9 p.m. when people wind down for the day." Most platforms provide you with insights and engagement analytics that you should monitor and reassess your strategy on the basis of.

Build a sharing schedule for each site, and see when you get the most contribution from your posts.

To better reach your audience, you will decide the day, time, and type of post you want to share. The more they connect with your posts, the more news feeds will feature your content.

Engaging with industry leaders and influencers

After listening to the 70:20:10 rule, you're probably thinking, "How do I get 20 percent of the traffic on my page if the traffic isn't really mine?" As I mentioned briefly earlier, engaging with industry influencers would be a great tool in improving your social media strategy and creating a big social media presence. These companies or individuals are the think leaders in your industry who are following your customers and target audience. Only tap the tool!

Follow professional industry content you are reading or watching and share it with your audience. It's likely that your audience will follow or engage with them, too.

Do you attend Annual Conferences or Events? Look up and communicate with the speakers. Start to have virtual discussions about the event or message you are eager to learn about it. If the speaker engages with you, then you just may be mentioned in a post that will also reach all their followers.

Or, tag your most loved influencer in a post and ask your followers to also chime their members on their go-to thought. It will open the door to connect with your audience and have conversations.

Mari Smith, a top Facebook marketing space influencer, spoke last year at IMPACT Live 2019 and was so excited to share her experience with her. She's a perfect example of an influencer who needs to connect with her fans and get involved.

The emergence of micro-influencer micro-influencers are individuals with members from 1,000 to 1,000,000 followers/audience, and are considered experts in their respective niches.

The value of micro-influencers for businesses lies in the dedication, relatability, and affordability that micro-influencers offer.

If you have a big name celebrity who endorses your brand on social media, they may carry a huge following, but you might not be looking for the following. A micro-influencer, on the other hand, offers a more niche audience that you can reach a much lower price point.

Plus, consumers searching for content in a niche market would have a better chance of trusting those influencers in the same niche compared to a big name influencer they have never really linked to. Again, everything is back to building trust.

Using hashtags

You have this awesome content and are reaching your audience, but how do you better organize your posts for new people to find?

Using matching hashtags!

The (#) hashtag or pound sign for old-schoolers is a quick refresher tool used on social media platforms to pool audiences towards specific content.

As with a website or blog article keyword, hashtags are used to help your social posts perform better in search results. Users can directly follow these hashtags or can check for similar posts.

Hashtags made their Twitter debut but have rolled out on all major platforms since.

What types of hashtags would I use?

The trick to using hashtags effectively is to recognize the ones most important and famous with your target audience.

For example, if you work for a homebuilding business, you could suggest using a hashtag such as "# homeremodeling," as it is relevant to what your audience is looking for and is likely to be consistent with the type of content you are posting and will be posting.

It is important to remember that your hashtags can and should adjust according to the content that you publish. Although the hashtags you use in your content would be repetitive, adding diversity will help you reach wider audiences already interested in your area.

Where do my posts have Hashtags?

The Swift Response? It is a complicated operation.

There's no single location or way to use hashtags, and it may depend on the site you're posting on. A simple rule-of-thumb is to define and use your most wanted hashtag directly in your message.

For similar or secondary hashtags that you want to catch, try using those at the bottom of the post or in a comment or thread so that they don't detract from your content but still work in search results for you.

I discussed keyword technology in a previous article that I published, as my article was about the relationship between workers and their technology. With that, I've been using # technology to try and appear on the website in more search results.

8. Now that you are up and running on your social media platform, it's time to take things one step further.

Organic views are only going to get you so far, and they are becoming increasingly hard to achieve. Why? For what? Because the networks are smart, and you want to pay to play to gain the elite status in social media.

Social media ads, however, is one of the most cost-effective ways of communicating with a modern, targeted audience.

Facebook advertising As you've learned, it 's crucial for users seeing your awesome content to build a following on social media. However, with the ' latest improvements to Facebook's algorithm, content shared by friends and family is now given preference over company sites.

Uh oh ... If users don't see my stuff, how do I ever create a Facebook that follows?

This is where advertisement comes into play on Facebook.

Owing to the vast number of users using the site and powerful targeting tools you have at your fingertips, Facebook ads can be immensely beneficial for your organization.

If you're trying to encourage users to like your page or want to spread unique content you're sharing; you have a fair chance of reaching the users you want to reach due to the ability of Facebook to target very specific factors beyond gender and place, like live events, purchasing habits and interests.

There's, though, a right and wrong way of using Facebook ads to get results.

If you really want to get more eyes on your posts, you'll get there by boosting them. So if you want to build up your follow-up and increase interaction with the right audience, you'll have to do a lot more precise and targeted ads to bring the right content to the right person.

Ali discussed why Facebook ads are so important in a conversation with Ali Parmelee; IMPACT's paid media specialist, and Facebook expert.

"This is something that's more long-term and advantageous. [Facebook ads] really do stuff like improving site traffic, raising page interaction, growing followers, and creating seed audiences to attract net new users. Let's say you're writing a blog and posting it on Facebook. It'll probably get limited engagement. Yet there's still a high interest in using Facebook ads.

Instagram advertising Instagram has been a highly successful advertisement medium for advertisers and consumers alike after it was acquired by Facebook.

There are many new features that Instagram has rolled out to be able to take advantage of on the advertising front companies to create a following and promote their goods/business.

Unlike any other social network, the Explore tool provides users with a fully personalized and exclusive interface to discover individuals, brands, developers, and more that might be of interest.

In 2019, Instagram launched Explore ads, which I believe is a win-win for both the brands and customers.

Brands can now get to more of the consumers they want in a tab designed to discover something new with the highly customized experience offered in Explore. This makes the discovery of products due to their appealing content and encourages people to adopt them organically.

On the other hand, customers can navigate through their Explore feed naturally, and discover a new brand or website they are interested in without disturbing their experience.

Sellable posts and stories It has been found that 72 percent of Instagram users made a buying decision based on what they saw on Instagram, so it's only fair that the company should find a way to make it easier for them to buy.

As we discussed earlier, the power of sellable (or shoppable) posts is a major differentiator for Instagram as a website. For influencers, in particular, it can dramatically raise the chances of users making a purchase on Instagram by showing their followers that they are using a certain product and giving them the chance to buy with a few clicks of a button.

LinkedIn Ads As I mentioned earlier, LinkedIn is the go-to social media site for B2B marketers, but it can take a lot of work to create a following.

As a forum, LinkedIn has thousands, if not millions, of influencers vying for your attention. This can make individuals and brands stand out very difficult.

With that in mind, in 2019, LinkedIn launched many promotional innovations to make the site more fruitful.

Two features particularly stand out for me when it comes to building up a following and having the right people to look at your content; Lookalike Audiences and Audience Models.

By integrating the main features of those customers with data collected by LinkedIn, the Lookalike Audiences feature lets you get in front of more of your ideal clients. This feature will help you find more people you want to interact with without all the usual heavy lifting.

Audience Models remove the pain and time-consuming method of building exclusive publics in LinkedIn advertising. Now, marketers may pick different pre-made markets and characteristics they want to target for their advertising.

For example, if you were an HR talent agency in the image below, creating a following using the Corporate HR Professionals, Audience Template can be a perfect market for you to target using the LinkedIn advertisement.

Twitter Advertising Advertisements that provide video were found to be cost-per-engagement 50 percent cheaper.

Twitter does an excellent job of not intervening with its ads with the user experience.

When you can see below, while the other material is blanked out, the quality of the video doesn't stand out as an obvious commercial. Rather, the post is designed to catch the user's eye and give them the option to avoid scrolling, instead of stopping for them.

This is a simple yet enticing way to pull someone into the eye of your audience and hopefully make them listen.

What's more, a fascinating (and potentially surprising) fact about Twitter is its very common video content sharing and viewing.

Twitter users are taking in more than 2 billion videos a day, and video tweets are seeing 10x interaction with only a typed tweet.

Engage with your audience

On social media sites; it can be easy to get swept up in the followers and likes. But once you're building your audience, you completely have to communicate with them to keep it going.

React to posts in which you're mentioned, answer questions when you're asked, and respond to comments about your content.

If you come across a question, you might not be sure of the answer, tag some leading thinkers and industry experts to get their opinion. Social media is meant to be private!

People love to connect socially with brands. The more I do so, the more likely they would be to support me or to hang around with me. Several companies have also been extremely popular in interacting with their fans and clients. For example, Take Netflix.

Netflix releases amusing snippets of data that they find and have some enjoyable experiences with their followers.

This amusing tweet had more than 72,000 retweets and more than 280,000 comments.

This tweet's sheer scale is shocking. You can only imagine the scope all those retweets have.

Furthermore, Netflix not only communicates with Amanda, but other followers also communicate with messages of follow-up!

Netflix's replies are receiving more than 1,500 retweets, as well as 26,000 comments.

In the success of this post, they are building up their following while also regularly communicating with their existing followers. This is a win-win!

Let's build an empire on social media!

Now that you've got the tools and the know-how to create your social media empire, you probably feel pretty geared up to go.

Conclusion

Social media can be developed anywhere with an Internet connection, and marketers, advertisers, and creators of online content should accept it as a fundamental part of their communications because social media affects all facets of the Internet and changes the role of the Internet in people's lives. Through social media, today, consumers are gaining a new position. Users are 'content producers' and, thus, interactive users rather than merely consuming, as in the past. Blogs, micro-blogging applications (such as Twitter), social networking sites (such as Facebook), podcasts, and video and photo sharing sites (such as YouTube and Flickr) are social media apps or platforms that facilitate this. Given this fact, the incorporation of social media into marketing and their marketing strategies is useful for businesses, especially marketers. This study attempted to describe the main advantages and disadvantages of social media marketing as defined by the advancement of Internet technology. Social media is the latest platform for advertisers who aim to get their message out to their target audiences with any means. Depending on their business, the tool has both benefits and drawbacks, and many businesses are still trying to find the best way to use it. The typical company owners or advertisers do not completely comprehend the threats and obstacles therein. The sector is still so new that the credentials of "experts" in social media who provide their expertise online are difficult to determine. And they have to complete thorough research on social media activities before an organization moves into the world of social media marketing. To succeed in the field of social media marketing, a company has to learn basic concepts and strategies of using social media as an effective tool. A business or organization's key objectives must attract consumers, protect the credibility of the business, provide good product and service quality to consumers, and meet the needs of customers.

Do Not Go Yet; One Last Thing To Do

I would be very happy if you would write a short review on Amazon if you liked or considered it useful. Your encouragement makes a difference, and I personally read all comments to get your input and make this book even better.

Thanks for your help and support!